THE RESOURCES OF
RATIONALITY

Studies in Continental Thought
John Sallis, general editor

THE RESOURCES OF RATIONALITY

A Response to the Postmodern Challenge

CALVIN O. SCHRAG

Indiana University Press

BLOOMINGTON • INDIANAPOLIS

The paper used in this publication meets the minimum requirements of American
National Standard for Information Sciences—Permanence of Paper for Printed
Library Materials, ANSI Z39.48-1984.

Manufactured in the United States of America

Library of Congress Cataloging-in-Publication Data

Schrag, Calvin O.
   The resources of rationality : a response to the postmodern challenge / Calvin O. Schrag.
      p.   cm. — (Studies in Continental thought)
   Includes bibliographical references and index.
   ISBN 0-253-35054-9 (alk. paper). — ISBN 0-253-20733-9 (pbk. : alk. paper)
      1. Reason.   2. Postmodernism.   I. Title.   II. Series.
   BC177.S335   1992
   128'.3—dc20   91-39551

1 2 3 4 5   96 95 94 93 92

To my grandson
Eric Michael Stampfl
Too young to understand
but old enough to inspire

Contents

Preface

Prefaces tend to be superfluous. They often comprise efforts to render an account of the emplotted story in the main text before it is told. To the extent that such an account would be successful, the reasons for going on would be significantly attenuated. If the essentials were to be embodied in the preface, then the main text itself would become superfluous and there would be little need to proceed further. But if, on the other hand, a comprehension of the consummate story being told requires a journey over the terrain of the assembled chapters, then any prefatory consolidation of the succeeding discussions becomes quite dispensable.

Prefaces also tend to be divisive. It is common practice to use the preface to acknowledge an indebtedness to all those who helped shape the project. But authors, being the mortals that they are, are prone to experience lapses of recall and invariably neglect to include individuals and groups who had a hand in what is being said. This is particularly the case with students, whose contributions tend to remain unacknowledged. Many of the issues that find their way onto the printed page have been worked through in sustained classroom and seminar discussions. The students involved in these discussions tend to remain the forgotten motivators when credits are assigned.

Yet, it is a requirement of the trade to provide some prefatory remarks; hence, the risks of superfluity and divisiveness need to be assumed. These remarks might best be confined to factors that occasioned the specific project before us. The nature of philosophical discourse is such that no particular work of an author stands as an island entire to itself. An author's current work is often an extension of a previous work, occasioned by problems that the previous work left unattended. To a large measure, it is this that explains the present study.

Critics of an author's work can be demanding taskmasters. Various respondents to my previous book, *Communicative Praxis and the Space of Subjectivity*, were of the mind that insufficient attention had been given to the role and resources of reason in my account of the texture and dynamics of praxis. In particular, there were concerns expressed about the relevance of rationality for what I came to call the rhetoric and ethic of the "fitting response." In what manner does the determination of that which is fitting in our discourse and our action solicit considerations pertaining to the claims of reason? The present volume has been designed to address this particular issue, and the wider ramifications of the relation of rationality to praxis, straightaway. The context in which these matters are addressed is the postmodern challenge to the resources of rationality itself.

Numerous individuals have contributed in one way or another to the thought experiments and discursive strategies that inform the current

project. Some of these are referenced in the text itself; others are acknowledged, directly and indirectly, in the notes. The contributions of
others, however, will remain undetected by the reader because the occasions for these contributions have been forgotten by the author himself.
This is particularly unfortunate, and to all those who have contributed
but have remained unnamed I offer my profound apologies.

There is, however, a more specific occasion that marked the initiation
of the current work. In 1986 the National Endowment for the Humanities
provided a grant for an Institute for College and University Teachers, to
be conducted at Purdue University, on the topic "The Linguistic Turn in
Recent Continental Philosophy." It was principally as a result of the dialogic exchanges that took place during the tenure of this institute that the
outlines of the present project began to emerge. It is thus that I am particularly indebted to the persons who comprised this distinguished collo-
quy of scholars. These persons included my very able assistant director,
Dorothy Leland, and a visiting faculty consisting of Hubert L. Dreyfus,
James M. Edie, Barbara Johnson, Joseph J. Kockelmans, and David Couz-
ens Hoy. They all in different ways helped to define the issues at stake
in the current work. However, of even greater relevance for the shaping
of the contours of the present study were the sustained critical discussions with the twenty selected participants, themselves faculty members
from sundry American colleges and universities, who were never satisfied with easy answers. To all of them I inscribe an acknowledgment; but
surely they are not to be held responsible for any indiscretions that might
appear on the subsequent pages.

The preparation of the final manuscript was entrusted to the competent
secretarial hands of Bonnie J. Memering and Joyce E. Whitman. To them
I owe a special thanks, for their patience, diligence, and good sense about
typographical details. John Michael Fritzman assisted in the reading of
galley proofs and in the preparation of the index. I wish to express my
gratitude to him for performing this very valuable service.

West Lafayette, Indiana
March 1992

THE RESOURCES OF
RATIONALITY

Introduction

The definition of the task of philosophy as the cultivation of reason and the portrait of the philosopher as the steward of rationality reach far back into the tradition of Occidental thought. The defense of this task of philosophy was at times undertaken with an accentuated earnestness. The existential pathos of Socrates' apologia for the life of reason, in the face of some rather dire consequences, became the touchstone for the philosophical way of life in the continuing tradition. It was simply taken for granted that the life of reason was to be defended at all costs, even if such a defense should imperil the life of the person who attests to reason's claims.

This image of the philosopher and the life of reason sketched by the thought and practice of the ancients issued from a spate of metaphysical ruminations on the interconnections of reason, knowledge, and truth. The very nature or essence of the human self was defined in Greek antiquity as a "living being having logos" (*zōon logon ekhon*) and later in Latin antiquity as a "rational animal" (*animal rationale*). Whether sketched against the backdrop of the Greek "logos" or the more narrowly circumscribed and more metaphysically restricted Latin "ratio," the essentially human became directly associated with resources for reasoning and the attainment of knowledge. These resources, it was alleged, issue from the very nature of what it means to be human. Aristotle makes this quite clear in the opening line of his *Metaphysics*: "All men by nature desire to know."

To observe that from time to time this classical portrait of the philosopher as the steward of rationality and the surveyor of the terrain in which knowledge claims are to be staked out has been called into question would simply be to call one's attention to the obvious. The history of Western philosophy is pretty much a history of conflicting interpretations on the understanding and use of reason. The story of the fifth-century Sophists in ancient Greece, as well as that of the rise of skepticism during the Hellenistic period, is of particular importance for a wider historical account of the travail of rationality already at the beginnings of Western thought. The common feature that these two schools of thought exhibited was a profound suspicion of what they considered the overextended claims of reason in the reigning Platonism and Aristotelianism of the day. The Sophists and the Skeptics were the most adamant and the most influential critics of rationality in the premodern age. Thus, already in the classical period of Occidental thought we find recurring voices of dissent, calling into question the rational resources of the human mind.

It is, however, in the ethos of modernity that one finds the most intensified philosophical self-consciousness of the peculiarly intertwined potentialities and limits of human reason. This involves specifically the contributions of Immanual Kant and more generally the encompassing story of modern rationalism. Certainly Kant, and the composite contribution of his three *Critiques*, deserves specific reference in any historical account of the claims of reason.

If Kant did not set the stage for the drama of rationality as it unfolded in the modern period, he clearly played a prominent role in the developing plot. Indeed, his tripartite "critique of reason" is very much center-stage, and it is difficult to overestimate the effects of his celebrated critiques upon the subsequent discourse of modernity. The grammar of critique, as it was fashioned by Kant, exhibited a bivalent case structure. On the one hand it was accusative, designed to displace the dogmatic metaphysical claims of reason by the tradition; on the other hand it was genitive, geared to a reflexivity upon the internal critical resources of reason wherewith to respond to the challenge of skepticism. It was thus that the modern programmatic of "critical rationality" was inaugurated to provide a passage through the philosophical straits so as to avoid at once the Scylla of dogmatism and the Charybdis of skepticism.

Kant's concept of critical rationality shared the properties of being transcendental and autonomous, forging a linkage of knowledge and freedom at the very heart of reason. His "critique" of reason, in its genitival, internal deployment, assumes a transcendental posture in that it proceeds by way of a demonstration of the universal and necessary conditions that make knowledge possible. Although knowledge begins with experience, it does not arise from experience. Knowledge has its genuine origin in the forms of intuition, the schema of the imagination, and the categories of the understanding, that reside a priori in the human mind. Without these forms, schema, and categories, knowledge would not be possible. According to Kant, it is precisely the operation of these transcendental determinants, which are themselves not experienced but function as indispensable conditions for the determination of knowledge within experience, that the skeptic overlooks. On the other hand, the dogmatist fails to recognize the limits to the resources of critical rationality in his or her efforts to comprehend reality as it exists in itself. The transcendental resources of reason, although they provide conditions for the knowability of the phenomenal world, remain within the strictures of human finitude. The substantive rationality of the premodern metaphysical tradition, with its claims for knowledge of transcendent forms and essences, gives way to the more limited achievements of a critical rationality.

The transcendental functions of reason in Kant's critical philosophy were coupled with a postulate of autonomy. Critical reason is at once transcendental and autonomous. Its autonomy, highlighted particularly in the domain of practical reason, is exemplified in reason's liberation from the socio-historical tradition and external moral authority. It was this particular exemplification of autonomy that provided the "Enlightenment" imprint on Kant's critical reason. Reason won its independence both from the fetters of ecclesiastical authorities and the imperatives of a state apparatus. The Protestant Reformation came to be seen as a cultural expression of the former and the French Revolution as a cultural expression of the latter.

There was yet another expression of autonomy in Kant's transcendental philosophy, within the economy of critical reason itself. Reason was distributed over a rather wide-ranging spectrum of human endeavors, including science, morality, art, and religion. The question of the exchange relations governing the use of reason in each of these spheres thus emerged as a special problem. Each sphere exemplified a certain autonomy in its deployment of critical reason. The critiques of pure reason, practical reason, and aesthetic judgment became differentiated. Max Weber spoke of this as a "stubborn" or "recalcitrant" differentiation, inviting a diremption of the three culture-spheres of science, morality, and art. It is important to remember, however, that there was a fourth culture-sphere named in Kant's economy of distributive reason—the sphere of religion. There is a long-standing tendency in Kant-interpretation to gloss the significance of Kant's *Religion within the Limits of Reason Alone*, which tends to be viewed at most as a kind of appendage to his three *Critiques*. Religion too for Kant was a sphere that was open to rational discourse—however limited the resources of reason in this sphere might be. In any event, the postulate of autonomy that regulated the domestic economy of Kant's resources of rationality problematized the requirement for unification that Kant himself had inscribed in the very telos of reason.

It was the challenge to find in the resources of reason the requisite power of unification, wherewith to bind the differentiated culture-spheres bequeathed in the legacy of Kant, that motivated the philosophical aspirations of Hegel. The design of Hegel's grandiose project took shape as a resituation and incorporation of transcendental reflection into a more encompassing dialectical reason that proceeded by way of a mediation of the opposites within the cultural spectrum of human affairs. It was the problem occasioned by Kant's diremption of the domains of science, morality, art, and religion, and Hegel's attempted resolution of this problem, that defined, to a large measure, both the grammar and the contents of modernity. Hence, any discussion of the issues pertaining to the widely publicized modernity/postmodernity debate requires attentiveness to the problems and discourses that emerged from the Kantian and Hegelian perspectives on rationality.

It is to the credit of Jürgen Habermas that he remains attuned to the historical backgrounds that informed at once the "discourse of modernity" and the counter-discourse of postmodernity.[1] As one who walks the fine line between defending and critiquing modernity, Habermas is at least insistent on the need to continue the conversation with the likes of

---

1. See particularly Jürgen Habermas, *The Philosophical Discourse of Modernity*, trans. Frederick Lawrence (Cambridge, MA: The MIT Press, 1987).

Kant and Hegel. This is not to say that "postmodernists," either self-proclaimed or suffering the fate of having the epithet assigned to them, do not continue the conversation (although admittedly at times it becomes rather strained!), but it soon becomes evident that the discourses of modernity and postmodernity move in different directions.

Habermas is of the mind that the problematic as defined by Hegel is one that requires serious attention. There was nothing amiss in Hegel's accepting the segmentation of science, morality, and art as a genuine state of affairs peculiar to modernity; nor was there anything wrong with Hegel's search for a way of unifying the separated spheres. What went awry in Hegel's philosophy, according to Habermas, was the way that he went about effecting the unification—particularly in his later works. The early Hegel (that of the Jena period) apparently was still on the right track. In his early reflections the notion of community was given prominence, and here Hegel still had the opportunity to work out a full-bodied, Habermasian-like "communicative rationality." But then, continues Habermas, Hegel took the wrong turn in proceeding to his later thought, in which rationality becomes grounded in a sovereign rational subject and Hegel's project culminates in an exaggerated claim for absolute knowledge.[2]

The task that Habermas thus lays out for himself is that of setting Hegel aright, using the early Hegel against the later, dredging his *Jena* period reflections on community, mutual acknowledgment, love, and freedom, to find connections with and support for a multi-tiered "theory of communicative action." Such a theory would unify the separated culture-spheres of science, morality, and art not from the vantage point of absolute knowledge, construed as a fulfillment of subject-centered reason, but rather along the lines of a "universal pragmatics" that employs the services of communicative reason.[3]

In the execution of this task, which by any measure is considerable in design and expectation, Habermas purports to stay with the philosophical discourse of modernity. However, he does not stay with this discourse *uncritically*. To the contrary, he launches some rather formidable criticisms of the founding concepts of modernity—and particularly the concept of subject-centered reason. Yet, one is repeatedly given notice that there is nothing "postmodern" about this criticism. It is directed toward a transformation of the discourse of modernity by way of a critical reassessment of the claims of reason and the prospects for a philosophy of the future.

Richard Rorty has taken up the conversation with modernity in such a way as to effect a somewhat different move than that recommended by

2. *The Philosophical Discourse of Modernity*, pp. 40 and 74.

3. Jürgen Habermas, *The Theory of Communicative Action: Volume One: Reason and the Rationalization of Society*, trans. Thomas McCarthy (Boston: Beacon Press, 1984), and Volume Two: *Lifeworld and System: A Critique of Functionalist Reason*, trans. Thomas McCarthy (Boston: Beacon Press, 1987). See also "An Alternative Way out of the Philosophy of the Subject: Communicative versus Subject-centered Reason," in *The Philosophical Discourse of Modernity*, pp. 294–326.

Habermas. Rorty responds to the discourse of modernity not via a Habermasian critical reconstruction of its philosophical platform, geared to a "transformation of philosophy"; instead he proposes a rupture with the discourse of modernity and proclaims that we are now at the "end of philosophy."[4] The accepted "givens" and paradigmatic constructs of modernity are brought under indictment. Rorty, like Habermas, initiates a conversation with the likes of Kant and Hegel, but he is of the mind that the "wrong turn" was taken even prior to Hegel's later philosophy. The wrong turn was negotiated not by Hegel when he took recourse to an inflated philosophy of subjectivity so as to unify the culture-spheres of science, morality, and art; the wrong turn was already taken by Kant in splitting up the culture-spheres in the first place.

> But whereas Habermas thinks that the cultural need which "the philosophy of the subject" gratified was and is real, and can perhaps be fulfilled by his own focus on a "communication community," I would urge that it is an artificial problem created by taking Kant too seriously. On this view, the wrong turn was taken when Kant's split between science, morals, and art was accepted as a *donnée*, as *die massgebliche Selbstauslegung der Moderne*.[5]

Rorty's central point is that things got off rather badly when Kant differentiated and congealed the three culture-spheres under the aegis of the telos of a unifying rationality. Hegel simply continued to make purchases on the received problematic of cultural differentiation and the requirement for unification. But to continue a preoccupation with this problematic in search of the correct solution is for Rorty to continue to scratch where it doesn't itch. Efforts to respond to this problematic via an epistemological reconstruction have outworn their usefulness. Such efforts are simply vestiges of an inclination to do *philosophy*, i.e., foundationalist and epistemological reflection that yearns for a reconstruction of knowledge. Philosophy thusly conceived, according to Rorty, has mercifully come to its end.[6] Having arrived at this liberating stage in our philosophical history, Rorty is of the mind that we now have better things to do than to carve out the domains of science, morality, and art—and then search for a grand, unifying perspective. With an even, pragmatist temperament, he

4. In their edited volume *After Philosophy: End or Transformation?* (Cambridge, MA: The MIT Press, 1987), Kenneth Baynes, James Bohman, and Thomas McCarthy have structured their format along the lines of representatives of the "End of Philosophy" movement (including Rorty, Lyotard, Foucault, and Derrida) as contrasted with representatives of the "Transformation of Philosophy" approach. The latter includes efforts to transform philosophy via "Systematic Proposals" (Davidson, Dummett, Putnam, Apel, and Habermas) or via "Hermeneutics, Rhetoric, Narrative" (Gadamer, Ricoeur, MacIntyre, Blumenberg, and Taylor).
5. Richard Rorty, "Habermas and Lyotard on Postmodernity," in *Habermas and Modernity*, ed. Richard Bernstein (Cambridge, MA: The MIT Press, 1985), p. 167.
6. For an extensive discussion by Rorty on the vagaries of epistemological foundationalism and the self-deceptive efforts in a rational reconstruction of knowledge, see his *Philosophy and the Mirror of Nature* (Princeton: Princeton University Press, 1979).

enjoins us to live with plurality, change, difference, and incommensurable discourse. Let us speak of all this as the Rortyian exemplification of postmodernism.

Surely there are family resemblances in what we have here named Rorty's postmodernism to that espoused by the commonly identified postmodern thinkers on the contemporary scene. One is of course straightaway reminded of Jacques Derrida's attack on logocentrism and his philosophy of *différance;* Jean-François Lyotard's assault on metanarratives and his celebration of plurality and paralogy; and Gilles Deleuze's use of "the multiple" against the hegemonic mind-set of royal science and the state apparatus. It would be difficult to pursue a discussion of postmodernism without a fair amount of attention being given to Derrida, Lyotard, and Deleuze. However, even a consolidation of the contributions of this current French philosophical triumvirate (if indeed such a consolidation could be achieved) would still fall short of providing a portrait of the postmodern mind. There are many other figures in the philosophical and literary world who have been implicated, either by choice or destiny, in the thought and activity of postmodernism. Indeed, it becomes increasingly difficult to "catch" someone *doing* postmodernism, mainly because the parameters of its discourse are so distressingly noodle-like.

Once one begins to devise a canon of postmodern thinkers (which would likely include the works of Derrida, Lyotard, Deleuze, Guattari, Bataille, Foucault, Baudrillard, Rorty, Feyerabend—and surely Nietzsche and Heidegger, among others) one quickly learns that postmodernism is a subversion of any and all strategies of canonization and that one would be well advised to abandon any such project. If one looks for a common set of beliefs or doctrines that bind the thought of the various contributors, one is again informed, and certainly with considerable evidence, that postmodernism is neither a theory nor a platform of doctrines. So again one is looking for perch in a trout stream.

Not uncommonly, the rejoinder to one's varied efforts to consolidate the discourses of postmodernity is that the discourses at issue have to do with innovative cultural perspectives—for example, the effacing of the boundaries between high culture and mass culture. But these cultural perspectives have neither edges nor a center. They are dispersed among the disciplinary activities of science, philosophy, literature, art, politics, economics, jurisprudence, and religion in such a manner as to render any stabilization of these activities and any designs for their unification and totalization useless and boring. This may indeed get us closer to the "facts of the case," but without considerably more elucidation of the *praxis* of such cultural renovation/innovation, the phenomenon that we are investigating remains pretty much a Schellingian night in which all cows are black. Pinning down the referent of "postmodernism" is indeed very much like pinning down a droplet of mercury.

Given such an unsettled state of affairs in efforts to make sense of the body politic of postmodernity, the reader of our current project may be inclined to question the sanity of an author who purports to define the topic of rationality against the backdrop of what we have named "the postmodern challenge." This, however, is precisely what is intended in the present volume. It will thus be required of us to tell the reader what it is that postmodernism challenges and how it does so. The main title of our current project, "The Resources of Rationality," of course, provides the central clue. It is rationality, and particularly rationality as it figures in the philosophical discourse of modernity, that has been challenged and problematized by postmodernism. This has the advantage of providing our project with a measure of specificity. We will attempt to tease out from the varied voices of postmodernity a spate of worries about the overdetermination of reason, and specifically as this overdetermination was played out in the modern epistemological paradigm. Our concern will be principally with the *philosophical* expression of postmodernity, and hopefully this will help to circumscribe the parameters of our own discourse somewhat. At the same time, however, we realize that philosophical considerations cannot be that easily separated from the wider cultural scene. Yet, so as to achieve an optimal management of the issues pertaining to rationality, we will contextualize our discussion against the backdrop of the philosophical reflections on the claims of reason that issue from modernity. Our project could thus be construed as an exploration of rationality *between* modernity and postmodernity.[7]

Our contextualization of the challenge of postmodernity in its relation to the contents and the forms of discourse of modernity turns out in the end to be quite in accord with one of the more heavily cited framers of the constitution of postmodernism—Jean-François Lyotard. In his oft-cited work, *The Postmodern Condition*, Lyotard responds to his own question "What, then, is the postmodern?" by informing the reader: "It is undoubtedly a part of the modern. . . . A work can become modern only if it is first postmodern. Postmodernism thus understood is not modernism at its end but in the nascent state, and this state is constant."[8]

Not only, however, does Lyotard assist us in attending to the to-and-fro movement between the modern and the postmodern; he also aids us in achieving some specification of the challenge of postmodernity within modernity. The challenge has to do with fostering an attitude of "incredulity toward metanarratives"; refining our "sensitivity to differences"; instructing us to "tolerate the incommensurable"; learning to live with "the inventor's paralogy"; and waging "a war on totality."[9] Although this may all add up to more than an ordinary mortal can stomach at a

---

7. Certain selected and highly condensed features of this wider project have already been addressed by the author in his contribution to the *Festschrift* for Fred R. Dallmayr: *Life-World and Politics,* ed. Stephen K. White (Notre Dame: University of Notre Dame Press, 1989). See Calvin O. Schrag, "Rationality Between Modernity and Postmodernity," pp. 81–106.
8. Jean-François Lyotard, *The Postmodern Condition: A Report on Knowledge,* trans. Geoff Bennington and Brian Massumi (Minneapolis: University of Minnesota Press, 1984), p. 79.
9. *The Postmodern Condition,* pp. xxiv, xxv, and 82.

single sitting, we will attempt to show how these pronouncements, coupled with ruminations in some of his other writings, evoke the requirement for a radical reconsideration of the received claims of reason. It is the problematization of rationality that falls out from all this—as it does also from Derrida's disparagement of logocentrism and from Deleuze's "anti-logos" literary machine—placing before us the challenge to respond. We will simplify this challenge by naming it the challenge of "the despised logos."

Although Paul Feyerabend may not consider himself a member of the extended family of postmodernists, he is rather frequently referenced in the literature. In any case, we find his recent book, *Farewell to Reason*, particularly helpful in formulating the challenge to which we are disposed to respond. According to Feyerabend, the multiple appeals to reason in the history of the philosophical enterprise have pretty much run aground. Reason (which he chooses to capitalize—and this itself may contain a message) is bereft of any universal content; is unable to dissociate itself from the particularities of human concerns and interests; invites monotony and boredom—and we had best bid it farewell.

> But rationalism has no identifiable content and reason no recognizable agenda over and above the principles of the party that happens to have appropriated its name. All it does now is lend class to the general drive towards monotony. It is time to disengage Reason from this drive and, as it has been thoroughly comprised by the association, to bid it farewell.[10]

The bidding farewell to reason; the disparagement of the logos; the jettisoning of the drive for unification; and the celebration of difference, plurality, and multiplicity—all these conspire to challenge us to respond anew to the question, "How does it stand with rationality as we attempt to make our way about in a postmodern world?"

The story that we intend to relate in response to this question unfolds as an extended preoccupation with rationality as a *praxis*. The notion of praxis at issue in the subsequent discussions, it will soon become evident to the reader, is not that referenced in the "Philosophy of the Praxis School," which took shape in the mid-twentieth century as a confluence of Marxist, existentialist, and phenomenological theories. It is rather the refigured understanding and use of praxis that we sketched in our recent *Communicative Praxis and the Space of Subjectivity*.[11] Whereas the Praxis School moved out principally from Marx's concept of labor, and more specifically

10. Paul Feyerabend, *Farewell to Reason* (New York: Verso Press, 1987), p. 13. Closely following this passage we are given a clue as to the existential motivation that informs this vigorous assault on the citadel of Reason: "The chapter will make it clear that my concern is neither rationality, nor science, nor freedom—abstractions such as these have done more harm than good—but the quality of the lives of individuals." P. 17.
11. Calvin O. Schrag, *Communicative Praxis and the Space of Subjectivity* (Bloomington: Indiana University Press, 1986).

as this concept was informed by his early ruminations on alienated consciousness that quickly lent themselves to an existential-phenomenological appropriation, our notion of praxis functions as an indicator of the amalgamated discourse and action that textures the space of human endeavoring, exhibiting a striving for an understanding and explanation of the configurations of experience through which such endeavoring passes. Within such a scheme of things, both the production-labor paradigm and the primacy-of-consciousness motif become problematized. Forms of labor and the subject of consciousness, either alienated or authentic, are seen as implicates of praxis rather than foundations for it.

The issue, however, that did not receive sufficient attention in our previous detailing of the performances of communicative praxis was the role of rationality within the interstices of its dynamics. This was particularly the case in our installation of the requirement for the "fitting response," demanded by the ethos of the rhetorical situatedness of our engaged discourse and action. The current project, properly understood as a self-critical continuation of our previous project, takes up the gauntlet of providing an account of the claims of reason in our communicative involvements and endeavors.

Our account relies heavily on a reformulated notion of transversality. If the reader already at this stage insists on a preliminary statement of thesis, it could be said that the proposed thesis is that rationality is transversal to the multiplicity of our discursive and nondiscursive practices. Somewhat expanded, our proposal is that reason is operative in and through the transversal play of discourse and action, word and deed, speaking and writing, hearing and reading, in the guise of three intercalated moments or phases of communicative praxis: (1) discerning and evaluative critique; (2) interactive articulation; and (3) incursive disclosure. Praxial critique, articulation, and disclosure constitute the coefficient dynamics of transversal rationality.

The general design is to address the challenge to rationality in postmodernism by tracking the performance of a transversal logos lying across the multiple forms of life that make up our communicative practices. This will provide an alternative to the concept of the universal logos that remained the bane of both premodern cosmological/metaphysical speculation and modern subject-centered epistemological reflection. It will also, if our argumentation is successful, rescue the resources of reason from a postmodern diaspora in which reason succumbs to a rhapsodic play of *différance* and a rampant pluralism. Situated between modernity and postmodernity, passing between the Scylla of a hegemonic and ahistorical universalism and the Charybdis of a lawless, self-effacing particularism and enervated historicism, transversal reason charts the course of comprehending the configurative practices and forms of life that comprise our socio-historical inherence.

The plotting of such a course of comprehension is not that of a smooth

linearity. Hence, it will require attentiveness to certain juttings and jog-
gings, byways and detours, as they are encountered along the way. We
have already alluded to the principal signposts—*critique, articulation,* and
disclosure—that mark out the terrain of reason. These signposts, however,
become intelligible only against the backdrop of solicitations by the challenge of postmodernism (chapter one); strategies in the theory and practice of critique (chapter two); the hermeneutical demand and the consequences of interpretation (chapter three); the claims of narrative (chapter
four); and the interface of rhetoric and rationality (chapter five).

The portrait of postmodernism that we sketch in the opening chapter
solicits a sustained focus on what we call "the despised logos" thematic.
We discuss this thematic in connection with a spate of philosophical aporias that have made their way into postmodernist discourse. These include indeterminacy and undecidability; plurality and paralogy; the politics of power and desire; and the problematization of presence in a new
historicism. An examination of the conditions that have conspired to produce these aporias hopefully will bring into somewhat sharper relief what
we understand by the postmodern challenge to the claims of reason.

Chapter two addresses rationality as praxial critique. In this chapter
an effort is made to think beyond the received theory/practice bifurcation
and the associated concept/fact dichotomy so as to make visible a performance of rationality within a dynamics of communicative praxis that antedates, if not subverts, the mapping apparatus of theory construction
and fact reification. The resultant praxial critique, it is claimed, comports
its own resources for discernment and valuation. It is at this stage that
the postmodernist jettisoning of "critique" (and specifically as this jettisoning occurs in the thought of Jean-François Lyotard) is confronted. An
effort is made to refigure the dynamics of critique as a discernment and
assessment of the play of discourses, beliefs, and institutional lines of
force with and against each other. The backdrop of this play is the dialogic, interactional, and agonistic life of our daily discursive and nondiscursive encounters. The upshot of our discussion in this chapter is a dismantling of the notion of critique informed by the modern theoretico-
epistemological paradigm and its foundationalist *Urteilstheorie,* without,
however, succumbing to a flat-out abandonment of the critical resources
of reason and the regulative demands of rational consensus. Thus a passage between the judgment-theoretical, foundationalist notion of critique
in modernity and the agonistic and interventionist strategies in postmodernity is opened up.

Chapter three situates the consequences of interpretation for a rational
comprehension of our assorted discursive and institutional practices. Two
competing models of interpretation—the hermeneutics of nostalgia and
the hermeneutics of affirmation—are sorted out and interrogated. The articulation of meaning as a manifestation of rationality is addressed, as is
also the consequence of interpretation for the notion of truth. The rele-

vance of structuralist criticism is discussed, particularly in connection with the alleged semiotic constraints within hermeneutics, and an effort is made to show how interpretive textuality brings into relief the limits of the signifier/signified matrix of semiology. The principal result of these different forays is a transmutation of interpretation as a mental act into interpretation as a discursive and institutional practice.

The fourth chapter isolates some of the main features of narration as they relate to the life of reason. The workings of the logos in the emplotment of the stories that we tell is examined; the issue of narrativity and knowledge is probed, particularly vis-à-vis the interplay of fact and interpretation; and the limits of the "world of narrative" in its confrontation with the praxis-oriented "lifeworld" are highlighted. This chapter is basically a continuation of the previous one, extending the tracking of delimitations as one moves from semiotic analysis to textual strategies to narrational configurations to the forms of life in the world of praxis. At each stage there is a delimitation of the previous one; and throughout this maneuver of delimitation, interpretation is seen as being at work. Interpretation does indeed go all the way down and all the way back. But this does not legitimate the inference that *everything is interpretation*. In the end, interpretation suffers its own delimitation. The travail of interpretation as the articulation of meaning is complemented by narrational reference, in the guise of rationality as disclosure, which occurs in the moment when narrative encounters that which is other-than-narrative— the alterity and incursivity of the socio-historical lifeworld. This comprises the "phenomenological moment" in the odyssey of rationality.

The topic of rhetoric and rationality defines our concerns in chapter five. The long-standing controversy among rhetoricians and philosophers concerning matters of reason, logic, argumentation, and truth is well known. Plato, of course, did not help matters much when he pegged rhetoricians as perpetrators of sham wisdom. Aristotle attempted to make the best of a bad situation by according rhetoric a place in his philosophical canon. In the medieval trivium, too, logic and rhetoric were able to live side by side. The relationship between them, however, became increasingly strained in subsequent Occidental thought, particularly as a result of the solidification of the theoretico-epistemological paradigm in modernity. We consider it as a not inconsequential contribution of postmodernism to question the received bifurcation of rhetorical and philosophical discourse, and we take this to be one of the salient features in its challenge that requires a response. Our response takes shape as an exploration of the possibility of incorporating rhetoric into a transfigured notion of rational discourse. This leads us to the binding topos of a "communicative rhetoric" in which the economy of reason remains activated in managing the affairs of everyday, public life. At this stage in the wider design of our investigations it will of course be already evident to the reader that this economy of reason is stimulated by the *vis a tergo* operations of discerning critique, interactive articulation, and incursive disclosure.

The sixth and concluding chapter strives for a consolidation of the networking and dynamics of critique, articulation, and disclosure by refiguring and expanding the concept/metaphor of transversality. The principal efficacy of reason is seen to reside in its gathering and binding performance, extending over, lying across, intersecting, and at times overturning the configurations of our communicative practices, which are at once critiqued, articulated, and disclosed. The hermeneutical circle of interpretation, circumscribing the understanding of meaning, and the phenomenological moment of displayed reference to an everyday life-world are reclaimed in this concluding scenario of a transversal rationality of praxis. However, the metaphorical use of the circle in hermeneutic understanding is delimited by the play of the diagonal in transversal comprehension; and phenomenological reference is liberated from the aporias of representation and the given. "Transversal Rationality" is the title of the last chapter; but insofar as first and last as episodes in ongoing philosophical exchange tend to be manifestly relative to each other—in want of absolute beginnings and final ends—the reader may profitably elect to begin with the last chapter so as to facilitate an anticipation of the end at the beginning.

ONE

The Challenge of Postmodernism

A MELANGE OF PORTRAITS

Anyone attempting to provide a sketch of postmodernism has to contend with a somewhat curious diversity of portraits on display both in the academy and on the wider cultural scene. This diversity is in part the result of grammatical variations in the identification of the phenomenon at issue. In the proliferating discussions of the topic the vocabulary often shifts from "the postmodern" to "postmodernity" to "postmodernism" without clear indications of what, if anything, is at stake in such shifts. Now it may be the case that no clear indications can be rendered, and one might be well advised not to make too much of these grammatical variations. Several authors, however, have made efforts to clear the air somewhat by offering certain lexical markers. A case in point is the following:

> "Postmodernity" is a social/technological condition; "postmodernism" is an aesthetic or philosophical subcategory within the larger problem of "the postmodern."[1]

Such is certainly a possible way to divide the terrain, utilizing "the postmodern" to indicate the more encompassing field of cultural thought and activity; defining "postmodernism" as an aesthetic/philosophical marking within this broader spectrum; and then restricting "postmodernity" to a more specific sociopolitical ethos or mind-set. The problem, however, is that this set of distinctions has not become normative for the literature. The three grammatical constructs register different senses as one moves from one expositor to the next. This, indeed, may be quite inevitable, given that each designator readily slides into the other. It is for this reason that we have decided not to devise lexical boundaries in advance, but rather to elucidate their different senses within their context-dependent usages. For the most part we will use "the postmodern

---

1. "Lexicon: Guide for the Perplexed II" (arranged by Robert Cheatham, J. W. Cullum, Glen Harper, Patrice McDermott, Angel Medina, and David Tinsley), in *Art Papers* 10, no. 1 (1986): p. 8.

challenge" and "postmodernism," banking on the context to manage the play of ambiguity in their usages.

Another feature contributing to the diversity of portraits of postmodern, postmodernism, and postmodernity is the global, multidisciplinary expanse of the terrain. One quickly learns that there is postmodern architecture, postmodern art, postmodern literature, postmodern politics, postmodern culture-studies, postmodern science, postmodern philosophy—and the list goes on. Postmodernism has spread its mantle over an extended spate of disciplines, and the task of finding a common thread running through and across the multiple disciplines in the wider postmodern curriculum is a formidable one indeed.

The enormity of the task, however, has not reduced those authors disposed to write about postmodernism to a state of despair; and from the growing literature on the topic there is indeed much to learn. We learn, for example, that postmodern architecture involves a dismantling of the division of inside and outside by decentering the space of our dwellings and destabilizing their relation to the environmental setting. Postmodern art, we are told, engineers a break with representation, realism, symbolism, and all claims of referentiality. Postmodern literature appears to fall out as a requiem for nostalgia and recollection and a celebration of experimentation and invention. Postmodern politics finds its telos in dissensus rather than consensus, intervention rather than litigation. Postmodern culture-studies problematize the distinctions between elite and popular culture. Postmodern science is viewed as an effort to manage instabilities in a milieu of incommensurability and shifting paradigms. Postmodern philosophy is anti-foundationalist, suspicious of theory, and distrustful of any universal claims of reason.[2]

Although there would admittedly be something to be learned from an elaboration of our one-line characterizations of the multidisciplinary expression of postmodernism, one would be sorely disappointed were one to expect a unifying perspective at the conclusion of such a project. There are too many conceptual and metaphorical shifts as one moves across the wider cultural curriculum. Postmodernism simply does not congeal into a unified system of beliefs or doctrinal formulations. It appears to be more like an assemblage of attitudes and discursive practices.

It is thus that Steven Connor's suggestion that we understand postmodernism as a *"discursive* function," the integrity of which derives from its "effects in different discursive operations, rather than from the consis-

2. For some of the more successful efforts toward consolidating the composite contribution of postmodernism across the disciplines, the reader is encouraged to look at Steven Connor, *Postmodernist Culture: An Introduction to Theories of the Contemporary* (Oxford: Basil Blackwell, 1989); David Harvey, *The Condition of Postmodernity: An Enquiry into the Origins of Cultural Change* (Oxford: Basil Blackwell, 1989); Vincent B. Leitch, *Deconstructive Criticism: An Advanced Introduction* (New York: Columbia University Press, 1983); and Gary Shapiro, ed., *After the Future: Postmodern Times and Places* (Albany: State University of New York Press, 1990).

tency of the ideas within it," would seem to hold some promise.[3] Viewing postmodernism as an assemblage of discursive practices rather than a system of beliefs or ideas would indeed seem to have certain advantages. However, this is at best a kind of stipulative starting point. What is required is an account of the *performance* of postmodern discourse, how it functions and what it is about. To render such an account a trustworthy guide to direct us along the way would indeed be worth much fine gold. The peculiarity of our predicament is that trustworthy guides for matters such as these are hard to come by.

A common approach to defining such elusive achievements of the human spirit like romanticism, idealism, positivism, existentialism, humanism—and the virtually endless "isms" that have invaded our academic vocabularies—is that of sorting out the formative historical influences that have conspired to produce them. This approach has never been all that successful in dealing with the standard fare of "isms." It may even be less promising for coming to terms with postmodernism. This is the case, first of all, because the particular historical figures referenced in the literature on postmodernism are as variegated in their discourses as are the portraits that emerge among the multiple disciplinary/departmental genres and practices.

Nietzsche and Heidegger may be the most commonly referenced architects of postmodernism. But even a cursory acquaintance with their thought makes it quite clear that there is no unified discourse that binds their philosophical ruminations. Also, it can be quickly discerned that the response to Heidegger has patterned itself along the lines of right-wing and left-wing developments. Gadamer, as a representative of right-wing Heideggerians, emphasizes the continuity of tradition and the requirement for a universal hermeneutics. Derrida, chief of the left-wing Heideggerians, radicalizes Heidegger's performance of an *Abbau* into a more accentuated strategy of deconstruction that leaves in its wake no tradition to be repeated and reclaimed.

There are other notables, alleged to have had a formative influence on postmodernism, who gain recognition from time to time. One interpreter situates John Dewey as "a postmodernist before his time."[4] Another author is of the mind that Ludwig Wittgenstein "became our greatest postmodernist philosopher after having authored the most exquisite masterpiece of modernist philosophy."[5]

It thus becomes readily evident that the precursors and propounders of postmodernism comprise a somewhat variegated collection. Nietzsche

3. *Postmodernist Culture*, p. 10. "Instead of asking, what is postmodernism?, we should ask, where, how and why does the discourse of postmodernism flourish?, what is at stake in its debates?, who do they address and how?" Ibid.
4. Richard Rorty, "Postmodernist Bourgeois Liberalism," in *Hermeneutics and Praxis*, ed. Robert Hollinger (Notre Dame: University of Notre Dame Press, 1985), p. 219.
5. Richard Shusterman, " 'Ethics and Aesthetics Are One': Postmodernism's Ethics of Taste," in Shapiro, ed., *After the Future: Postmodern Times and Places*, p. 115.

and Heidegger, Dewey and Wittgenstein, are alleged to have had a hand in its formation. Add to this list the likes of Marx and Freud, or more specifically their neo-Marxian and neo-Freudian interpreters, and the base of the historically informative influences on postmodernism continues to expand. This of course is not to deny that the members of this somewhat heterogeneous group in different ways made contributions to the ethos of postmodernity, but it does point up the difficulty of locating a continuum of historical influences.

The situation does not change much when one moves to the more current exemplars of postmodern discourse. The thought of Lyotard would appear to comprise a fairly clear-cut case, and it may well be that in the field of philosophy he more than anyone else is responsible for giving "the postmodern" the currency that it presently enjoys. Deleuze, Guattari, and Baudrillard too give notice in their writings that they would not resist the postmodernist label. Also the French feminists, particularly Julia Kristeva and Luce Irigaray, with their concerns about the marginality of the feminine, can be linked with postmodern critical discourse. But even among these no consistent pattern of themes emerges. And matters become somewhat disconcerting when one invites Foucault into the company of postmodernists—and clearly there are those who believe that that is where he belongs. In an interview with Gerard Raulet, Foucault was asked to respond to the issue of postmodernity and quite straightforwardly replied: "What are we calling postmodernity? I'm not up to date."[6]

Any identification of a common set of concerns, uniformity of discourse, or historical self-understanding in postmodernism thus continues to elude us. How is postmodernism similar to and how is it different from the other competing "isms" that have appeared in earlier and recent times? It would be helpful to know this. Yet, an imaginary interlocutor might raise an objection to our very question, in that it presupposes some species of commonality and consensus in the self-understanding of postmodernism, which would then secure for it a differentiating form and a historical periodization. Such presuppositions, our imaginary interlocutor might remark, are simply unwarranted. After all, does not postmodern discourse celebrate dissensus rather than consensus, difference rather than sameness, heterogeneity rather than solidarity? How can such congeal into a common platform of concerns, a confluence of discursive strategies that make up a movement or historical period? Indeed, according to at least one commentator it is precisely such periodization of human thought and practice that is called into question by the postmodernists, requiring that we view postmodernism as roughly synonymous with "postperiodization."[7]

6. Michel Foucault, *Politics, Philosophy, Culture: Interviews and Other Writings 1977–1984*, ed. Lawrence D. Kritzman (London: Routledge, Chapman, & Hall, 1988), p. 33.
7. Such is the view expressed by Gary Shapiro when he writes: "Postmodernism is engaged in a difficult and ambitious struggle with the project of periodization. It might be more aptly if barbarously named postperiodization. Such a term, a deliberate oxymoron, would have

The refusal to be defined by historical influences and categories of periodicity has some direct consequences for the postmodernist attitude toward the uses and *non*-uses of history. We will need to examine some of these consequences in our subsequent discussion of the "new historicism" of postmodernism. At this juncture, however, it is sufficient to recognize that postmodernists are not unaware of the need to ascribe some intelligibility to the "post" in postmodernism. Lyotard is surely a case in point, having duly informed us that the postmodern remains a part of the modern and that it is indeed modernism in its nascent state.[8] It is thus that the discourse of modernity remains within the web of the discourse of postmodernity. Wolfgang Welsch has made an effort to put a face on this peculiar intertextuality of the modern and the postmodern by suggesting that "postmodern" be properly construed neither as "trans-modern" nor as "anti-modern" but rather as a radicalization of the modern *(radikal-modern)*.[9] This proposal may indeed get us as far as any, particularly with regard to the somewhat tenuous role of historical understanding in the discourse of postmodernity.

Recognizing the formidable obstacles along the path of exploring the terrain of postmodernism, we will attend to certain portions of philosophical discourse, situated within the space between modernity and postmodernity, in an effort to determine how the purported radicalization plays itself out. Possibly the most for which one can hope is the recognition of certain family resemblances that obtain in the recurring topics and strategies of postmodern discourse. We will focus principally on the philosophical twists and turns in the postmodern effort to radicalize the modern, as this effects a philosophical challenge that may be difficult to avoid. If our response to this challenge indeed leads us to the "end of philosophy," as has been proclaimed by some, then we will at least have arrived at this result by going *through* it. At this stage of our discussion, however, it would be premature to speculate.

THE DESPISED LOGOS

The discourse of Occidental science and philosophy is a discourse deeply entrenched in the grammar and the concept of the logos. This most an-

the virtue of suggesting that what is at issue are alternatives to the sequential, developmental, and unitary emplotments of modern consciousness." *After the Future: Postmodern Times and Places*, p. xiii.

8. Jean-François Lyotard, *The Postmodern Condition: A Report on Knowledge*, trans. Geoff Bennington and Brian Massumi (Minneapolis: University of Minnesota Press, 1984), p. 79.

9. "In Wahrheit jedoch ist, was unter 'Postmoderne' sinnvoll zu verstehen ist, weder eine Trans-Moderne noch eine Anti-Moderne. Es handelt sich vielmehr gerade um Einlösungsformen spezifisch moderner Gehalte. Die Postmoderne ist—vorgreifend und pauschal gesagt—zwar nachneuzeitlich, aber keineswegs post-modern, sondern radikal-modern. In ihr kommt es zur exoterischen Einlösung der einst esoterischen Gehalte der Moderne." Wolfgang Welsch, "Vielheit ohne Einheit? Zum gegenwärtigen Spektrum der philosophischen Diskussion um die 'Postmoderne.' Französische, italienische, amerikanische, deutsche Aspekte." *Philosophisches Jahrbuch* 94 (1987): p. 111.

cient concept of Greek culture, which played such a decisive role in Greek philosophy, continued to inform the grammar and the self-understanding of knowledge pursuits throughout the medieval period and well into the modern. Along the way it charted a multidisciplinary map of knowledge ranging from the study of the physical and chemical properties of inert substances (mineralogy) to speculations about the existence and nature of divine substance (theology). In this progressive disciplinization the grammar and conceptuality of the logos became ubiquitous and pervasive. All knowledge endeavors were seen as expressions of an encompassing networking of the logos.

This disciplinization of the logos comprised efforts to take up the slack in the rich polysemy of the ancient Greek concept in the interests of methodological design. In advance of such disciplinization, the Greek concept of the logos remained open to a multiplicity of senses and usages, including logos as utterance, conversation, oration, rendering an account through a story, measure, proportion, general principle or rule, argument, and definition.[10] In the development of Greek philosophy these senses became illustrative of the binding rationality that united the human soul with the cosmos. It is this that Gadamer has aptly named the "grand hypothesis of Greek philosophy," addressing rationality as "not first and foremost a property of human self-consciousness but of being itself," whereby "human reason is far more appropriately thought of as a part of this rationality instead of as the self-consciousness that knows itself over against an external totality."[11] Within such a scheme of things rationality is accorded an explicit ontological determination. The human mind is rational insofar as it participates in the rational structure of the cosmos. The logos articulates the bonding of the human mind with reality.

The slide of this ontological construal of rationality into technical/methodological rationality, the shift from logos to logic, illustrates a dominant mark of modernity. Ontological rationality becomes transmuted into "scientific rationality," in which concerns about method, measurement, algorithmic formalization, and effective prediction and control become uppermost. Hegel's grandiose effort to rechart the course of ontological reason notwithstanding, the tendencies in modernity toward a universalization of technical and scientific reason, in the guise of a *mathesis universalis*, moved steadily onward and congealed into what came to be called variously "positivism" or "scientism." Modernity's central problematic of the differentiation of the culture-spheres of science, morality, and art received a putative resolution by investing scientific rationality with an uncontested sovereignty.

10. W. K. C. Guthrie has provided a detailing of these senses of the logos as they came to prominence during the fifth century of ancient Greece. See *A History of Greek Philosophy*, Volume I (Cambridge: Cambridge University Press, 1962), pp. 419–24.
11. Hans-Georg Gadamer, *Reason in the Age of Science*, trans. Frederick G. Lawrence (Cambridge, MA: The MIT Press, 1981), p. 81.

It is against this backdrop of an encroaching *mathesis universalis* that the contribution of Husserl's epochal work, *The Crisis of the European Sciences and Transcendental Phenomenology*, needs to be assessed. Husserl's central argument in this work was that the positivistic ideal of rationality has brought us into a veritable crisis situation, in which the concrete intentionality of our everyday praxis-oriented preoccupations has become occluded by a stultifying objectivism. This objectivism has eviscerated not only the content of our moral and artistic concerns but the body of scientific knowledge itself, severing the abstracted results of scientific inquiry from their source in the pre-theoretical, doxic perceptions and cultural practices that make up our quotidian lifeworld. He set his project in *The Crisis* as that of disavowing the hegemony of scientific rationality and its accompanying objectivism through a recovery of the concrete, functioning (*fungierende*) intentionality that is operative in the lived-through, intersubjective understanding of everyday life. He flagged this project as "a return to the lifeworld" (*Rückgang auf die Lebenswelt*). This return and recovery yielded a reinstatement of the orientation toward understanding in the realm of *doxa*. In a piquant passage Husserl characterizes the ethos of modern scientific rationality as tributary to the aegis of "the despised doxa" (*die verächtliche Färbung der δόξα*).[12]

Husserl's request for a revitalization of doxa received an unexpected response by the philosophical contingent of postmodernism. Subjected to a serendipitous radicalization, Husserl's problematic was turned back upon itself, shifting the scene from that of a "despised doxa" to a *despised logos*. Postmodernism has indeed remedied the disparagement of doxic discourse, but only at the expense of scuttling the logos. We thus move from the despised doxa of modernity to the despised logos of postmodernity—and it may well be that in this move the proverbial baby has been pitched out with the proverbial bath water.

It clearly is the case that the radicalized return to doxa illustrated by postmodernity outstrips Husserl's philosophical intentions. In his attack on the hegemony of scientific rationality Husserl never so much as intimated the abandoning of the resources of reason. Indeed, his aim was precisely that of rescuing reason from its rationalistic/scientistic distortions by reminding us of its origins in a concrete lifeworld.[13] Postmodernists, however, find Husserl's project of recovery flawed and ineffectual, ensnared within aporias of rational reconstruction.

A rather explicit disenchantment with any efforts to reactivate an interest in rational reconstruction surfaces in Lyotard's consummate assessment that we have no guide other than that of opinion (*doxa*). "There is no politics of reason neither in the sense of a totalizing reason nor in that

---

12. Edmund Husserl, *Die Krisis der europäischen Wissenschaften und die transzendentale Phänomenologie*, ed. Walter Biemel (The Hague: Martinus Nijhoff, 1954), p. 127.
13. See particularly Husserl's essay "The Origin of Geometry," included as Appendix III in the Biemel edition of *Die Krisis*, pp. 365–86.

of the concept. And so we must do with a politics of opinion."[14] Even
more to the point is Lyotard's direct assault on the logos as the main-
spring of theory and critique. The linkage of theory and critique, which
provided the platform of modern rationalism, is for Lyotard the implaca-
ble bugbear that needs to be dispelled. The function of theory is not only
to provide a rational comprehension but also to criticize, to question, and
to overturn. The battle for reason becomes a fight for consistency and
commensurability, the adjudication of differences, and the unification of
diversities. But this battle can never be won because the presupposed
logos principle always offers more than it can deliver. It thus remains
useless—it gets us nowhere; and this state of affairs obtains because "such
a battle is still a battle for reason, for unity, for the unification of diversities, a quibbling battle which no one can win for the winner is already
and has always been reason."[15]

Lyotard's broadside against the uses of reason in the service of theory
construction is reinforced by his ruminations on the uses and misuses of
narrative set forth in his postmodernist manifesto, *The Postmodern Condition*. This manifesto, unlike that of Marx and Engels, calls for a rally by
storytellers rather than workers—and more specifically, storytellers who
relate little narratives (*petits récits*) rather than grand narratives, local narratives instead of metanarratives. The coefficient of gain is that in doing
so we have nothing to lose but our metanarrational chains. What is more
specifically at issue here are the metanarratives of modern philosophy
that are intent upon integrating theory and critique within the designs of
a totalizing logos. Although Lyotard's list of such metanarratives is not
complete, he does highlight some of the more consequential ones. The
list includes Hegel's grand narrative of the dialectic of spirit; the emancipatory narrative of the Age of the Enlightenment; the account of the hermeneutic of meaning; and the encompassing story of the creation of
wealth.[16]

A similar challenge to the resources of rationality is posed by Gilles
Deleuze's proclamation of "the bankruptcy of the Logos" and the ensuing
appeal to the "anti-logos" workings of "the literary machine."[17] The literary machine at issue here is principally that illustrated in Proust's *Re-*

14. Jean-François Lyotard and Jean-Loup Thébaud, *Just Gaming*, trans. Wlad Godzich (Minneapolis: University of Minnesota Press, 1985), p. 82. It is important to note, however, that
Lyotard's use and understanding of "opinion" is not that of the Sophists. Indeed, he makes
a point of the need to free opinion "from the overly empirical context that many Sophists
(and even Aristotle) have given to it," and to relate it to Kant's peculiar use of judgment as
"the capability of thinking outside of the concept and outside of habit." Ibid. Although
Lyotard admittedly learned much from the Sophists, it simply will not do to define him as
a member of the clan.
15. Jean-François Lyotard, *Driftworks*, ed. Roger McKeon (New York: Semiotext(e), Inc., 1984),
p. 11.
16. *The Postmodern Condition*, p. xxiii.
17. Gilles Deleuze, *Proust and Signs*, chapter VIII: "Antilogos, or the Literary Machine,"
trans. Richard Howard (New York: George Braziller, 1972), pp. 93–157.

membrance of Things Past, in which, according to Deleuze, the anti-logos posture takes shape as a rupture with Platonic recollection construed as a recovery of stable and invariant essences. The economy of Proustian reminiscence is one of a production of new viewpoints rather than a reproduction of that which is timeless and changeless. In such an economy the classical notion of the logos suffers bankruptcy. There is no atemporal and universal logos to be instantiated. The recollection of stable and unchanging essences gives way to the surge of invention and creation within a flux of becoming. "To remember is to create." [18] To be sure, there are traces of repetition in this dynamic reminiscence as it moves across various viewpoints in the landscape of memory; but these traces follow the lines of difference. There is only a repetition *with difference* and never a repetition *of the same*. With this novel notion of repetition Deleuze is able to provide a new slant on Proustian reminiscence while advancing a new reading of Nietzsche's doctrine of eternal recurrence. [19]

In the case of Deleuze as in the case of Lyotard we are challenged to inquire if the displacement of the logos as an unchanging, atemporal essence, or a totalizing metanarrative, scuttles the logos in all senses imaginable. Does the "bankruptcy of the logos" entail a divestiture of all its previous holdings, or are there some ventures of reason that manage to keep their capital intact? This becomes a particularly pertinent question against the backdrop of the proposal by Deleuze and Guattari for a *nomadology*, which sets "the war machine" in counter-position to "the state apparatus." [20] The war machine illustrates the model of a "nomad science." Nomad science valorizes the traversing of space, movement, becoming, multiplicity, and heterogeneity. Royal or state science yearns for that which is stable, eternal, unitary, and constant. Nomad science is heterarchical and inventive; state science is hierarchical and hegemonic. "The fact is that the two kinds of science have different modes of formalization, as State science continually imposes its forms of sovereignty on the inventions of nomad science." [21]

What interests us at this particular juncture in our statement of the postmodern challenge is the reemergence of the vocabulary of the "logos" and a discourse about "science" after the declared "bankruptcy of the logos." What manner of logos is operative in *nomadology*? What are the scientific features of a *nomad science*? Apparently, what has gone bankrupt is the logos of the state apparatus, but not the logos of the war machine. What has gone awry is the hegemonic science of royal or state imperatives, but not the nomadic science of movement and becoming. Whither the logos after its dehegemonization?

18. *Proust and Signs*, p. 99.
19. Gilles Deleuze, *Différence et répétition* (Paris: Presses Universitaires de France, 1968).
20. Gilles Deleuze and Félix Guattari, *A Thousand Plateaus: Capitalism and Schizophrenia*, trans. Brian Massumi (Minneapolis: University of Minnesota Press, 1987). See particularly chapter 12, "1227: Treatise on Nomadology:—The War Machine," pp. 351–423.
21. *A Thousand Plateaus*, p. 362.

A similar sort of challenge follows in the wake of Derrida's assault on "logocentrism." Here too we find that a dissemination of the logos as "centric" does not entail a jettisoning of the grammar of the logos per se. Indeed, Derrida's attack on logocentrism is launched from a platform of "grammatology," the strategy of which is detailed in a rather massive 354-page discourse, *Of Grammatology*.[22] What is learned from this remarkable volume is a lesson in deconstruction as both an art of writing and reading. Grammatology is a form of writing that deconstructs the semiotic constraints of the signifier/signified dyad and opens the text to a multiplicity of meanings, in turn requiring of the reader that she or he approach the text in such a way as to avoid closure and the reduction of its contents to a central meaning, idea, or theme. It is thus that grammatology, the logos of writing (*écriture*), does battle with logocentrism—which has its sights firmly fixed on an underlying and centralized idea or conceptual scheme. The logos, despised as a centralizing agency, is allowed to reenter the scene of writing. Now the effect of such an entwined deconstruction and reutilization of the logos upon the fate of rationality would appear to remain moot. In a passage, not entirely free of ambiguity, Derrida puts the matter as follows:

> The "rationality"—but perhaps that word should be abandoned for reasons that will appear at the end of this sentence—which governs a writing thus enlarged and radicalized, no longer issues from a logos. Further, it inaugurates the destruction, not the demolition but the de-sedimentation, the deconstruction, of all the significations that have their source in that of the logos.[23]

The main difficulty resides in pinning down the logos that falls under indictment, the logos as the source of significations, the logos that congeals into "logocentrism." This indicted logos is apparently the one that has stood in the service of classical metaphysics and modern epistemology—the logos modeled after the spoken word, representing that which is present in speech, congealing into a phonocentrism. The logocentrism of the tradition, both classical and modern, appears in the form of a phonocentrism. All of this is undermined by the deconstructionist strategy of grammatology. Yet, as we have observed, grammatology displays its own logos—its own radicalized rationality—and we are again challenged to inquire how it stands with such a refigured logos and radicalized rationality.

In this section we have begun to sketch our portrait of the postmodern challenge by attending to what we have named "the despised logos." We have made an effort to specify what is at issue in this feature of our por-

22. Jacques Derrida, *Of Grammatology*, trans. G. C. Spivak (Baltimore: Johns Hopkins University Press, 1974).
23. *Of Grammatology*, p. 10.

trait by highlighting Derrida's assault on logocentrism; Deleuze's declaration of the bankruptcy of the logos; and Lyotard's proposed substitu-
tion of a politics of opinion for a politics of reason. That the consummate
contributions of these three representatives of postmodernism may not be
cut from the same cloth need not concern us at this point. What is apt,
however, is that all three illustrate "the despised logos" motif. Derrida
exemplifies the motif through his strategy of deconstruction, which de-
centralizes the determinations of meaning and the claims of reason. Deleuze (and Guattari) get at it via a celebration of the anti-logos of nomadic
becoming. Lyotard addresses the theme in his radicalization of doxa, in
his accentuation of the heterogeneity of our language games, and in his
recommendation for incredulity toward metanarratives. Pretty much in
concert, we are advised to have done with classical and modernist overarching metaphysical designs and unifying epistemological principles that
purport to tell the whole truth and nothing but the truth about our insertion in the world. The question that remains is whether after such a radical overhaul of our traditional philosophical habits of thought there is
indeed any truth left to tell.

UNDECIDABILITY AND INDETERMINACY

The disparagement of the traditional concept of the logos in postmodernism proceeds hand in glove with a problematization of modern theories
of meaning and reference. To write the history of modern philosophy is
to write about issues of meaning and reference. Preoccupations with these
topics have been particularly pronounced in the continental tradition from
Kant to Husserl and in the Anglo-American tradition from the British em-
piricists to Russell. The representatives of these traditions have been particularly concerned to analyze conditions and structures of meaning and
to secure the referents of our discourse. The continuing preoccupation
with these issues in modernity was a quite natural consequence of the
epistemological turn inaugurated by Descartes. If the epistemological paradigm indeed provided the touchstone for modern philosophy, then one
ought not be surprised at the studied attention given to meaning and
reference. Inquiring minds will want to know *what* our discourse means,
and they will want to determine the *that* to which it refers.

One of the dominant features of the postmodern philosophical challenge resides in its reaction against the epistemological paradigm of modernity. The knowledge claims issuing from a Cartesian ego-cogito, the
reflections of a Kantian transcendental ego, and the perceptions of the
sensorial subject of British empiricism have all become problematized. The
quest for epistemic certainty and the search for unimpeachable foundations of knowledge fall under indictment. Indeed the very project of
epistemology, as a *logos* of *epistēmē*, as a rational reconstruction of the

conditions for knowledge, is written off as being philosophically incoherent.

Among those commonly consigned to the postmodernist camp, Richard Rorty has been the most ardent spokesperson for the poverty of epistemology. He finds it difficult to imagine what a rational reconstruction of knowledge would look like, purporting as it does to provide us with a species of "knowledge" about knowledge. Rorty links the epistemological project with a search for foundations that seeks to underwrite the knowledge claims in science, morality, and art—the three culture-spheres of modernity. Such a project, however, is doomed to fail, according to Rorty, principally because it succumbs to the aporias of representationalism. Accurate representations are allegedly made possible by a mind mirroring the structures of reality. But for Rorty both the modern "invention of mind" and the ontological weight ascribed to the metaphor of mirroring remain insufficient for the task and in the end need to be seen as philosophical constructs that have no redeemable cash value. They simply do not help us in deciding what to believe and what to do.

It is mainly because of their disenchantment with the vocabularies of mind, mirroring, and representation that Wittgenstein, Heidegger, and Dewey come off as heroes in Rorty's quite remarkable treatise, *Philosophy and the Mirror of Nature*. All three began their philosophical careers attempting to make philosophy foundational and then came to recognize their earlier efforts as self-deceptive. Against the backdrop of the accomplishments of Wittgenstein, Heidegger, and Dewey, it is recommended by Rorty that we make a move "from epistemology to hermeneutics" and learn to live with a philosophy "without mirrors." [24]

With this move beyond epistemology the fates of meaning and reference appear to be sealed. There no longer is a secure space in which decisions about meaning and determinations of reference can be made. The space that epistemology staked out for its explorations was the space of representation. It was the task of the cognitive subject, the knowing mind, to represent as accurately as possible the objects-as-known. To accomplish this feat, the knower, whose traits were predefined by either Cartesian, transcendental, or empiricistic constructs, was required to search for those privileged representations that provided the most direct access to the known. Depending upon one's philosophical orientation, these privileged representations assumed a variety of forms, including the clear and distinct ideas of Descartes, the a priori categories of Kant, the general ideas of empiricism, the logical forms of Russell, the intuited essences of Husserl, the protocol statements of positivism—and the garden varieties of each of these. The master plan in each of these endeavors was to match the representations with the "objects" as putatively given. In short, the goal of the enterprise was to picture, mirror, or reflect reality via one's

24. Richard Rorty, *Philosophy and the Mirror of Nature* (Princeton: Princeton University Press, 1979).

favorite representation.[25] With this achievement, the problems of meaning and reference would be solved.

The response of postmodernism to the epistemological imperative and its model of representational knowledge has taken the form of a frontal attack. The principal target that is isolated for attack is the postulate of presence as it informs the episteme of re-presentation. Derrida works this out by sparring with his formidable mentor, Edmund Husserl.[26] In Husserl's phenomenological program, meaning is attained by representing (*Vergegenwartigen*) the object-as-meant. According to Derrida, this procedure of representing leads one into an aporia because both the presence of the represented object and the self-presence of the representing subject (the ego as transcendental consciousness) succumb to *différance*—they are perpetually deferred. That which is represented is no longer the object in its originary presence but rather an *idealized* object, which stands in wait for an infinite recall within a multiplicity of changing perspectives. Likewise, the self-presence of the epistemological subject is displaced, no longer determined vis-à-vis its relationship with an object, but now postulated as a peculiar presence-to-itself within an interiority of transcendental subjectivity. It is thus that the claim for presence, which alone can anchor meaning and reference, remains unredeemed. Neither the presence of the object nor the presence of the subject can be secured. The effort of representation to capture presence ends in failure. The epistemological presentation/re-presentation dyad remains caught up in the throes of a circularity of endless deferral.

The shift to language, and more specifically to the semiotic dyad of signifier/signified, does not help matters much. Semiotics is unable to rescue the enterprise of knowledge that epistemology apparently botched. Through the instrumentation of the signifier/signified matrix we have pretty much a repeat performance of what happened in the use of the representation model of classical epistemology. The signifiers of our grammar are simply too lame to identify the properly signified. Not only does the signified escape a fixed determination of reference because of the evident polysemy of our language, the identity of the signifier and the signified is threatened as a result of the facile transportation of the one to the plane of the other. The representative idea can be called upon to function either as signifier or signified, depending upon circumstances.[27] Signifiers and signifieds are thus seen as playing off against each other within a vicious

---

25. For a concentrated discussion of the aporias in such a plan, see *Philosophy and the Mirror of Nature*, chapter IV, "Privileged Representations," pp. 165–212.

26. See particularly Jacques Derrida, *Speech and Phenomena: And Other Essays on Husserl's Theory of Signs*, trans. David B. Allison (Evanston: Northwestern University Press, 1973).

27. Derrida finds that it is particularly in metaphor that this play and exchange of signifier and signified is operative. "Metaphor must therefore be understood as the process of the idea or meaning (of the signified, if one wishes) before being understood as the play of signifiers. The idea is the signified meaning, that which the word expresses. But it is also a sign of the thing, a representation of the object within the mind." *Of Grammatology*, p. 275.

circularity of closure, yielding neither decidable meaning nor determinable reference.

The quandaries about meaning and reference, first occasioned by the epistemological imperative and then continued in the semiotic turn, become intensified in Lyotard's ruminations on the *différend*. Differends are occasioned by disputes in which no criteria for adjudication are available. As such they need to be distinguished from litigations, which are responses to conflict situations in which there is an agreement on the applicability of a rule for resolving the conflict.[28] The proverbial fly in the ointment in attempting to deal with the differend, struggling to bring it under the conditions of litigation, is the recalcitrant heterogeneity of phrase regimens—descriptives, prescriptives, exclamatives, interrogatives, commands, etc. In all these different phrase regimens varying senses are articulated, even though their referents are not signified according to a predetermined rule. Whatever the regimen of a particular phrase, the identity of its sense and the reality of its referent can be determined only in response to the particular question that is at issue in the phrase. "The addressor of an exclamative is not situated with regard to the sense in the same way as the addressor of a descriptive. The addressee of a command is not situated with regard to the addressor and to the referent in the same way as the addressee of an invitation or of a bit of information is."[29] The identity of senses within phrases and their claims for reality are contingent upon the manner in which the addressor and the addressee, speaker and hearer, rhetor and interlocutor, are stationed within the particular discursive situation.

The mistake of the epistemologists of sense and reference, from Frege onward, was their failure to recognize the dependence of sense and reference upon the discursive context and the peculiarities of the addressor/addressee interaction. Different phrase regimens involve different manners of addressing the interlocutor and different responses by the interlocutor to the addressor. This heavy accentuation of context-dependency and heterogeneity of phrase regimens has some far-reaching consequences for the fate of modern theories of meaning and reference. Chief of these is the result that the decision on the identity of meaning and the determination of reference "is not established once and for all. It has to be affirmed 'each time.' "[30] Another consequence is the untranslatability of phrase regimens. "Phrases obeying different regimens are untranslatable into one another."[31] A third result of the heterogeneity and contextuality of phrase regimens—and this may be the most consequential re-

28. "As distinguished from a litigation, a differend [*différend*] would be a case of conflict between (at least) two parties, that cannot be equitably resolved for lack of a rule of judgment applicable to both arguments." Jean-François Lyotard, *The Differend: Phrases in Dispute*, trans. Georges Van Den Abbeele (Minneapolis: University of Minnesota Press, 1988), p. xi.
29. *The Differend*, p. 49.
30. *The Differend*, p. 43.
31. *The Differend*, p. 48.

sult of all—is the undermining of the telos of litigation and its appetition for consensus. "This heterogeneity, for lack of a common idiom, makes consensus impossible."[32]

Lyotard's radicalization of the ventures of meaning and reference against the backdrop of his philosophy of the differend undercuts not only the modern epistemological doctrine of representation but hermeneutical theories of meaning as well. In *The Postmodern Condition* Lyotard flags "the hermeneutics of meaning" as one of the metanarratives (along with those of the dialetical idealism of Hegel, the materialism of Marx, the rationalism of the Enlightenment ideal of emancipation, and the individualism of capitalism) that has become subject to our incredulity.[33] Although it is not all that clear who the specific targets of Lyotard's attack on the hermeneutics of meaning are, the motivation of his attack is clear enough. As one cannot arrive at stable, self-identical meanings through a strategy of representation, so also one cannot deliver invariant and transcultural meanings by working one's way through layers of interpretation so as to arrive at rock bottom. Interpretations are as undecidable as are representational ideas. There is no interpretation that can be picked out as the correct one. It all depends upon what language game one is playing at the time, how our phrase regimens are constituted, which story one purports to tell. The specter that lurks in the background of all this is that of a hermeneutical anarchy and relativism. If all interpretations are localized, irremediably context-dependent, and each has an equal claim to thrive, any determinations of correct or incorrect or better or worse (to say nothing of true or false) interpretations exceed the limits of our discourse.

The challenge herewith posed to a hermeneutic of meaning requires an investigation of the many faces of Hermes from Aristotle's *Peri hermēneias* to Gadamer's *Truth and Method*—and beyond. The history of hermeneutics from its Greek origins to its contemporary expressions is not that of a serene and untroubled unfolding. Aristotle's hermeneutics is significantly different from that of the moderns, and within the modern period itself a variety of interpretive practices were set forth. During much of its life in the modern period hermeneutics remained under the influence of *Erkenntnistheorie* and borrowed rather freely from the more popular epistemological models that happened to be around. Schleiermacher aligned hermeneutics with a romanticist version of understanding, construed as a divination of the thoughts in the mind of an author by way of empathic identification. Dilthey, as is well known, was unable to suppress his enchantment with Kant's definition of the problem of knowledge. For both Schleiermacher and Dilthey, hermeneutics came to be understood principally as a method of reconstruction. In the case of Schleiermacher it was viewed as a method for reconstructing the meaning of a text by gaining entrance to the life and intentions of the author. In

32. *The Differend*, p. 55.
33. *The Postmodern Condition*, pp. xxiii–xxiv.

the case of Dilthey the range of the project of reconstruction was somewhat broader, geared to an excavation of meanings behind their textual
expressions, embedded within the various cultural forms of human existence.

The agenda, sometimes hidden and sometimes explicit, in this figuration of hermeneutics as a method was that of securing a space for the
human sciences *(Geisteswissenschaften)* as distinct from that of the natural
sciences *(Naturwissenschaften)*. This agenda became explicit in the thought
of Dilthey, who sought to secure a methodological foundation for the
human sciences in an operation of understanding *(Verstehen)* that parted
company with the explanatory procedures of the natural sciences. Whereas
nature is subject to explanation, human culture is amenable to understanding. Yet, Dilthey's concerns with method invited a borrowing from
the epistemological constructs that informed the apparently successful
ventures in the special sciences of nature. It was thus that the modern
epistemological imperative continued to inform the hermeneutical project, providing it with a measure of objectivity in its interpretive understanding. In seeking to locate the target of Lyotard's assault on "the hermeneutics of meaning" as a grand narrative, it may well be that it is this
particular species of reconstructive hermeneutics, inspired by a Kantian
Erkenntnistheorie and classical German idealism more generally, that he
has in mind.

But reconstructive hermeneutics, either of the Schleiermachian or Dil-
theyian sort, is not the only kind that has been made available to us.
There is also Nietzsche's hermeneutics of suspicion, which undercuts any
methodological-epistemological foundations for interpretation and places
into question any project for the reconstruction of meaning.[34] According
to Nietzsche, a hermeneutics of reconstruction, be it a reconstruction of a
meaning in the mind of an author or the reconstruction of meanings
embedded in the cultural forms of religion, morality, or art, reduces to a
grand cover-up, a hermeneutical Watergate, in which the interplay of power
and desire remain disguised. In its continuing appeals to the notions of
intellect and truth, a hermeneutics of reconstruction engages the intellect,
the "master of deception," in a "planking of concepts," a conceptual construction and reconstruction, that occludes the source of human striving
and endeavor. The intellect forgets that concepts have their origin in a
"primitive world of metaphors" and masks the sensuous apprehension
of self and world. Meaning and truth become reified and objectified, cut
off from their origins in metaphor and drained of their sensuous force.[35]

34. Paul Ricoeur has identified three hermeneutical "masters of suspicion": Nietzsche, Freud,
and Marx. Each, according to Ricoeur, utilized hermeneutics not as a means for restoring
meaning but rather as a strategy for unmasking the power, desire, and exploitation that
escape the vigilance of ordinary consciousness. See *Freud and Philosophy: An Essay on Interpretation*, trans. Denis Savage (New Haven: Yale University Press, 1970).
35. Friedrich Nietzsche, "On Truth and Lies in a Nonmoral Sense," in *Philosophy and Truth:*

Above the din of this dispute between hermeneutical reconstruction-ists and hermeneutical suspicioners, Gadamer, like any postmodernist in good standing, will have no truck with the reconstructionist models of classical hermeneutics and emphasizes the openness of the text, proclaiming that everything we understand, we understand *differently*.[36] Yet, Gadamer is not ready to relinquish all evaluative judgments about the propriety or fittingness of interpretations. Another voice heard above the din is that of Paul Ricoeur, who in effecting a graft of the hermeneutic problem onto the phenomenological method steers a path through the "conflict of interpretations."[37] In a related work, John Caputo has designed a "radical hermeneutics" that combines features of deconstruction and restoration, made possible by a Derridean reading of Heidegger and a Heideggerian reading of Derrida.[38] None of these recent hermeneutical approaches have much to do with an epistemological and representational theory of meaning, nor are they cast in the form of a metanarrative. Yet, the search for a satisfactory perspective on meaning is not cut off at the pass.

It is thus that we encounter another feature of the postmodern challenge to which we will need to respond in the subsequent chapters. Does the postmodern radicalization of the theses of undecidability and indeterminacy disqualify all efforts toward reaching an understanding of meaning and a tracking of reference? Is undecidability total and clean cut, or does it have fuzzy edges, twilight zones where the decidable and the undecidable meet? Does the displacement of epistemological theories of meaning and reference jettison meaning and reference in all manners conceivable? Can meaning and reference be in some fashion refigured, circumventing the aporias of epistemological construction and hermeneutical reconstruction whilst rendering an account of the sense of our communicative practices and providing indicators of that which our discourse and action are about?

PLURALITY AND PARALOGY

A related feature in the postmodern declaration of the bankruptcy of the logos and the dissolution of modern theories of meaning and reference is the concentrated preoccupation with plurality and paralogy. One would not be far afield in defining postmodernism as an inscription of the con-

Selections from Nietzsche's Notebooks of the Early 1870's, ed. Daniel Breazeale (Atlantic Highlands: The Humanities Press, 1979), pp. 86–91.

36. "Not occasionally only, but always, the meaning of a text goes beyond its author. That is why understanding is not merely a reproductive, but always a productive attitude as well. . . . It is enough to say that we understand in a different way, if we understand at all." *Truth and Method* (New York: The Seabury Press, 1975), p. 264.

37. Paul Ricoeur, *The Conflict of Interpretations: Essays in Hermeneutics*, ed. Don Ihde (Evanston: Northwestern University Press, 1974).

38. John Caputo, *Radical Hermeneutics: Repetition, Deconstruction, and the Hermeneutic Project* (Bloomington: Indiana University Press, 1987).

sequences of pluralism. The vocabulary of pluralism has become standard fare in the postmodern literature, used to flag the plurality of signifiers and signifieds, the plurality of language games, the plurality of narratives, and the plurality of social practices. Plurality, it is attested, infiltrates our grammar, our concept formation, our social attitudes, our principles of justice, and our institutions. Veritably, plurality appears to have become a global phenomenon of postmodern life.

Students of the history of American culture and philosophy may be a bit puzzled about this postmodern celebration of pluralism, as though it marked the advent of something profoundly innovative or radically new. They would be inclined to point out that plurality, diversity, and heterogeneity have characterized American culture from its very beginnings. American society has been able to accommodate a multiplicity of races and ethnic groups, religious persuasions, and political institutions. Throughout its history it has unfolded as a veritable laboratory for experimentation with different modes of thought and different styles of life. Plurality and heterogeneity have been indigenous features of the American experience. Indeed, one might get significant mileage from the claim that *difference* has been for some time the distinguishing character trait of American culture. So what is all the noise about?

The role that American philosophy has played in the theater of pluralism—whether as a central character or as a stage manager behind the scenes—needs to be given some consideration. The fact that William James, one of the deans of classical American philosophy, chose to title one of his more influential works "A Pluralistic Universe" would seem to have some relevance to the matter at hand. If no more, it would at least provide an opening for a comparison or even an interface of American pragmatism with postmodernism relative to the nature and consequences of pluralism.

It might be pointed out, however, that the rhetoric of plurality and multiplicity goes back somewhat farther than the arrival of either pragmatism or postmodernism. The pre-Socratics thought profoundly about the problem of the one and the many, which quickly became linked with the problem of permanence and change. The position-taking on these related philosophical concerns congealed into a rather impressive array of competing schools. The Eleatics (Parmenides and Zeno) argued for unity and permanence; the Pythagoreans were the apostles of plurality; and Heraclitus lined up the forces for flux and becoming. Their successors, Empedocles and Anaxagoras, tried to accommodate the seemingly disparate demands for unity and permanence on the one hand and multiplicity and change on the other hand.

Given these achievements of early Greek reflection on unity and plurality, permanence and change, it might be submitted that pragmatism and postmodernism have unwittingly engaged themselves in the reinvention of the wheel. This in itself would not be a decisive criticism, if indeed the wheel that is reinvented is a better one. Whether better or not, there is some evidence that the wheel is different. The inventive thinking of the Greeks issued explicitly from cosmological-metaphysical concerns. The reinventions of pragmatism and postmodernism arise principally from sociopolitical-historical considerations.

This again brings us back to the "end of philosophy" agenda, which is one of the more determinate marks of postmodernity. Although postmodernists beg to differ among themselves about many things, there appears to be a general agreement among them that at least the metaphysical tradition of Occidental philosophy has outworn its usefulness. From Heidegger's "destruction" of the history of Western metaphysics, to Derrida's "deconstruction" of the metaphysics of presence, to Lyotard's indictment of metaphysics as a metanarratology, to Deleuze's portrayal of metaphysics as a solidification of arborescent thinking, this much becomes clear: metaphysics has little to offer for an understanding of our socio-historical inherence in a world of language, labor, and human associations. Although postmodernists may submit different accounts for their disenchantment with metaphysical categories and their binary logic, they all agree that our commerce with the world can proceed jolly well without heavy investments in a metaphysical enterprise.

The ruminations of Gilles Deleuze and Félix Guattari on the matter may be peculiarly apt for initiating the discussion. According to Deleuze and Guattari, metaphysics from its inception has been informed by arboreal metaphors. The "tree of knowledge" metaphor has captivated the minds of metaphysicians particularly from the third century "tree of Porphyry" to Descartes's depiction of metaphysics as the tree roots from which the trunk of physics and the branches of the special sciences issue. The use of this tree root image in devising "grammatical trees" (Chomsky's transformational linguistics) or matrices of binary oppositions (structuralist linguistics) is simply a methodological version of an arborescent metaphysics. The result of this privileging of arborescent metaphors is seen by Deleuze and Guattari as a subordination of multiplicity and difference to unity and totality.

> The tree is already the image of the world, or the root the image of the world-tree. This is the classical book, as noble, signifying, and subjective organic interiority (the strata of the book). . . . But the book as a spiritual reality, the Tree or Root as an image, endlessly develops the law of the One that becomes two, then of the two that become four. . . . This is as much as to say that this system of thought has never reached an understanding of multiplicity.[39]

What the times require, according to Deleuze and Guattari, is the introduction of a new metaphor wherewith to subvert the hegemony of

39. *A Thousand Plateaus*, p. 5.

arborescence. This new metaphor is named "the rhizome." Rhizomes, unlike tree roots, follow no predetermined lines of development and growth. Their potentialities, unlike those of the acorn, are not fulfilled in the organic unity and symmetry of a mature and sturdy oak, but are rather dispersed and dissimulated into a multiplicity of directions and forces. Apparently the unpredictable and serpentine crabgrass has more to teach us about the ways of the world than does the measured unity and stability of the towering oak. We thus seem to be offered a new proverb: "Go to the crabgrass, thou sluggard, consider its ways and be wise!"

The use of the rhizome metaphor to accentuate the play of multiplicity provides to a large extent the binding textuality of *A Thousand Plateaus* by Deleuze and Guattari. Although their plea for multiplicity often approaches a quasi-metaphysical program, granting a privileged ontological status to the multiple, the shift from metaphysical to sociopolitical concerns becomes clear enough. What is principally at issue is the rhizomatic arrangements of our social and institutional practices. The assemblages of our discursive and political practices exhibit a multiplicity of discursive strategies and political lines of force. This does not mean that considerations of unity and totality are straightaway ruled out of court. It means rather that every project of unification and totalization is delimited by the ever present-becoming of multiplicity.

It is in another collaborative endeavor, a series of discussions with Claire Parnet, that Deleuze makes explicit the praxial dimensions of the multiple. "Proclaiming 'Long live the multiple' is not yet doing it, one must do the multiple."[40] A recognition of the rhizomatic becoming of our variegated practices occasions a call to action, a requirement to respond to the effects of multiplicity. The dominant concerns about becoming and multiplicity are no longer metaphysically motivated but issue rather from a recognition of our insertion into a sociopolitical world. It is thus that Deleuze and Parnet are comfortable following Félix Guattari's maxim, "before Being there is politics."[41]

The recognition and accentuation of plurality and multiplicity as indelible marks of the assemblages of our social practices again brings to the fore the question of the consequences of pluralism for the resources of rationality. Concerns about whether indeed reason may still have something to offer become intensified when we observe the slide of plurality and multiplicity into heterogeneity and then into paralogy. It is this facile transition from the multiple to the heterogeneous and the paralogic that requires some attention.

There would appear to be a worrisome categorial inmixing in the discussions of the issues at hand. Consequential distinctions within the as-

40. Gilles Deleuze and Claire Parnet, *Dialogues*, trans. Hugh Tomlinson and Barbara Habberjam (New York: Columbia University Press, 1987), p. 16.
41. *Dialogues*, p. 17.

sembly of these closely related terms tend to be glossed, leaving the impression that they are convertible each into the other. Although plurality and multiplicity are required for heterogeneity, it is surely not the case that every instance of plurality or multiplicity is an instance of heterogeneity, nor does heterogeneity necessarily entail paralogy and its implicatory dissensus. A multiplicity of discursive and nondiscursive practices can be assembled in such a manner that lines of similitude remain operative and a binding of multiple discourses and modes of action remains possible. Dissensus, incommensurability, irretrievable conflicts of interpretation, and hermeneutical nihilism—all of which are features of a strong sense of paralogy—are not necessary consequences of plurality and multiplicity.

It is at this point that the challenge of postmodernism becomes acute. When Lyotard informs us that "consensus is only a particular state of discussion, not its end. Its end, on the contrary, is paralogy,"[42] any claims of reason for the unification of human experience, either from the side of the subject or the side of the object, and any hopes for communicative solidarity, appear to be undermined.

The issues at stake in Lyotard's oblique universalization of paralogy are very much the central ones in the celebrated Lyotard/Habermas dispute concerning consensus and communicative action. Lyotard counters Habermas's project of solving the legitimation crisis through critical discourse by pointing out what he considers to be two flawed presuppositions in Habermas's approach. The one presupposition is that criteria are available for assessing validity claims across the multiple language games. This presupposition, according to Lyotard, simply belies the fact "that language games are heteromorphous, subject to heterogeneous sets of pragmatic rules."[43] The counter-assumption on Lyotard's part appears to be that multiplicity strictly entails heterogeneity. Habermas's second presupposition that Lyotard contests is that the proper goal or aim of discourse is consensus. This presupposition is met with the counterclaim that the "end" of discourse is paralogy, dissensus, incommensurability, and the disclosure of instabilities.

It would be difficult to define the issues separating Habermas and Lyotard more sharply. They are set in terms of antipodal expectations of what discourse as argumentation can achieve and in terms of diametrically opposed views on the nature of language and thought. According to Habermas, even though language is subject to multiple usages it still has the resources to shape up into common discourse; and thought has the power to discern the criteria of universal validity operative in discourse and to liberate it from any bondage to the merely local or situational. For Lyotard the heteromorphous character of our language games

42. *The Postmodern Condition*, pp. 65–66.
43. *The Postmodern Condition*, p. 65.

precludes any common discourse; thought remains bound to particularities; the emancipation ideal of modernity is but another incredulous metanarrative; and consensus "has become an outmoded and suspect value."[44]

The lines of battle that are drawn in this recent Lyotard/Habermas dispute find their traces in the development of modern philosophy going all the way back to Kant, who bequeathed to his successors the task of unifying the three culture-spheres of science, morality, and art—which he left in a somewhat troubled state of differentiation. Habermas is not ready to abandon this inherited problem of modernity, and after seeking to rechart Hegel's wrong turn in addressing this problem he fashions a program of "communicative rationality" that is designed to accommodate the Enlightenment rhetoric of emancipation within the bounds of a new critical theory. This provides Habermas with a standpoint for cultural critique that transcends the particularities of our socio-historical situatedness. Lyotard sees this move on the part of Habermas as little more than a resuscitation of one of the more glaring vagaries of modernity—its appeal to "critique" in the service of cultural criticism. This is a vagary that has dominated particularly the school of "critical theory" from Adorno onward. The "critical relation" that grounds the critical theorists' vision of emancipation suffers entanglement within its own dialectics and remains unable to reach its intended object.

> The critical relation cannot criticize itself, it can only parody itself in the derision of autocritique. And in this impossibility, it shows that it is still an authoritarian dominating relation, that is negativity as power. This power is that of language, which annihilates what it speaks of. Criticism can only redouble the empty space where its discourse plunges its object, it is cloistered in this space of vacuity, it belongs to language and to representation, it can no longer think the object, the work and history, except as language.[45]

This telling passage, a veritable epitaph for critical theory, highlights the Achilles' heel of every project of critique. Criticism is unable to break out of its linguistic cocoon. It remains stuck within the aporia of a representational theory of language, unable to address its object for there is no object for it to represent. It can never move beyond the representational schemata of thesis and antithesis as linguistically constituted. The only power that it has is that of negativity, the annihilating power of language. If we then ask Lyotard how one might extricate oneself from this aporia, we are told that the appropriate recourse is that of "a deployment of libidinal investment."[46] Desire replaces dialogue and intervention stands in for communication. Consensus and solidarity become fugitive ideals, and we are advised to shed our nostalgia for emancipation and live life as a perpetual interregnum.

44. *The Postmodern Condition*, p. 66.
45. Jean-François Lyotard, "Adorno as the Devil," *Telos* 19 (1974): p. 135.
46. "Adorno as the Devil," p. 136.

The challenge of postmodernism at this particular juncture, where one is instructed on the consequences of plurality and paralogy as they pertain to a problematization of the resources for critique, emancipation, and solidarity, motivates us to explore a possible space for dialogue and communication in which criticism can proceed without the underwriting by a theory of critical principles, a representational view of language, and a metanarrative of emancipation. It should be noted that a gesture toward the exploration of such a space has already been made by Richard Rorty in his suggestion for "splitting the difference between Habermas and Lyotard," whereby one would retain a sense of community and solidarity without the backup of metanarratives and epistemological theories of critique.[47]

One may indeed be reluctant to abandon efforts to criticize and assess the social practices that contextualize our thought and action; and one may still place a value on the achievement of mutual understanding. However, such cultural criticism and orientation toward understanding need not make purchases on the modern, theoretico-epistemological, foundationalist project of grounding and justification. In our continuing story we will propose an alternative to the foundationalist and theory-grounded perspective on the claims of reason as we plot a transversal rationality that displays intercalated moments of evaluative discernment, interactive articulation, and incursive disclosure.

POWER AND DESIRE

The rational resources for critique and emancipation are challenged not only by the postmodern celebration of plurality and paralogy but also by the emphasis placed on the insinuation of power and desire. Our education on the latter has been facilitated principally by the contributions of Michel Foucault and Gilles Deleuze. Foucault has sketched for us a politics of power and Deleuze has provided a politics of desire.

Although Foucault has expressed misgivings about being included in the company of postmodernists, he has suffered the fate of such an inclusion principally because of his heavy indebtedness to Nietzsche and Heidegger. "My entire philosophical development," Foucault informed us in his last interview several weeks before his death, "was determined by my reading of Heidegger. I nevertheless recognize that Nietzsche outweighed

47. "One could try to create a new canon—one in which the mark of a 'great philosopher' was awareness of new social and religious and institutional possibililities, as opposed to developing a new dialectical twist in metaphysics or epistemology. That would be a way of splitting the difference between Habermas and Lyotard, of having things both ways. We could agree with Lyotard that we need no more metanarratives, but with Habermas that we need less dryness. We could agree with Lyotard that studies of the communicative competence of a transhistorical subject are of little use in reinforcing our sense of identification with our community, while still insisting on the importance of that sense." Richard Rorty, "Habermas and Lyotard on Postmodernity," in Richard J. Bernstein, ed., *Habermas and Modernity* (Cambridge, MA: The MIT Press, 1985), p. 173.

him."[48] This acknowledgment of a profound Nietzschean influence on his own thought does much to explain his preoccupations with power. Foucault's politics of power is admittedly not simply a French version of Nietzsche's *Wille-zur-Macht*; yet, it was Nietzsche's integration of will and power that provided the backdrop for Foucault's perspective on the linkage of the will to truth with a politics of power.

Deleuze's politics of desire, like Foucault's politics of power, also needs to be contextualized against the backdrop of certain formative influences. Here too Nietzsche plays a decisive role.[49] But there is also Deleuze's spirited conversation with Freud, a veritable *agon*, in which Freud's doctrine of the libido suffers considerable punishment. Deleuze's politics of desire has little in common with the libidinal economy of Freudian psychoanalysis; however, in both cases the claims of reason confronting the insinuation of desire become problematized. We thus encounter a new wrinkle in our effort to respond to the postmodern challenge. How does it stand with rationality in the wake of a recognition of the inroads of power and desire?

Foucault's politics of power provides a portrait of a power/knowledge nexus that pervades our personal and social existence. This sketching of the ubiquity of power relations within the fabric of society approximates a veritable *ontology* of power. No structures of personal and social life escape the predicates of power. The human subject, with its strategies for achieving knowledge, is a *product* of power. Foucault is quite clear about that.

> We should admit rather that power produces knowledge (and not simply by encouraging it because it serves power or by applying it because it is useful); that power and knowledge directly imply one another; that there is no power relation without the correlative constitution of a field of knowledge, nor any knowledge that does not presuppose and constitute at the same time power relations. These 'power-knowledge' relations are to be analyzed, therefore, not on the basis of a subject of knowledge who is or is not free in relation to the power system, but on the contrary, the subject, who knows, the objects to be known and the modalities of knowledge must be regarded as so many effects of these fundamental implications of power-knowledge and their historical transformations.[50]

The power/knowledge nexus thus registers its inscriptions across the whole scene of human endeavor, creating disciplinary regimes or regimes of knowledge that condition and constrain our multiple social and institutional practices. Foucault's principal interest resides in detailing the op-

48. Michel Foucault, "Final Interview," *Raritan: A Quarterly Review* 5, no. 1 (1985): p. 8.
49. See particularly Gilles Deleuze, *Nietzsche and Philosophy*, trans. Hugh Tomlinson (New York: Columbia University Press, 1983).
50. Michel Foucault, *Discipline and Punish: The Birth of the Prison*, trans. Alan Sheridan (New York: Random House, 1979), pp. 27–28.

eration of this nexus in the disciplinary practices of the history of the asylum, the prison, and patterns of sexuality. In his *Discipline and Punish* he is particularly concerned to link the exercise of power and the production of knowledge to a panoptical surveillance and control. He uses Bentham's Panopticon as the decisive architectural symbol and illustration of the inmixing of power and knowledge in a carceral society. The view of the supervisor in the central tower of Bentham's Panopticon is encompassing and constant. He sees but is not seen. The prisoners, on the other hand, are seen but do not see. They are objects for observation and information but never subjects in a communicative interchange. However, the Panopticon is not simply an observation tower. It is also a "laboratory of power" designed to carry out experiments, alter habits, and correct wayward behavior.[51]

What specifically interests Foucault in the surveillance model of Bentham is the virtually indefinite generalizability of the mechanisms of panopticism. "Panopticism is the general principle of a new 'political anatomy' whose object and end are not the relations of sovereignty but the relations of discipline."[52] And "discipline," as understood in this context, is to be "identified neither with an institution nor with an apparatus; it is a type of power, a modality for its exercise, comprising a whole set of instruments, techniques, procedures, levels of application, targets; it is a 'physics' or an 'anatomy' of power, a technology."[53] The levels of application of this physics or anatomy of power, referenced in the above passage, are spread across the domains of military institutions, the police apparatus, clinics and hospitals, religious organizations, and economic and governmental units. Possibly of greatest significance is the extension of the panoptic principle to the micro-practices of everyday life. The networking of the power/knowledge nexus indeed appears to be global and pervasive.

Numerous challenges addressed to more traditional views of reason surface in Foucault's politics of power. If the logos is itself an effect of power, then any appeal to theory for a comprehension and management of the constraints of power would become useless. If the rational subject is a product rather than an agent of power, then the grammar of autonomy and emancipation is deprived of any significant function. If everything, from our specialized disciplines of knowledge to our pre-reflective everyday practices, is imbued with power, there is neither resource nor standpoint to combat the specter of ideology that always hovers over the power relations in a given society. If no rational discernment of the forms and uses of power is available to us, any distinctions between power, domination, oppression, and violence would seem to be imperiled.

To this list of challenges, already quite considerable, one might add

51. *Discipline and Punish*, p. 204.
52. *Discipline and Punish*, p. 208.
53. *Discipline and Punish*, p. 215.

yet another—one pertaining to the disciplinary maneuvers that define our institutions of higher learning. Although Foucault has chosen to focus primarily on the insinuation of power in the disciplinary practices within the history of the asylum, the prison, and sexuality, the implications of all this for the modern/postmodern university are plain enough to see.[54]

We are disposed to define our centers of learning as localities where reason resides and where the discovery and communication of knowledge comprise the central task. Yet, what is often overlooked is the degree to which these citadels of knowledge are subject to the play of power relations. The constellations of power in the life of the university are most clearly discernible in its organization as a separation and intended balance of power invested in the deliberating bodies of administration, faculty, clerical staff, and students. The much-cited arenas and forms of conflict—disputes between faculty and administration; the formulation and exercise of hiring and firing policies; decisions on tenure and promotion; territorialization in curriculum design; and the affirmation of departmental autonomy and authority—are concrete institutional expressions of an explicit and pervasive power nexus in the governance of the university.

There is, however, a more subtle and less explicit expression of power in the knowledge business. This involves the very definition, consolidation, distribution, and valuation of knowledge. Knowledge is defined along the lines of disciplinary matrices and regimes—schools, departments, areas of concentration—that function as political units with their designated seats of authority, prescribed techniques, and systems of rewards and punishments. This regimentation of knowledge receives expression in the canonization of selected texts and in the legitimation of certain investigatory procedures. Certain texts and procedures become "authoritative" while other texts and procedures are marginalized or indeed outlawed. Often this leads to situations in which local narratives about gender, race, minorities, and non-Western modes of life are relegated to the margins of academic discourse.

The postmodern challenge to the present-day university is that of recognizing the play of power in the disciplinary practices and the regimentation of knowledge operative in academe. As this regimentation continues to make purchases on logocentric principles of totalization, formalization, unity of discourse, and hierarchical structuring, one can

---

54. Some of the implications of the assorted power relations that govern the contemporary American university have been addressed by Bruce Wilshire in his recent book, *The Moral Collapse of the University: Professionalism, Purity, and Alienation* (Albany: State University of New York Press, 1990). Taking as his guiding theme the threats of academic professionalism, Wilshire demonstrates, with the help of illuminating cases, the effects of the insinuation of power for the segmentation, excessive specialization, and self-isolation of technical vocabularies. This he sees as being accompanied by rites of purification and exclusion that lead to an alienation among faculty and students alike, producing a profound loss of personal and institutional self-identity.

read the postmodern challenge as an invitation to engage in a subversive intervention. The very idea of a *uni*-versity as an unbroken solidarity of unified discourse becomes problematized and is challenged by a *pluri*-versity of knowledge practices. But this challenge presupposes that there are resources for discerning the *misuse* of power in the academy, bent toward the establishment of hierarchically ordered regimes of marginalization, and we again return to our question concerning the role of reason as critical discernment and normative assessment.

It would surely be premature to characterize Foucault's consummate project as a facile bidding farewell to the logos, a simple identification of power and knowledge, and a glossing of the distinction between power and domination. In *Discipline and Punish* Foucault is concerned to avoid a reduction of either power to knowledge or knowledge to power; rather "the formation of knowledge and the increase of power regularly reinforce one another in a circular process."[55] In the interview "The Ethic of the Care for the Self as a Practice of Freedom," Foucault cleared the record on the distinction between power and domination: "One cannot impute to me the idea that power is a system of domination which controls everything and which leaves no room for freedom."[56] In this same interview he speaks of a political and ethical subject, attuned to a Socratic-like imperative: "Care for yourself," an imperative involving "the assimilation of *logoi*."[57]

It is thus that there are hints of a reclaimed logos and a resituated subjectivity in the wake of Foucault's assault on a totalizing and hierarchical rationality. Clearly, Foucault will have no truck with logocentrism and its epistemological privileging of the ocular in a panoptic construal of knowledge. Yet it remains a moot question as to what figuration/refiguration of the logos remains intact in his *genealogy*. A tracking of the genesis of our discursive and political practices could hardly proceed effectively without some rational capacities for discerning the various constellations produced by the power/knowledge nexus. Also, we have noted the emergence of certain ethical imperatives in Foucault's "care for the self" project, indicating that genealogy may have normative resources wherewith to critique the constellations of power that slide into domination and oppression. Contrary to some interpreters, the vocabulary of critique, emancipation, and creative self-formation may not be all that foreign to Foucault's thought.[58] Admittedly, the place and function of critique in

---

55. *Discipline and Punish*, p. 224.
56. *The Final Foucault*, ed. James Bernauer and David Rasmussen (Cambridge, MA: The MIT Press, 1988), p. 13.
57. *The Final Foucault*, p. 5.
58. Jürgen Habermas, for example, discerns clearly enough the general problem of combining a Foucauldian genealogical approach with normative ethics and social criticism, but he surely overstates the negative facts of the case in his parodic assessment of Foucault's accomplishment. "To the extent that it retreats into the reflectionless objectivity of a nonpar-

genealogy and its possible strategies for achieving emancipation from power under the conditions of domination are somewhat scantily addressed by Foucault. It is not all that clear what resources he has in dealing with these questions. It is undeniable, however, that he has provided the challenge to ask them.

Closely allied with the challenge of finding a place for critique and normative assessment in the midst of the network of power relations embedded within our discursive and institutional practices is the challenge of desire confronting the claims of reason. The body politic of the postmodern world is at once a politics of power and a politics of desire. As Foucault has been the dominant voice regarding the former, Deleuze is the principal spokesperson for the latter. The complementarity of Foucault and Deleuze on the particular points at issue becomes readily discernible. Power slides into desire and desire slides into power. Both Nietzsche and Freud, to whom references in the writings of Foucault and Deleuze abound, recognized this clearly enough. They directed our attention to the ambiguous phenomenon of the entwinement of power and desire, soliciting approaches to the phenomenon either by way of power (Nietzsche) or by way of desire (Freud). Deleuze appropriates this general insight common to both Nietzsche and Freud concerning the power/desire nexus. However, in fleshing out his portrait of humans as desiring machines, assemblages of libidinal rhizomes, Deleuze rather quickly leaves behind the conceptual constructs of Freud's psychoanalytical model.

The first Freudian conceptual prop to go, one that provided considerable support for Freud's metapsychology, is the postulate of unification—the "reduction to the One," the tracing of all constellations of desire back to "a single Father," the sublation of everything into the Oedipal relation—a postulate that remains reminiscent of the royal science and arborescent reflection of modernity.[59] The central issues here boil down to a problematization of the modernist privileging of certain concepts and strategies: royal science over nomad science; unity over multiplicity; arborescent metaphors over rhizomatic metaphors; logos over nomos; the state apparatus over the war machine; the mathematical model over the hydraulic model; the theorematic over the problematic; territorialization over deterritorialization; and the majoritarian principle over minoritarian praxis.[60] Although Freud initially recognized the rhizomatic character of

ticipatory, ascetic description of kaleidoscopically changing practices of power, genealogical historiography emerges from its cocoon as precisely the *presentistic, relativistic, cryptonormative* illusory science that it does not want to be." *The Philosophical Discourse of Modernity,* trans. Frederick Lawrence (Cambridge, MA: The MIT Press, 1987), pp. 275–76.

59. "Freud himself recognizes the multiplicity of libidinal 'currents' that coexist in the Wolf-Man. That makes it all the more surprising that he treats the multiplicities of the unconscious the way he does. For him there will always be a reduction to the One: the little scars, the little holes become subdivisions of the great scar or supreme hole named castration; the wolves become substitutes for a single Father who turns up everywhere, or wherever they put him." *A Thousand Plateaus,* p. 31.

60. *A Thousand Plateaus,* pp. 351–74.

desire, he quickly took refuge in arborescent construction, privileging the former terms in the Deleuzian almanac of polarities and subordinating the latter. This took shape in Freud's theory of psychoanalysis in the guise of the primacy and hegemony of "the complex." "Oedipus, nothing but Oedipus, because it hears nothing and listens to nobody."[61]

The proposed path around the reduction of desire to the category of "the One" and its confinement within the conceptual schemes of royal science moves across the terrain of desire construed as a multiplicity of political-libidinal assemblages. In *Anti-Oedipus* Deleuze and Guattari give an account of desire by utilizing the vocabulary of "desiring machines" and "bodies without organs."[62] The grammar of bodies without organs provides a sheet anchor against any philosophy of subjectivity that is still disposed to search for a principle of individuation within a centered subject. A body without organs is never individuated as *yours* or *mine;* it is an anonymous configuration that extends beyond all nodal points of self-identity. Also, speaking of desiring machines as bodies without organs dissociates desire from an organicism and a holism that understands the libidinal lines of force as gathered up into an organic unity of functioning parts.

In *A Thousand Plateaus* there is a perceptible shift of vocabulary from desiring machines and bodies without organs to that of "assemblages of desire."[63] In this work the notion of assemblage or arrangement *(agence-ment)* is made prominent for articulating the politics of desire. The language of assemblages accents the sociopolitical contextualization of desire and highlights the rhizomatic play of multiplicity in opposition to the unity and totality of the arborescent principle that remained in force in Freudian psychoanalytical theory.

The specific challenge of Deleuze's and Guattari's rhizomatic politics of desire for our general project of reclaiming and refiguring the resources of rationality turns on the question concerning the commerce between reason and desire and the issue of the fate of the Western concept of the logos more generally. Assuredly this question, and the more general issues pertaining to the logos, is reminiscent of Plato, who proposed a resolution to the problem of the relation of reason and desire in his celebrated doctrine of the tripartite soul. The threefold structure of the human soul, according to Plato, afforded a perfect analogy to the tripartite structure of society, whereby the rational part of the soul and the guardian

61. *A Thousand Plateaus*, p. 34.
62. Gilles Deleuze and Félix Guattari, *Anti-Oedipus: Capitalism and Schizophrenia*, trans. Robert Hurley, Mark Seem, and Helen R. Lane (Minneapolis: The University of Minnesota Press, 1983).
63. *A Thousand Plateaus*, pp. 22–23. In their collaborative project, *Dialogues*, Deleuze and Parnet speak of "an assemblage of enunciation" to describe the configurative becomings that characterize the style of conversation and writing (p. 4). The vocabulary of assemblages plays a more central role in Deleuze's later writings, applicable not only to the economy of desire but also to the dynamics of discourse.

class are viewed as correspondingly entrusted with the responsibility of governance in accordance with the four cardinal virtues of wisdom, courage, temperance, and justice. This grand design of the strictly correlative structures of the soul and society under the guidance of a reason informed by a transcendent logos is not much in vogue today, but the questions that Plato asked in designing his republic are still with us—and may indeed be inescapable. Even a deconstruction of Plato's rational psychology and class-structured politics does not displace the question of how it stands with the relation of reason to desire and power.

The challenges of Deleuze's politics of desire and Foucault's politics of power thus intersect at the crossroads of an interrogation of the fate of the logos. There are differences between these challenges, and the differences are of some consequence. Deleuze's nomadology charts a course other than that of Foucault's genealogy. Indeed, Deleuze proclaims that "The rhizome is an antigenealogy . . . a short-term memory, or antimemory."[64] The grammar of genealogy, for Deleuze, still smacks too much of a philosophy of origins and reminiscence. Nomadology apparently has done with all that. But however one sorts out the differences between Foucault's genealogical politics of power and Deleuze's nomadological politics of desire, the point of some interest is that referenced vestiges of the logos remain in both projects. Apparently the logos is still at work *in some fashion* in a genealogy as well as in a nomadology.

The question remains: "In what fashion is the logos at work in a genealogy and in a nomadology"? Admittedly, we can be satisfied that for Foucault and Deleuze the logos as a logocentric principle of unification and totalization is out. This sense of the logos is disallowed in Foucault's close association of knowledge and power and in Deleuze's valorization of multiplicity and libidinal assemblages. Yet, the displacement of this sense of the logos does not entail a jettisoning of the logos in every sense you please. We are of the mind that both Foucault and Deleuze might well accede to this assessment. But they appear to be reluctant to go public on this matter. They thus challenge us to tease out from their texts, albeit through some species of subversive reading, an acknowledgment of the fortunes of rationality in the aftermath of their assaults on logocentrism.

A NEW HISTORICISM

Historicism was one of the principal consequences of modernity, coming to maturity during the latter part of the nineteenth century. The conceptual framework of historicism was informed by specific attitudes toward the three dimensions of time. The attitude toward the past was one of theoretical detachment, and the motivation for a study of the past was

64. *A Thousand Plateaus*, p. 21.

that of describing and explaining historical events as they actually occurred. The past was viewed as a fertile field for historical research, and
the implied requirement was that of an objective determination of historical fact. The attitude toward the future was one of unbridled optimism,
nurtured by a profound faith in the resources of science and technology
to deliver us from all social ills. Predictability and progressivism were
linked and virtually accepted as axiomatic, congealing into a vision of the
perfectibility of human potential. The attitude toward the present was
that of a happy relativism, a relativism without anxiety or *Weltschmertz*.
Although there were no obliging claims forthcoming from morality, religion, or art, this was of no concern because the capital of science and
technology, coupled with the inevitable perfectibility of humanity, would
see that things worked out in the end. The "heavenly city of the eighteenth-century philosophers" would soon become an empirico-historical
reality.[65]

The historicism of modernity was thus informed by a set of rather
specific attitudes toward the three modes of temporality and by accompanying procedures and goals for historical investigations. Jean Baudrillard, in his contribution to the recent edition of the French *Encyclopaedia
universalis*, writing on the topic of *"Modernité,"* unpacks three character-
izing features or dimensions of the modern concept of time. He names
these the *chronometric, linear,* and *historic* dimensions, respectively.[66] The
chronometric dimension provides the matrix for a quantitative measurement of time. The linear dimension fixes time as an irreversible succession of instants moving across a continuum of past, present, and future.
The historic dimension, which Baudrillard sees as providing the dominant expression of the modern concept of time particularly since Hegel,
portrays time as a dialectical becoming that actualizes the potentialities of
a beginning in a consummatory end.

It was the imprint of the historic dimension of time that directed the
gaze of modernity to the future and to the envisionment of perfectibility.
However, according to Baudrillard, the workings of this historic dimension led to an ironic reversal of the futural intentionality of time, turning
the anticipation of the future into a preoccupation with the present. "After
first privileging the dimension of progress and the future, it seems to
confound itself more and more today with the present, the immediate,
the everyday—the reverse, pure and simple, of historical duration."[67]

The story of the breakup of the historicism of modernity has a number
of overlapping subplots. Nietzsche's philosophy was one of the formative

65. The phrase is that of Carl L. Becker, used as the title for his parodic and witty reflections
on the Age of Reason. See *The Heavenly City of the Eighteenth-Century Philosophers* (New Haven:
Yale University Press, 1932).
66. *Encyclopaedia universalis,* Volume 12 (Paris: Encyclopaedia universalis France, 1985), pp.
424–26. An English translation of Baudrillard's essay by David James Miller appears in the
Canadian Journal of Political and Social Theory 11, no. 3 (1987): pp. 63–72.
67. *Canadian Journal of Political and Social Theory,* p. 66.

factors in the breakup, as also was early and mid-twentieth-century existentialism. In his essay "The Use and Abuse of History," Nietzsche
launched a scathing attack on the pretensions of historicism in its effort
to reconstruct an objectified knowledge of the past, indicting its insensi-
tivity to the creative aspirations of the human spirit. The charge against
historicism in this essay needs to be contextualized against the backdrop
of one of his major philosophical doctrines—the teaching of the eternal
recurrence. It was with this doctrine in particular that Nietzsche was able
to dismantle the chronometric, linear, and progressivistic framework of
the modern historicist use of the past to advance the future.

Nietzsche's dissatisfaction with the historicism of modernity was taken
over and given a new expression in the loosely defined philosophical
platform of existentialism. The central ingredients of the existentialist protest against historicism were its new attitudes toward the three regions of
historical time. The attitude toward the past became that of participatory
involvement and engaged recollection, countermanding the attitude of
objectivity and theoretical detachment that characterized the historicist
approach to the past. The attitude toward the future was tempered with
an anxiety occasioned by the recognition of the contingency and unpredictability of historical developments and trends. The attitude toward the
present took on a stance of commitment, an orientation to action, a pre-
hension of the present as the moment of decision. These three new attitudes toward time in existentialism can be read as a virtual subversion of
the correspondent attitudes of modern historicism. Theoretical detachment from the past is supplanted by participatory involvement; the pre-
dictable progressivism of the future gives way to unpredictability and un-
certainty; and the relativization of all contents of the present is disavowed
by a stance of commitment and a call for decisive action.

Somewhere at the center of the existentialist rejoinder to historicism
was its doctrine of "the existential subject." With this doctrine existentialism was able to express its dissatisfaction with the multiple uses of the
subject in modern philosophy. It problematized the epistemologically insulated thinking subject of Cartesian thought, the abstracted transcendental subject of Kantian philosophy, and the vapid sensorial subject of British
empiricism. However, its assault was leveled more specifically against the
rational world-historical subject of Hegelian idealism. What emerged from
all this was the secured space of a concretely existing subject, shouldered
with the awesome responsibility of constituting itself through the travail
of inner-directed decision and action. Through a rather encompassing
maneuver, both the sovereign epistemological subject and the dialectical-
historical subject of modernity were transmuted into a radically individuated existing subject. The rational consciousness of the modern world-
historical subject became a consciousness of personal crisis.

It was thus that the existential subject, which had already made its
debut in the philosophy of Søren Kierkegaard, provided an alternative to

the subject as the foundation of epistemological reason on the one hand and as the bearer of historical reason on the other hand. Kierkegaard's notion of "infinitely interested passion"; Sartre's privileging of engagement *(engagé)*; Jasper's philosophy of praxial activity *(Handlung)*; and the celebration of resoluteness *(Entschlossenheit)* in the early Heidegger—all collaborated in an assault on the subject of modernity. That there were tendencies toward irrationalism in the existential posture cannot, of course, be denied. Yet, the platforms of its various exponents did not demand a rejection of reason per se, but rather recommended a notion of reason more attuned to the concerns and preoccupations of everyday life.

Along with the philosophy of Nietzsche and the varieties of existentialism there were other voices raised in protest against the postulates of historicism. The philosophy of Karl Popper in England and certain currents of pragmatism in the United States are cases in point. But in addition to the various philosophical rejoinders to historicism there were certain socioeconomic-political events of the early decades of the twentieth century that issued their own indictments of the historicist doctrines of inevitable progress and indefinite perfectibility. A worldwide economic depression, two world wars, the horrors of the Holocaust, and recurrences of famine and deprivation across the globe brought to the world's attention the fact that the indefinite perfectibility of the human species proved to be "indefinite" indeed! The projected historical embodiment of "the heavenly city of the eighteenth-century philosophers" turned out to be a mirage. The realities of our social existence supplied strong indicators that any progressivistic view of human nature is a flirtation with an impending metaphysical disappointment.

Hopefully our brief sketch of the principal features of modern historicism, and the late-modern reaction against it, can provide a working context for addressing some postmodern perspectives on history. We have already proposed that it might be more fruitful to think of postmodernism as a radicalization and retrenchment of modernity (and particularly in conjunction with the late-modern reactions within the modern itself) than as a period of history that comes "after" the modern. It is especially important to keep this in mind as one broaches the issue of the "new historicism" of postmodernity.

It would be relatively easy to spot postmodern affinities with the existentialist revolt against the totalizing rationality of Hegel's metanarrative of the dialectics of Absolute Spirit. Also, postmodernism and existentialism would appear to be on common ground in their shared dissatisfaction with the Cartesian invention of mind and the hegemony of the theoretico-epistemological paradigm. There are similarities between existentialism and the postmodern anti-logos motif. There is a place for minoritarian thought in existentialism and postmodernism alike. Both existentialism and postmodernism are interested in securing a place for discourse about the human emotions. To be sure, Kierkegaardian "passion" is not Deleuzian

"desire" or Lyotardian "libidinal deployment"; yet, there is a commonality of interest in attending to those features of human existence that have
been marginalized by royal science and its obsession with mind and intellect. There is a sense in which existentialism and postmodernism provide a common challenge to the design of our current exploration, namely
that of finding a new slant on the dynamics of reason on the hither side
of the unredeemable promissory notes of modern rationalism.

It would appear, however, that at this point the convergence of existentialism and postmodernism comes to a halt. Postmodernism will have
no truck with the existentialists' resolve to salvage the "existential subject" in the aftermath of the demise of the sovereign rational subject. Not
only the epistemological subject of Cartesianism, the transcendental subject of Kantianism, and the dialectical-historical subject of Hegelianism,
but the subject in pretty much every sense whatever suffers the fate of
erasure. The break with all philosophies of the subject seems to be abrupt
and final. The existential subject goes the way of all the rest. What remains are reactive and active forces, lines of affect and effect, assemblages
of desire, and ensembles of micro-practices. But there is no identifiable
subject from which these reactions and actions, desires, and practices
proceed. It were as though the smiles of Lewis Carroll's Cheshire cat remain, even though the cat itself has disappeared.

As postmodernism problematizes the historical subject, so also does it
problematize the notions of origin and telos that provide the span of historical actualization for the subject. Both archaeology and eschatology become suspect. Each is indicted for failing to have overcome the urge to
provide a unifying perspective and a metanarrational account. Yet, it should
be noted that a peculiar sense of the historical remains after the historical
subject and the determinations of beginning and end have been dissimulated. The Deleuzian assemblages of desire are intrinsically social; Foucault's micro-practices are always situated in political and institutional power
relations; and Lyotard's play of plurality and paralogy is borne by historical circumstances. The effects of socio-historical forces are thus rather
prominently inscribed. As structuralism fell out as a transcendentalism
without a transcendental subject, so postmodernism can be viewed as a
historicism without a historical subject. This defines the "new" historicism of postmodernity.

It might be maintained by some that to speak of historicism without a
historical subject is to speak, at most, of a quasi-historicism. In any case,
to sketch the contours and directions of such a new historicism, be it
quasi or full blown, shoulders the sketcher with certain idiosyncratic obstacles. This is so, not only because it is difficult to conceive of what
history without a subject who undergoes and makes it would look like,
but also because it is not clear how postmodernism comes to terms with
the phenomenon of historical time. It would appear that the displacement
of the historical subject is principally the consequence of postmodern

worries about "presence." A historical subject, either in the mode of acting or being acted upon, would be installed within the interstices of a present, as the centralized locus for centrifugal and centripetal forces. But such a present, according to the lexicon of postmodernism, is perpetually deferred, ever remains fugitive, is always invaded by absence, buffeted by the play of difference.

But if there is no place for presence, what about the past and the future? In short, what is the postmodern attitude toward the three modes of temporality, and how does this attitude differ from that of the historicism of modernity as well as that of the late-modern reaction to it by Nietzsche and by existentialism? Without some sense of presence there can be no vibrant notion of the past and little appreciation for the role of tradition. That postmodernity should register some uneasiness about the past and tradition comes as no surprise, as it is the tradition that has provided a congenial home for logocentrism, royal science, authority, hegemony, and grand narratives. Thus there remains in postmodernism a desire to be traditionless, to stand outside of all traditions and view the play of heterogeneous discourses with an attitude of neutrality if not outright "indifference."

Now if the past is to carry such little weight, then what is one to make of the future? The future within a postmodern scheme of things makes few demands, issues no call for decisive action, and appears to afford little in the way of possibilities for an emancipation from oppressive power relations and distorted communication. As the past is the residuum of authority, hegemony, and ideology, so the future is viewed principally as a projection of utopian dreams and unrealizable ideals. Here the break with the attitudes toward the future, as expressed both by modern historicism and the late-modern reaction against it, becomes pronounced. The postmodern attitude toward the future neither comports a secular eschatology of human perfectibility and inevitable progress nor is inscribed as a call for decision and commitment.

The new historicism of postmodernity devalues both the past and the future in its decentering of the present. At most we are left with an evanescent present, a present pulverized into a "present-becoming." One of the more straightforward pronouncements of the credo of the new historicism has been delivered by Gilles Deleuze and Claire Parnet:

> Future and past don't have much meaning, what counts is the present-becoming; geography and not history, the middle and not the beginning or the end. . . . In becoming there is no past nor future—not even present, there is no history. In becoming it is, rather, a matter of involuting; it's neither regression nor progression.[68]

Thusly framed, the new historicism comprises a virtual exit from history, not via a transhistorical appeal, but rather via a reduction of history

68. *Dialogues,* pp. 23 and 29.

to geography. What remains is a thin and eviscerated sense of the historical, a devalued past and future that limp along with an evanescent present. One finds in this devaluation of a robust sense of historical presence, required for a reclamation of the past and an anticipation of the future, echoes of Hegel's "unhappy consciousness"—a consciousness that is unhappy because it has nothing to remember and nothing for which to hope.

It is at this juncture that the challenge of postmodernism reaches its highest pitch of intensity, eliciting from some of its critics a barrage of vigorous rebukes. One of the more articulate among such critics, John O'Neill, sees the consequences of the new historicism of postmodernity, for which "the return to history is rather an escape from history," as leading pretty much straightaway to "the dead-end of history, the foreclosure of community, and the trivialization of the self."[69] On the issue of the new historicism, the postmodern challenge assumes its boldest relief.

Our sketch of the new historicism of postmodernity may be somewhat overdrawn. There may indeed be some resources within postmodern thought itself for addressing this most intense feature of its challenge. Specifically, we have in mind the suggestive notion of transversality that intermittently appears in the postmodern literature. Nevertheless, our sketch does point to some of the more distressing tendencies in the challenge of the new historicism that require a corrective. The nerve center of this challenge pertains quite directly to our more general interest in refiguring the resources of rationality. A historicism of present-becoming, sans historical subject, lacking tradition and futurity, without a standpoint for critique and evaluation, challenges us to ask again the question as to the claims and efficacy of reason.

Alasdair MacIntyre, in his recent work, *Whose Justice? Which Rationality?*, has argued for the impossibility of extricating oneself from the tradition and establishing a neutral standpoint. Thought and action, he maintains, are never traditionless. And it is precisely in our engagements with the tradition that the claims of reason are exercised.[70] It is against the background of this general thesis that MacIntyre situates his critique of postmodern perspectivism and its denial of tradition-imbued rationality, citing Nietzsche's and Deleuze's abandonment of rational communicative practices and the uses of argumentation.

Socrates is not to be argued with; he is to be mocked for his ugliness and his bad manners. Such mockery in response to dialectic is enjoined in the aphoristic paragraphs of *Götzen-Dammerung*. And the use of aphorism is itself in-

69. John O'Neill, "Postmodernism and (Post) Marxism," in Hugh J. Silverman, ed., *Postmodernism—Philosophy and the Arts* (New York: Routledge, 1990), pp. 70 and 73.
70. "There is no standing ground, no place of enquiry, no way to engage in the practices of advancing, evaluating, accepting, and rejecting reasoned argument apart from that which is provided by some particular tradition or other." Alasdair MacIntyre, *Whose Justice? Which Rationality?* (Notre Dame: University of Notre Dame Press, 1988), p. 350.

structive. An aphorism is not an argument. Gilles Deleuze has called it "a play of forces" (and see more generally 'Pensée Nomade' in *Nietzsche aujour-d'hui*, Paris, 1973), something by means of which energy is transmitted rather than conclusions reached.[71]

If it is the destiny of rational inquiry to stay with the tradition, even when it purports to deconstruct its concepts and contents, then it may well behoove us to give studied attention to our historical inherence to monitor how the logos is operative in it. In following such a path, or a line of force, as postmodernists would be inclined to put it, it may well be that a firmer sense of the historical awaits us, and that incommensurability, conflict of perspectives, paralogy, and dissensus do not have the final word. Without suppressing the recognition that these lexical designators of postmodernism elicit, there would nonetheless still be available some positive resources for dialogue and communication. We would be left with something more than a multiplicity of irreconcilable discursive and social practices and a war of all against all. The communicative practices of our historical inherence would be seen to provide possibilities for rational critique, articulation, and disclosure as these are geared to an understanding of shared experiences, evaluation, and emancipation.

71. *Whose Justice? Which Rationality?*, p. 368.

TWO

Rationality as Praxial Critique

RATIONALITY, THEORY, AND CRITIQUE

It was modern philosophy that issued the birth certificate for the off-spring of a rationality defined by the twin traits of theory and critique. Kant was to a great extent responsible for the shaping of this particular contour of modernity. The critical and transcendental philosophy of Kant portrayed critique as the telos of reason in its deployment of an internal criticism within the bounds of a self-reflexive delimitation. The general design of this formidable project unfolded as a series of investigations of the finitude of human reason displayed in a critique of pure reason, a critique of practical reason, and a critique of aesthetic and teleological judgment. These critiques moved about within the space of theory, remaining cognizant to be sure of the finite resources of human reason, but geared nonetheless to a discovery of the principles of transcendental grounding in the domains of science, morality, and art.

The formative influences of this critical and transcendental philosophy were broad and deep. As a comprehensive response to British empiricism and continental rationalism, Kant's critical and transcendental philosophy veritably shaped the portrait of philosophical modernity. The skepticism about knowledge of things in themselves was blended with an affirmation of the autonomy of reason in its pursuit of an understanding and explanation of the phenomenal world. It was in this manner that Kant became a principal figure in the shaping of the modern theoretico-epistemological paradigm.

The appropriation of critique within a project of theoretical, transcendental grounding and epistemological foundationalism set the stage for the dividing up of the three culture-spheres of science, morality, and art in such a manner that each was entrusted with its own epistemic responsibilities in awareness of the natural cleavages that set them apart. It was this division of culture into separable but yet related theoretical domains that comprised the distinctive problematic of modernity—a problematic that all philosophers subsequent to Kant were forced to address. Hegelians, Marxists, existentialists, and positivists were summoned to respond, and the responses offered introduced a colorful variety of answers to the modern preoccupation with rationality.

Of special concern in dealing with the problem of the relation of the three culture-spheres was the determination of the role of reason in each of the spheres, as well as its efficacy in addressing a possible unification of them. Further complications got into the picture through the install-ment of yet a fourth sphere—that of religion. Kierkegaard in particular played a rather decisive role in this, but the move toward a demarcation of a fourth sphere was already set by Kant's "fourth critique," *Religion Within the Limits of Reason Alone.* Within the variations of the post-Kantian response to the problematic, the drive for a unification of the culture-spheres remained in force.

This was particularly the case, albeit in quite different ways, in the responses of Hegelianism and positivism. Given the successes in the sphere of science, it was perhaps inevitable that scientific rationality would make overtures toward hegemony. "Rational," "scientific," and "objective" be-came virtually identified and, in concert, provided the touchstone for fleshing out the epistemological requirement of modernity in its quest for certainty—a requirement that had already been set in place by Descartes. Thus, if there was to be any unification of the culture-spheres forthcom-ing, it would likely have to find its theoretical foundations in the ratio-nality of science. In any event, it was such a unified field theory of knowl-edge that was proposed in the positivistically oriented "unity of the sciences" movement of the later nineteenth and early twentieth century.

A development in the continuing saga of modernity relating to matters of rationality, which is particularly pertinent to the story that we have to tell, was the emergence of the School of Critical Theory. It was in the thought of the proponents of this school that the binding of "critique" and "theory" was given a distinctive expression. This was the case both in the early and the later stages of its development. The early phase of critical theory, flagged in the thirties as "the Frankfurt School," and spearheaded by Max Horkheimer, Theodor Adorno, and Herbert Mar-cuse, was postured principally as a *critique of ideology,* designed to attack the ideological sedimentations within bourgeois society. A rather pro-nounced Marxist thrust informed these early developments. Indeed, the Frankfurt School became the intellectual conscience of the left-wing re-formers of traditional Marxism and assumed the mission of sensitizing the world to the suppressed presuppositions of bourgeois science and culture that were at the root of both individual and social alienation. It was thus quite understandable that the Frankfurt School would become one of the parties in the celebrated *Methodenstreit* of the thirties and for-ties, a controversy that pitted critical theorists against positivists on the issue concerning the possibility of a value-free science.

The contributors to the later phase of the critical theory movement, directed chiefly by Jürgen Habermas and Karl-Otto Apel, were less interested in a Marxist critique of ideology (although the theme persisted in modified form) and more concerned to fashion a dialogue with hermeneutical thought, analytical philosophy, and American pragmatism.[1] The main issues in this later phase of the movement turn on the theory/praxis relationship; transcendental pragmatics; the consensual theory of truth; and communicative action. Although more theoretical than the early phase of the movement—principally because it was not as politically oriented toward the displacement of fascism as was the earlier phase—it nonetheless did display a disdain for "pure theory" (which in part, and rightly or wrongly, was attributed to the philosophy of Edmund Husserl) and sought to realign theory construction with the variegated configurations of communicative action.

Although the Critical Theory School has clearly transformed the Kantian legacy of rationality as theoretically grounded critique, its general posture has remained "modernist." The mind-set of modernity surfaces at crucial points in the grammar of its discourse as it relates to the requirement for a theoretical adjudication of the disparate claims in the culture-spheres of science, morality, and art; to the demand for a justification of validity claims; to the autonomy-of-reason motif; and to the legitimation of knowledge through consensus.[2] In all this, overtones of a modernist notion of theory, canons for epistemic justification, and the Age of Enlightenment ideal of autonomy become discernible. It was thus that critical theory was forced to proceed to another phase of philosophical inquiry and debate, this time in its confrontation with the proponents of postmodernity. We will attempt to isolate one of the more salient features of this confrontation of critical theory by the postmodernists as it relates to the matter of the intertwining of critique and criteria.

CRITIQUE AND CRITERIA

The linkage of critique and theory in the modern conception of rationality had its counterpart in the linkage of criteria and method. These comple-

1. See particularly Jürgen Habermas, "The Hermeneutic Claim to Universality," in *Contemporary Hermeneutics*, ed. Josef Bleicher (London: Routledge & Kegan Paul, 1980); Karl-Otto Apel, *Analytic Philosophy of Language and the Geisteswissenschaften*, trans. Harold Holstelilie (Dordrecht: Reidel, 1967); and Karl-Otto Apel, *Charles S. Peirce: From Pragmatism to Pragmaticism*, trans. John M. Krois (Amherst: University of Massachusetts Press, 1981).
2. It should be remembered that at no point does Habermas abandon the uses of theory, epistemological and social, in the service of rational comprehension. The title of his recent work, *The Theory of Communicative Action: Reason and the Rationalization of Society*, Volume One (trans. Thomas McCarthy [Boston: Beacon Press, 1984]) was not haphazardly chosen. What we are offered in this volume (and its sequel, Volume Two: *Lifeworld and System: A Critique of Functionalist Reason*) is a theoretical account of the relation of forms of rationality to social action and historical configurations. The stated goal is the development of a universal pragmatics of communication designed to function as a foundation or grounding for societal understanding and interaction. "What can lead us to this goal," we are told, "is not a history of ideas but a history of theory with a systemic intent" (p. 140).

mentary linkages spawned what can be properly called the criteriological conception of rationality. This conception found its inaugural moment in Descartes's *Discourse on Method*, which set the tone for modernity in matters of knowledge and truth. In Part II of the *Discourse*, "The Principal Rules of the Method," the criteriological basis for the achievement of knowledge and truth is unequivocally set forth. The "rule of certainty," which leads the pack, legislates the criteria for the attainment of indubitable knowledge—the criteria of clear and distinct ideas.[3] Two features of this classical criteriological conception of rationality were thus made evident in its initial design: (1) its procedural trait of rule-governedness and (2) its function as a tribunal for epistemic justification.

The linkage of criteria and method issues a directive for the application of rules and provides the foundations for epistemic justification and legitimation. To be "methodical" is to work with rules, and more specifically with rules that have been laid down in advance. These rules incorporate criteria. Descartes's rule of certainty, for example, incorporated the criteria of clarity and distinctness. One will achieve certainty when one lands on ideas that are clear and distinct. These criteria, embodied within the rules of method, at once provide the foundations for epistemic justification. Hence, criteria in the criteriological conception of rationality function in the dual capacity of providing rules and affording a justificatory tribunal.

It is important to recognize that these methodological criteria are laid out in advance. They antedate the data selected for investigation. Forms and rules of thought precede content. Theory of judgment guides the questioning of the issues and affairs under examination, whether the issues or affairs have to do with the motion of physical particles, human behavior, social reality, or the existence of God. This pre-delineation of criteria, as Richard Rorty in particular has pointed out, may well provide an explanation as to why the modern, criteriological conception of rationality tended to look to the natural sciences for its touchstone of what it means to be rational. "If to be rational means to be able to lay down criteria in advance, then it is plausible to take natural science as the paradigm of rationality."[4] But if this is the case, Rorty continues, it leaves the humanities, and particularly poets and painters, in the proverbial lurch. "If the humanities are concerned with ends rather than means, then there is no way to evaluate their success in terms of antecedently specified cri-

3. "The first rule was never to accept anything as true unless I recognized it to be certainly and evidently such: that is, carefully to avoid all precipitation and prejudgment, and to include nothing in my conclusions unless it presented itself so clearly and distinctly to my mind that there was no reason [or occasion] to doubt it." *Discourse on Method and Meditations*, trans. Laurence J. Lafleur (New York: The Liberal Arts Press, 1960), p. 15.
4. "Science as Solidarity," in *The Rhetoric of the Human Sciences: Language and Argument in Scholarship and Public Affairs*, ed. John S. Nelson, Allan Megill, and Donald N. McCloskey (Madison: The University of Wisconsin Press, 1987), p. 40.

teria."[5] Poets and painters do not know in advance the standards of creativity that are to be achieved in their poems or their paintings.

Jean-Paul Sartre makes a similar observation when he writes: "It is clearly understood that there are no *a priori* aesthetic values, but that there are values which appear subsequently in the coherence of the painting. . . . Nobody can tell what the painting of tomorrow will be like. Painting can be judged only after it has once been made."[6] But does this relegate poetry and painting to the netherland of the irrational, or more generously, the "non-rational"? Such would seem to be the implication of a strict adherence to the criteriological conception of rationality. But poets and painters are prone to demur on this problematic implication because of the questionable premise from which it is alleged to follow. "The painter interprets . . . ," retorts Cézanne. "The painter is not an imbecile."[7]

The prioritizing of method with its pre-delineated criteria may well skewer the data and inhibit the inquiries and practices not only of the arts and humanities but of the social and natural sciences as well. The delimitation of method may well be orthogonal to both the social and the natural sciences as well as to the arts and humanities. Gadamer's attack on the overdetermination of method in the arts and the human sciences (*Geisteswissenschaften*) finds its counterpart in Feyerabend's problematization of method in the natural sciences.[8] It would seem that the humanities and the sciences alike have finally taken to heart the wisdom of the celebrated one-liner commonly attributed to Hermann Lotze: "The constant sharpening of the knife is tedious if there is nothing to cut!"[9]

The flip side of the privileging of method and its predelineation of rules in the modern criteriological conception of rationality is the platform of theoretico-epistemological foundationalism. The pre-delineated markers of certitude guide the quest for the justification of our beliefs. The criteriology of rules travels with a criteriology of justification. Stanley Cavell has deftly articulated matters concerning the modern criteriological conception of rationality and has offered some revisionary tactics from a Wittgensteinian perspective.

> When epistemology raises the question of knowledge, what it asks for are the grounds of our certainty. But we are reminded that what we call knowledge is also related to what we call getting to know, or learning, e.g., to our

5. "Science as Solidarity," p. 40.
6. *Existentialism*, trans. Bernard Frechtman (New York: Philosophical Library, 1947), p. 50. Sartre's position is that a similar state of affairs occurs in ethics. As there are no a priori rules for aesthetic endeavors so there are no a priori rules for moral behavior. There is creation and invention in both cases.
7. Quoted by Merleau-Ponty in "Cézanne's Doubt," in *The Essential Writings of Merleau-Ponty*, ed. Alden L. Fisher (New York: Harcourt, Brace & World, 1969), p. 240.
8. See Hans-Georg Gadamer, *Truth and Method* (New York: The Seabury Press, 1975), and Paul Feyerabend, *Against Method: Outline of an Anarchistic Theory of Knowledge* (Atlantic Highlands: The Humanities Press, 1975).
9. *"Das beständige Wetzen der Messer aber ist langeweilig, wenn man nichts zu schneiden vorhat."*

ability to identify or classify or discriminate different objects with and from one another. Criteria are criteria of judgment; the underlying idea is one of discriminating or separating cases, of identifying by means of differences. . . . In the modern history of epistemology, the idea of judgment is not generally distinguished from the idea of statement generally, or perhaps they are too completely distinguished. The problem is not that in focusing upon those forms of utterance which are characterized by their exclusive possession of truth or falsity a philosopher fails to attend to other 'uses' of language. One may presumably study what one chooses. The problem is to see whether the study of human knowledge may as a whole be distorted, anyway dictated, by this focus. The focus upon statements takes knowledge to be the sum (or product) of true statements, and hence construes the limits of human knowledge as coinciding with the extent to which it has amassed true statements of the world.[10]

Cavell proposes to undermine the epistemological-criteriological conception of rationality from the perspective of a Wittgensteinian revisionism. "Criterion" is divested of its affiliation with "theory of knowledge" and is refigured so as to fit its ordinary usages in the multiple language games of our variegated forms of life. What this all boils down to is "just the ordinary rhetorical structure of the ordinary word 'criterion.' "[11] No longer is there an appeal to incontrovertible evidence or unimpeachable truth conditions. Instead we are enjoined to exercise a sensitivity to the varying circumstances in which we show that something "consists in" or "counts as" something.[12]

This Wittgensteinian appeal to the performativity of our linguistic usages in assigning criteria also informs Lyotard's pragmatically construed "agonistics of language," in which criteria are seen to be at war with each other because they issue from disparate language games (denotative, deontic, interrogative, evaluative, etc.). The plurality and paralogy of language games precludes any unifying and epistemically binding criteria that would transcend the varying linguistic usages. Criteria are bound to the narratives that the various institutions in society tell, and there is no metanarrational standpoint from which the criterial conflicts might be adjudicated. "Thus the narratives allow the society in which they are told, on the one hand, to define its criteria of competence and, on the other, to evaluate according to those criteria what is performed or can be performed within it."[13]

In his effort to rescue a narrative-function of criteria Lyotard distances himself from the modernist concept of critique as it stands in the service of theory. Noting the traditional linkage of theory and criticism, Lyotard writes: ". . . the function of theory is not only to understand, but also to

---

10. *The Claim of Reason* (New York: Oxford University Press, 1979), pp. 16–17.
11. *The Claim of Reason*, p. 8.
12. *The Claim of Reason*, p. 7.
13. *The Postmodern Condition*, trans. Geoff Bennington and Brian Massumi (Minneapolis: University of Minnesota Press, 1984), p. 20.

criticize, i.e. to call in question and *overturn* a reality, social relationships, the relationships of men with things and other men, which are clearly intolerable." [14] This instrumentation of critique as a supplement to theory turns out to be not only useless but ends up in a parody of its own resources within critical reflection. We already have had the occasion in the previous chapter to quote the pivotal portion of text in Lyotard's assault on criticism and critique:

> The critical relation cannot criticize itself, it can only parody itself in the derision of autocritique. And in this impossibility, it shows that it is still an authoritarian dominating relation, that is negativity as power. This power is that of language, which annihilates what it speaks of. Criticism can only redouble the empty space where its discourse plunges its object, it is cloistered in this space of vacuity, it can no longer think the object, the work and history, except as language. [15]

A number of features need to be sorted out in Lyotard's agonistics directed against the modernist notion of theory-oriented critique. Four observations in particular need to be made. First to be noted is Lyotard's general disenchantment with rationalism, which he interprets as equating reason with the drive toward unification and totalization. Lyotard's agonistics plays itself out as a "war on totality." [16] Second, there is the more specific point having to do with the delimitation of the self-reflexivity of critique. Critique remains immune to self-criticism. It is unable to move outside the space occupied by its object and continues to employ the presuppositions and the telos of the discourse about the object. Critique is unable to establish a distance from itself, remaining circuitously enclosed within its own vacuous space. Third, its space remains vacuous because it is unable to locate its "object." More precisely stated, critique is able to think its object only as represented in language. It linguisticizes its object and thus is unable to think the otherness of its object as "work and history." Finally, there is, according to Lyotard, the failure on the part of critical theory to recognize the intrinsic connection of power and knowledge, which determines every knowledge relationship as an assumption of power and a drive for domination. "Where do you criticize from?" Lyotard asks. "Don't you see that criticizing is still knowing, knowing better? That the critical relation still falls within the sphere of knowledge, of 'realization' and thus of the assumption of power?" [17]

It is principally these four limiting features in the project of critique as theory that motivate Lyotard to make a paradigm/metaphor shift to another space of discourse, a narrational space that enables a "drifting" across

---

14. *Driftworks*, ed. Roger McKeon (Columbia University: Semiotext(e), Inc., 1984), p. 19.
15. "Adorno as the Devil," *Telos* 19 (1974): p. 135.
16. *The Postmodern Condition*, p. 82.
17. *Driftworks*, p. 13.

a multiplicity of narratives with their disparate language games. What Lyotardian agonistics calls for is a rupture, a breaking away, from the space of critique. "Critique must be drifted out of. Better still: *Drifting is in itself the end of all critique.*"[18]

Now whether indeed the metaphor of "drifting" and the narrational discourse of *Driftworks* is indeed adequate to the task of overcoming the modern theoretico-criteriological standpoint requires extensive discussion. More immediate circumstances, however, demand a recognition of the challenge of Lyotard's postmodern agonistic discourse as it concerns matters of theory, criteria, and critique.

PRAXIAL CRITIQUE AS DISCERNMENT

Our response to the postmodernist assault on theory-grounded critique and criteria takes the route of an exploration of a possible praxial refiguration of critical rationality. The displacement of critique in the interests of purely conceptual and theoretical grounding does not, in our view, entail a displacement of critique as such. We propose, in short, a resituation of critique within the space of our communicative practices and the dynamics of our lifeworld involvements. Rather than a centripetal activity issuing from the subject-centered rationality of an isolated epistemological, moral, or aesthetic subject, we understand critique as a centrifugal deployment of discursive and nondiscursive social practices. Critique, thusly contextualized, falls out as a communicative project, a praxis that finds its resources in the dialogic transactions and institutional forms that make up the fabric of our socio-historical existence. Critique is inseparable from the practices and projects of the various communities of investigators and interpreters as they attempt to understand and explain the various configurations of meaning in the personal and public worlds. Rationality as praxial critique fills the void that results from the displacement of the theoretico-epistemological paradigm of modernity.

Critique, refigured as *praxial* critique, enjoys neither modernity's zeal for foundations nor its hopes for the attainment of certainty. It rests content to discern and assess the play of forms of thought and action against the background of changing and historically conditioned patterns of signification. The relevance of a postmodern agonistics of intervention for the changing patterns of praxis needs to be acknowledged. Beliefs and practices are modified, recharted, or indeed overturned through intervention. But this need not be an intervention devoid of discernment; and it is precisely the discernment in our discursive and institutional engagements that defines critique as a praxial accomplishment.

The grammar of "praxis" in our notion of praxial critique is not without its own strictures and invitations to misunderstanding. "Praxis" is not

18. *Driftworks,* p. 13.

to be identified with "practice," and particularly not with practice as the application of pure and contextless theory. Clearly "praxis" encompasses the varied spate of social practices, both discursive and nondiscursive, in our personal and public existence. However, "praxis" does not reduce these practices to effects or in some manner consequences of theory application. "Praxis" refigures social practices as performances of meaning, displays of intentionality that exhibit their own insight, comprehension, and sense-constitution. Thusly refigured, social practices do not need to wait on the determinations of theory to provide them with intelligibility. Through this move "praxis" is able to "save the phenomena," that which "shows itself" in the performativity of discursive and nondiscursive practices.

The flip side of this saving of the phenomena as intentionality-imbued social practices is the "saving of theory" as contextualized concept formation. There is no escape from theory. The task is to see theory as itself embedded in the texture and dynamics of praxis. The theory/practice bifurcation, as a legacy of modern epistemology, is indeed jettisoned, but this does not catapult us into a situation in which practices somehow by themselves (whatever this would mean) remain blind, and theories by themselves (whatever this would mean) remain empty. The interwoven fabric of praxis allows for no such clean-cut incisions. Theory and practice alike are context dependent. A recognition of this context-dependency will provide a sheet anchor against any privileging of beliefs over actions, or vice versa. "Beliefs" and "actions" are post-analytic markers that are solicited by a communicative form of life that contextualizes both. The projects of a "theory of belief" and a "theory of action" that continue to buy into the epistemological paradigm, so as to secure the "conditions under which" as a backup for the "truth" of our beliefs and actions, lead at best to a vacuous formalism and at worst to an occlusion of the praxial intentionality of our living discourse and action.

The widely indexed "problems of philosophy," particularly as a legacy of the modern era, have for the most part been set with the prospect that they will be solved by pure and contextless theory. The later Wittgenstein had already shown, almost without effort, that this "problem/solution" matrix of thought is the principal occasion for our conceptual bamboozlement. He thus recommended linguistic analysis as a "cure" *from* the problems rather than a theoretical solution *of* them. Heidegger, from another perspective, more deconstructionist in nature, urged something similar in his project of the dismantling of traditional metaphysical and epistemological theory. This, however, does not imply a facile farewell to the philosophical discourse of the tradition. Rather it invites new readings of the classical philosophers in an effort to recover the contributions of their more praxis-oriented discourse, which for the most part remained marginalized in the formation of the philosophical canon.

Richard Zaner, working with the texts of Descartes, has shown how the celebrated Cartesian "mind/body problem" takes on a different face when it is reinterpreted against the background of Descartes's medical writings and letters, all of which display a more praxis-oriented response to the issue at hand.[19] It were as though Descartes got the mind/body connection right in his medical discourses but then screwed it up in his formal epistemology!

In undermining the theory/practice dichotomy, the refigured notion of praxial critique as discernment is allowed to make its contribution to the overcoming of logocentrism, methodologism, criteriology, and totalization—and it is able to do so without sacrificing rationality. It has the resources to address the vagaries and aporias of logocentrism without jettisoning the claims of reason. Indeed, it provides an opening for an understanding of what may well be the root vagary in the deconstructionist-postmodernist posture itself, namely the unspoken presupposition that unless there are logocentric foundations all knowledge and all rational contents of culture are undermined and overturned.

It is not without a measure of irony that the deconstructionist frame of mind, in its subversion of all contents of meaning and reference, makes purchases on the very logocentric belief system that it purports to undermine. It presupposes that claims of reason, performances of meaning and reference, and a standpoint for critique can be secured only on the basis of logocentric and foundationalist premises. But there is no necessity that ties rational and critical discourse to such premises. Indeed, there are philosophical discourses in the tradition that make do without logocentric foundations. The sweeping indictment of the tradition as logocentric and foundationalist is based on a conveniently selected canon. There are resources for rational critique and assessment other than those of a logocentric sort.

In securing a space for praxial critique one is able to navigate between the Scylla of a randomization of criteria and the Charybdis of a unified methodology by marking out a strategy of discernment that is "methodic" without succumbing to the a priorism of antecedently specified methodological rules. It keeps matters of method from solidifying into methodolatry. Criteria are liberated from the rule-hegemony of criteriology and are reformulated as strategies for discriminating and assessing the transversal configurations of discourse and action.

Praxial critique teaches us how to be systematic, while abhorring the constraints of "the System"—as both Kierkegaard and Nietzsche had already recommended. It is sensitive to the requirement for totalizing, so as to maintain the requisite coherence in the web of our beliefs and practices, but it abjures claims for finality and totality. It recognizes the play of epistemic commitments while avoiding the philosophical incoherence of epistemology as a special discipline designed to supply a putative

19. Richard M. Zaner, *Ethics and the Clinical Encounter* (Englewood Cliffs: Prentice Hall, 1988), p. 110.

knowledge of knowledge. It acknowledges the role of judgment in what we say and do, but it also is sensitive to the meaning formation already at work in our Gadamerian-like "pre-judgments" *(Vorurteile)*.

Rationality without logocentrism, the methodic moment without methodology, criteria without criteriology, systematic intent without system building, totalizing without totalization, and knowing without a theory of knowledge are the consequences of our refiguration of theoretical critique as *praxial* critique. This all boils down to an identification of discernment as it is operative within the manifold of our praxial engagements.

The refiguration of rationality as praxial critique can be facilitated and further elucidated via an etymological recovery of the sense of the originative Greek notion of *krino* (κρινω). David James Miller's study on this topic affords a particularly illuminating contribution. Miller has tracked the etymological origins of the English term "criterion" back to the Greek term *"krino,"* which, as he observes, offers a superabundant polysemy of both ordinary and technical usages. "The term 'criterion' enters into English parlance in the seventeenth century, initially from the Greek, as κριηριον *(kriterion)*. το κριηριον *(to kriterion)* stems from the root verb κρινω *(krino)*, the progenitor of an interesting array of semantic offspring."[20]

Krino, for the Greeks, transported a number of related senses, pertaining both to qualities of the soul and forms of behavior. It had to do with the capacity to distinguish, separate, sort out, and discriminate, but it also involved the volitional and actional comportment of assessing, deciding, and choosing.[21] It was thus that *krino* came to function as the etymological root of both "critique" and "criterion," but all this in advance of their epistemologization as protocols of theoretical cognition.

Critique as a performance of *krino* plays itself out as a discernment that draws upon the wider functions and faculties of the soul in its response to the social practices that extend transversally across the *polis,* providing at once an assessment of these practices and criteria for decision and action. These criteria are not rules legislated by an epistemologically oriented "theory of judgment." They are more like provisional and case-oriented maxims for assessing what is to be believed and what is to be done in particular situations.

Again, it is important to keep in mind that criteria, praxially construed, are not antecedently defined. They are not legislated in advance. They are a progeny of the transversal play of perspectives and practices. Feyerabend hits upon this central point when he informs us that "criteria do not merely *judge* events and processes, they are often constituted by them and they must be introduced in this manner or else research will

---

20. "Immodest Interventions," *Phenomenological Inquiry* 2 (October 1987): p. 109.
21. "The radical sense of κρινω *(krino)* is 'separating,' 'putting asunder,' 'distinguishing.' From this comes that of 'picking out,' 'choosing,' or, more commonly, 'deciding,' 'judging,' 'assessing,' as well as other senses." "Immodest Interventions," p. 109.

never get started."[22] A similar point, albeit from another perspective, is made by Deleuze and Guattari: "Although there is no preformed logical order to becomings and multiplicities, there are *criteria,* and the important thing is that they not be used after the fact, that they be applied in the course of events, that they be sufficient to guide us through the dangers."[23] *Krino,* as a performance of praxial rather than theoretical critique, is a discernment and assessment of thought and action as this thought and action play in the practical and public affairs of the *polis.*

This gathering of senses in *krino* as praxial critique was still present in the Latin rendering of *krino* as *cerno,* the etymological root of the English *discern.* The rhetoric of the ordinary English word "discern" retains its solvency for cashing in a variety of usages that span the economy of public discourse. One discerns not only the truth of propositions, one also discerns the pain in the shriek, the love in the caress, the anger in the shaking fist, the beautiful and the sublime in the artist's creative work, the fitting response to an ethical dilemma, and the proper conduct in a situation of social conflict. Discernment is itself a multiplex phenomenon that displays a variety of noetic and noematic profiles. It sets forth and brings into relief states of affairs, intensities of feeling, configurations of social behavior, avenues for moral choices, and possibilities for public action.

In the philosophical grammar of modernity, however, this praxis-oriented discernment was taken up into an epistemological quest for certainty, facilitating the slide of *cerno* into *certo.* The rich polysemy in the rhetoric of *cerno* as discernment became sedimented and confined within the bounds of certainty. The bounds of sense were identified with the bounds of certainty. The closely related notions of "critique" and "criterion" simply became fellow travelers in the quest for certainty, providing the tribunal of epistemic justification by clear and distinct ideas issuing from an insular *res cogitans.* All this gave birth to the modern theoretico-epistemological paradigm, in which critique and criterion fuse into an impossible epistemological requirement that demands unimpeachable foundations for certain knowledge.

The move from *cerno* to *certo,* from discernment to certainty, proved to be one of the more consequential moves in modern epistemology. The whole history of modern skepticism hinges on this move. If it would not have been for the proclamation of certitude in matters of knowledge and truth, the modern-day skeptics would have had little to be skeptical about. Postmodernism, like modern skepticism, was also to a considerable degree shaped by a reaction to the claim for certainty in modern epistemology; indeed, one might well make a case for the definition of postmodernism as a culturally expanded version of skepticism. The modern citadel

22. Paul Feyerabend, *Farewell to Reason* (New York: Verso Press, 1987), p. 283.
23. Gilles Deleuze and Félix Guattari, *A Thousand Plateaus: Capitalism and Schizophrenia,* trans. Brian Massumi (Minneapolis: University of Minnesota Press, 1987), p. 251.

of certainty may indeed have provided a secure resting place for Western logocentrism. Yet, as we have argued, shaking the foundations of this citadel does not entail a jettisoning of the resources of rationality. Rationality as praxial critique need not collapse into logocentrism and apodicticity. The resources of praxial critique, and its utility for discernment, assessment, and a fitting response to the inmixing of consensus and conflict in the diversification of our social practices, remain intact.

PRAXIAL CRITIQUE AND COMMUNITY

The interconnection of critique and community has been implicit throughout the preceding discussion. This interconnection needs now to be made explicit. Praxial critique is critique *in* the community, *by* the community, and *for* the community. A viable notion of rationality must come to terms with the social sources and the communal backgrounds of critique and criteria.

The communal context for critique and criteria has been intermittently acknowledged in both current Anglo-American and continental thought. Stanley Cavell, working out from a later Wittgenstein perspective, has consolidated some of the central features of a communal approach to the claims of reason.

> The philosophical appeal to what we say, and the search for criteria on the basis of which we say what we say, are claims to community. And the claim to community is always a search for the basis upon which it can or has been established. . . . *The wish and search for community are the wish and search for reason.*[24] (Italics mine.)

Jürgen Habermas arrives at a quite similar conclusion, moving out from his perspective of a universal pragmatics. Habermas's particular concern is to show how "communicative reason" leads us to the way out of the philosophy of the subject and its "subject-centered reason." This involves something like a paradigm shift in which the locus of inquiry moves from an interrogation of the knowing subject's relation to a world of objects or states of affairs to an exploration of criteria and validity claims that issue from a mutual understanding and intersubjective recognition.

> Subject-centered reason finds its criteria in standards of truth and success that govern the relationship of knowing and purposively acting subjects to the world of possible objects or states of affairs. By contrast, as soon as we conceive of knowledge as communicatively mediated, rationality is assessed in terms of the capacity of responsible participants in interaction to orient themselves in relation to validity claims geared to intersubjective recognition. Communicative reason finds its criteria in the argumentative procedures for

24. *The Claim of Reason*, p. 20.

directly or indirectly redeeming claims to propositional truth, normative rightness, subjective truthfulness, and aesthetic harmony.[25]

Both Cavell's Wittgensteinian linguistic community and Habermas's more action-oriented community provide contexts for the tracking of the claim of reason and its associated strategy of praxial critique. Each from his own perspective makes the linkage of rationality and community explicit. The task that they bequeath to their successors, and it is a task to be assumed time and again, is that of further articulating the peculiar connection of the performance of reason with our communal discourse and our communal action.

A determination of the connection with the help of a linear model provides neither an account of the two terms in the relationship, reason and community, nor an identification of the points of intersection. The linear model simply juxtaposes rationality and community within a serial succession and ends up in an aporia of origins. The hierarchical model is equally unsuccessful. The use of this model dictates a subsumption of the one under the other, a subordination of either rationality to community or community to rationality. Following this route we again end up in an aporia, the aporia of ultimate grounding. Both of these models still buy into the classical, metaphysically oriented *logos* versus *nomos* problematic, in which the issue is construed as a cosmic struggle of an abstracted, universal logos with the particularized and changing scene of custom and convention.

The current task requires an experimentation with a new form of questioning and a fresh paradigm—neither that of linear nor hierarchical ordering but rather that of transversal interplay.[26] The claims of reason are transversal to the claims of community; they intersect, lie across each other, converge without becoming coincident. We will attempt to show how in the performance of praxial critique they intersect by dint of a dialectical play of participation and distanciation.

The notions of dialectic, participation, and distanciation are admittedly not without their own problems and limitations. They have a history of involvement with the metaphysical/epistemological position-taking that has driven us into the current situation of crisis. Yet, an effort needs to be made to revitalize in some manner the grammar of these terms so that they can open up a new space of inquiry. We have named this new space the space of "communicative praxis," textured as an amalgam of discourse and action, in which the traces of a hermeneutical reference, a hermeneutical self-implicature of a decentered subject, and a hermeneu-

25. *The Philosophical Discourse of Modernity*, trans. Frederick Lawrence (Cambridge, MA: The MIT Press, 1987), p. 314.
26. It is in the concluding chapter of the present study that the dynamics of transversality is detailed and consolidated, after the consequences of interpretation, narrativity, and rhetoric have been sorted out in the following chapters.

tical rhetoric are discernible.[27] This wider space of communicative praxis is proposed as a displacement of the ethereal metaphysical regions of the ancients as well as the narrow epistemological straits of the moderns. It is within this new space of inquiry, post-metaphysical and post-episte-mological, that rationality undergoes its recovery and the workings of the dialectics of participation and distanciation become manifest.

Praxial critique, as the first moment of rationality within the dynamics of communicative praxis, aligns itself with the *pre*-judgments operative in our communal existence. These pre-judgments display our inherence in a linguistic community, our involvement and participation in a world of delivered and changing social practices. There is no discernment without these pre-judgments. It is by virtue of them that one is installed in the world in such a manner that one is already oriented toward an under-standing of it. This understanding is *pre*-theoretical insofar as it is not derived from an application of theory, and it is *pre*-cognitive in the sense that it is not a cognitive act proceeding from a translucent cogito. It is a *pragmatic* understanding, issuing from a comprehension through doing, an entwined knowing how and knowing what, a responsiveness within our discourse and action as this discourse and action take shape within our everyday involvements, habits, projects, and social practices. In short, it is an understanding that issues from our participation in the ongoing life of our intercommunal situatedness in the world.[28]

As there is no discernment decontextualized from the background of prejudgments, habits, and skills that inform our participation in the com-munal world, so also there is no discernment apart from a placing of these prejudgments, habits of thought, and action into question. The ac-tivation of such questioning requires the performance of distanciation, a stepping-back, as it were, to discern what it is that has been going on behind our backs. It is this performance of distanciation that provides the distinctively "critical" moment of rationality as praxial critique.[29] Partici-

27. See particularly Calvin O. Schrag, *Communicative Praxis and the Space of Subjectivity* (Bloomington: Indiana University Press, 1987).

28. Heidegger's notion of "fore-having" *(Vorhabe)*, Gadamer's recognition of the play of "prejudices" *(Vorurteile)*, and Dewey's insistence on "habit" all become relevant at this junc-ture. With his neologism of "fore-having" Heidegger was able to underscore the importance of the background of skills and everyday engagement with tools and utensils that at every step inform our self and world comprehension. Gadamer's "prejudices" also highlight the importance of background practices in our projects of interpretive understanding, but these "prejudices" (always to be understood in the non-pejorative sense of accepted prejudg-ments) take on a more linguistic orientation than do Heidegger's circumspect dealings of "fore-having." Prejudices make up the warp and woof of the tradition, which is principally literary and linguistic, and in which we always stand when we interpret either a text or ourselves. Dewey's notion of "habit" plays basically in the same arena, although the role of habit in Dewey's thought neither stands in the service of a Heideggerian fundamental on-tology nor is aligned with a Gadamerian notion of the tradition, construed along the lines of a "linguisticality of Being."

29. Paul Ricoeur is pretty much single-handedly responsible for the introduction of distan-ciation as an obligatory interpretive category. See particularly his essay, "The Hermeneutical Function of Distanciation," in *Paul Ricoeur: Hermeneutics and the Human Sciences*, ed. John B.

pation without distanciation congeals into traditionalism and conservativism, paving the way to a tyranny of custom. It is thus that the "critical" moment of praxial critique, which carves out a space for disagreement and dissent, needs to be secured. Although distanciation without participation remains bereft of its background conditions, participation without distanciation remains blind to resources for critical assessment and evaluation. One can best capture these twin moments of praxial critique by speaking of a *dialectics* of participation and distanciation.

The grammar of dialectics immediately raises philosophical eyebrows. This is particularly the case when one deals with the postmodernist challenge, in which the principal targets in the perpetration of dialectics are Hegel and Marx. According to Lyotard, the dialectics of Hegel and Marx simply provide examples of metanarratives that have succumbed to the urge for totalization. In these metanarratives, origin and end, *archē* and *telos*, are bound into an architectonic unity that is visible only from the hither side of history. Within such a scheme of things, the plurality of local narratives and the multiplicity of language games that inform them are glossed. The significance of local narratives and situated language-use cannot be discerned from the end of history.

Such an attack on dialectics (particularly Hegelian dialectics) had, of course, already been witnessed before. The chief brunt of Kierkegaard's philosophical rhetoric of irony was the Hegelian "system," in which, according to Kierkegaard, the categories of essence and existence were confused in such a manner that one had difficulty telling the one from the other. To all this, Kierkegaard responded with his ironical portrait of the Hegelian as one who erects an immaculate mansion of dialectically mediated philosophical categories and then lives in a dog kennel alongside it.[30] But Kierkegaard's disillusionment with the Hegelian dialectic did not compel him to reject the uses of dialectics cart blanche. Indeed, he used the occasion of his blistering attack on Hegel to transmute Hegel's dialectical idealism, as a dialectic of abstract thought, into an "existential dialectic."[31]

Thompson (Cambridge: Cambridge University Press, 1981). The phenomenological legacy in this concept, of course, is quite evident. Distanciation is a refiguration of the Husserlian *epoché*, the performance of bracketing, suspending, putting out of play. However, it is a *refiguration* of this classical phenomenological notion in that it separates the performance of the *epoché* from its classical alignment with the requirement for a "reduction," which putatively leads back to the transcendental ego as the primordial source of intentional consciousness. Distanciation is the phenomenological *epoché* incorporated into the hermeneutical turn.
30. *The Sickness Unto Death*, trans. Walter Lowrie (Princeton: Princeton University Press, 1951), p. 68.
31. Kierkegaard also referred to his dialectic as "qualitative" in an effort to distinguish it from the "quantitative" or modal dialectic of Hegel's *Logic*. Writing in his *Journals*, Kierkegaard underscores the point at issue: ". . . everything depends upon making the difference between quantitative and qualitative dialectic absolute. The whole of logic is quantitative or modal dialectic, since everything is and everything is one and the same. Qualitative dialectic is concerned with existence." *The Journals of Søren Kierkegaard*, ed. Alexander Dru (New York: Oxford University Press, 1938), entry 584.

In a similar vein of refiguration, we propose a situating of the workings of dialectics within the play and interplay of our social practices and
communal concerns. The grammar of dialectics thus falls out as an articulation of the entwined moments of participation and distanciation as they
configure our discourse and action in the public world. Hence, we may
do well to speak of a *socio-pragmatic* dialectics, a dialectics that unfolds
within our socio-historical becoming and that charts the odyssey of our
comprehension of self and world.

Within the interstices of this socio-pragmatic dialectics of participation
and distanciation, the voice of the subject continues to be heard, and its
actions continue to be registered. A displacement of the centripetal, subject-centered reason does not entail a jettisoning of rationality. The flip
side of this is that a displacement of reason as engineered by a centripetal
subject does not entail a jettisoning of subjectivity. On this point the legitimacy of the postmodern attack on the subject becomes overextended.
The discourse, interest, and action of the speaking, listening, writing,
reading, and agentive subject continue to register their inscriptions on the
participatory and distanciating performance. Admittedly, this subject, in
its multiple profiles, is no longer the hegemonous authority for what is
said, written, and done. The monarchical subject is dethroned, but the
subject as such is not expelled from the kingdom. The subject is decentered and resituated within the space of communicative praxis. As decentered, the subject no longer functions as foundation, ultimate ground, or
sole legislator in matters of discourse and action; it is rather an emergent
from the patterns of meaning and lines of force that comprise the socio-
historical republic.[32]

The subject-term needs to remain in play in the participatory relationship. The self/other structure of participation honors the integrity of both
parties. If the reciprocality within this polar structure is violated, then
participation collapses into a group substantiality on the ontological level
and into a collectivism on the political level. Participation is not absorp-
tion. The "identity" of the subject, which is of course never the modal
identity of self-sameness, needs to be protected if the participatory relation is to remain a genuine relation.

This identity of the subject is given an even heavier accent in the performance of distanciation. The space of the subject in the performance of
distanciation, like that of the subject in the participatory relationship, is
never absolute, but it does mark out a conditional standpoint from which
the discourse and action of the "other" can be tested and contested. The
space that is carved out by distanciation is the space of self-assertion and
self-affirmation, the space from which arguments are launched and strategies of contention and dissent are deployed.

32. For an extended discussion of the recovery of the subject in the wake of its decentering
and the dissolution of the modernist paradigm of subjectivity, see Part II, "The New Horizon of Subjectivity," of the author's *Communicative Praxis and the Space of Subjectivity*.

The affirmative feature in this confrontation with the other, however, is sacrificed if dissension and dissent reduce to a contextless negativity.[33] The background solicitations of mutual understanding and solidarity in communal endeavors, inscribed within the participatory relationship, remain dialectically bonded with the assertion of self in the distanciating performance. It is this that allows one to say "we" in the same space that one says "I."

33. Cavell makes this point well when he writes: "Dissent is not the undoing of consent but a dispute about its content, a dispute within it over whether a present arrangement is faithful to it." *The Claim of Reason,* p. 27.

THREE

The Consequences of Interpretation

NOSTALGIA VERSUS AFFIRMATION

The dynamics of praxial critique, sustained by the dialectics of participation and distanciation, solicits at every stage considerations pertaining to the workings of interpretation. Rationality as praxial critique proceeds hand in glove with rationality as interpretation. The discernment operative in participation and distanciation is linked with the practice of interpretation. Rationality is thus forced to come to terms with the consequences of interpretation. It is required to forge a response to the hermeneutical demand.

Interpretation is at work both in our participation in a tradition and in the self-affirmative moments that occasion a distanciation from it. This double performance of interpretive praxis is often portrayed as a polarization of two quite distinct types, a hermeneutics of nostalgia versus a hermeneutics of affirmation. It is such an opposition that Jacques Derrida finds to be solicited by the peculiar constellations of structure, sign, and play.

> There are thus two interpretations of interpretation, of structure, of sign, of play. The one seeks to decipher, dreams of deciphering a truth or an origin which escapes play and the order of the sign, and which lives the necessity of interpretation as an exile. The other, which is no longer turned toward the origin, affirms play and tries to pass beyond man and humanism, the name of man being the name of that being who, throughout the history of metaphysics or of ontotheology—in other words, throughout his entire history—has dreamed of full presence, the reassuring foundation, the origin and the end of play.[1]

---

1. Jacques Derrida, "Structure, Sign, and Play in the Discourse of the Human Sciences," in *Writing and Difference*, trans. Alan Bass (Chicago: University of Chicago Press, 1978), p. 292. These two types of interpretation are directly related to the two forms of deconstruction that Derrida discusses in his essay "The Ends of Man" (in *Margins of Philosophy*, trans. Alan Bass [Chicago: University of Chicago Press, 1982]). The hermeneutic of nostalgia would seem to be linked quite directly with what Derrida in this essay calls "a deconstruction without changing terrain, by repeating what is implicit in the founding concepts and the original problematic"; whereas the hermeneutic of affirmation travels with that form of deconstruction that makes an effort "to change terrain, in a discontinuous and irruptive fashion, by brutally placing oneself outside, and by affirming an absolute break and difference" (p. 135).

These two types of interpretation—one a hermeneutics of nostalgia and the other a hermeneutics of affirmation—are presented by Derrida as "absolutely irreconcilable," forcing us to "acknowledge and accentuate their difference and define their irreducibility."[2] It would seem to be of some import that rather quickly following Derrida's delineation of the two economies of interpretation, we are offered a third interpretation, something like an interpretation of the two initial interpretations—namely, that they are irreconcilable and irreducible. Now quite independent of whether sufficient justification has been provided for this third interpretive claim, putatively establishing the irreconcilability of interpretation one with interpretation two, we appear to be instructed, already at this early stage of our discussion, in a rather consequential truth about the hermeneutical economy. Interpretation seems to have a way of going on and on, remaining open-ended, resulting in a succession of interpretations of interpretations. One might be tempted to say that interpretations, like William James's turtles, go all the way down—were it not for the problematic metaphoricity of "down." Apparently there is no rock-bottom "down," no *Letztebegrunding* on which interpretation itself rests. It is more like an unending spiraling of interpretations, enclosed within themselves. Hence, the putative aptness of talk about "the hermeneutical circle."

It may be advisable, however, not to proceed too rapidly at this stage. There are a number of things that need to be sorted out. There is first the task of locating the proponents of the two types of interpretation that Derrida has set in opposition. It would seem that a likely candidate for the nostalgic view would be Friedrich Schleiermacher. It is common to tag Schleiermacher's perspective as a "romanticist" hermeneutics, bent toward the recovery or retrieval of the meaning of a text or an activity by way of an empathic identification with the mind of the author or the actor. Hermeneutics, thusly construed, falls out as a project of *reconstruction*, nurtured by a nostalgia for a lost origin, a fugitive essence in the mind of an original writer or actor who is no longer with us.

There are, however, other features at work in Schleiermacher's hermeneutics that significantly qualify this alleged romanticist posture. As Paul Ricoeur has shown quite clearly, Schleiermacher bequeathed to his hermeneutic successors a genuine aporia, occasioned by a tension between two forms of interpretation that reside within the parameters of his own project. On the one hand, Schleiermacher proposed a "grammatical" interpretation, objective in character, concerned with the linguistic features of the text rather than with the mind of the author, geared to a correction of errors and misunderstandings that arise from linguistic deformation. On the other hand, he appealed to a "technical" interpretation that aimed for the subjectivity of the author or speaker and that sought to deliver the originative thought that produced the discourse.[3] The her-

2. "Structure, Sign, and Play," p. 293.
3. Paul Ricoeur, "The Task of Hermeneutics," in *Paul Ricoeur: Hermeneutics and the Human*

meneutics-of-nostalgia approach thus seems to lose its clear lines of de-marcation and becomes a blurred genre, blending with other demands in the project of interpreting. At best, it functions as an "ideal type," ab-stracted from the actual practice of interpreting, indicating a tendency or orientation that may well be operative to a greater or lesser degree in a variety of hermeneutical approaches.

We are confronted with a similar quandary in attempting to locate the proponents of Derrida's second type of interpretation, defined as a her-meneutics of the affirmation of play and becoming sans origins and ends. Nietzsche is cited by Derrida as the principal proponent of this view, and it must be granted that for the most part Nietzsche does seem to fit the mold. Yet, it is not all that difficult to recognize a nostalgic coloring in certain facets of Nietzsche's philosophy. Such is evidenced particularly in his admiration of Greek style in advance of Socratic morality and Platonic metaphysics. Also, Nietzsche's reclamation of the Dionysian motif in Greek mythology and religion to flesh out his thematic of the will-to-power ex-hibits its own nostalgic reminiscence. So there are indications that also in this second type of interpretation we are dealing with a blurred genre rather than a clean categorial cut.

Both the hermeneutics of nostalgia and the hermeneutics of affirma-tion appear to be subject to a measure of inmixing. They interplay in the concrete project of interpretation as a praxis. They exhibit both reciprocity and tension—and this may be the long and short of Derrida's interpreta-tion of the two interpretations, namely that even given their irreconcila-bility there can be no question of *choosing* the one over the other.[4] In any case, we offer this "fourth" interpretation (an interpretation of Derrida's interpretation of the two initial interpretations) as a means for continuing the conversation. And we further suggest that this inmixing of nostalgia and affirmation can be given additional clarification by situating it within the dynamics of the dialectics of participation and distanciation. The nos-talgic moment becomes discernable particularly in the participatory pos-ture; the affirmative moment comes to the fore principally in the wake of the performance of distanciation.

There are some other matters that need to be sorted out in tracking the consequences of the hermeneutical demand. Not the least of these is the effect of nostalgia and affirmation on the concept of truth. Truth and rationality have traveled side by side in the history of Occidental philos-ophy, a history in which the temptations of "pure theory" have been difficult to resist. Theories of truth abound in the philosophical literature. The correspondence and coherence theories, as the proverbial every schoolboy knows, have been particularly influential. Under the guise of

Sciences, ed. and trans. John B. Thompson (Cambridge: Cambridge University Press, 1981), pp. 46–47.
4. "Structure, Sign, and Play," p. 293.

theory, it is not sufficient simply to tell the truth. One is required to furnish a theoretical account of the truth that is being told.

Now where does one place truth in the designs of hermeneutics? Does hermeneutics provide us with another "theory of truth"? Or does it *displace* truth, possibly by radically deconstructing its signifying function in such a manner that it becomes either something other than itself or indeed nothing at all? Did we not learn from Nietzsche that "everything is interpretation" and that "we have art so as not to die of truth"? Does hermeneutics transform truth into art? If not eliminated with the help of a Nietzschean-like aestheticism, can the grammar of truth in some way be salvaged and kept within the philosophical lexicon? Is truth but a vestige of logocentric nostalgia, or can it be rethought in some manner—possibly through a Heideggerian retrieval of a poetic world-disclosure, in which the *veritas* of the classical *adequatio intellectus et rei* is dismantled and dredged to yield a more originative *aletheia* as the unconcealment of Being?[5]

That hermeneutics has been able to align itself with different theories of truth throughout its history, from Aristotle's *De Interpretatione* to Gadamer's *Wahrheit und Methode*, becomes rather plainly evident from even a cursory examination of the literature. In response to this, it might be surmised that hermeneutics is basically a strategy that is content-neutral and is thus able to work in the service of any number of different theories of truth. It would take little effort to show that Aristotle's use of hermeneutics is more compatible with the notion of truth within a realist epistemology, whereas Dilthey's hermeneutical ventures make purchases on a Kantian-idealist perspective on truth. Equally it could be shown that romanticism, which clearly inspired the "technical" side of Schleiermacher's hermeneutics, is absent in the ontological hermeneutics of Heidegger. It might thus appear that hermeneutical approaches are different not because of different strategies but because of the varying theories of truth and conceptual schemes that accompany them. The method remains the same; only the truth-content varies.

The tendency to think of hermeneutics as a neutral method or contextless strategy has been particularly fashionable since the invention of the modern epistemological paradigm and its subject-centered, criterio-

5. Short of engaging in yet another interpretation of Heidegger on the question of truth and Being—of which a vast number already exist in the literature—we simply wish to suggest that Heidegger himself may have been led to a more radical redefinition of the issues involved than most of his interpreters would concede. What needs to be investigated is the possible emergence of a *second Kehre* in Heidegger's thought, consequent to the first, which maneuvered the shift from the question as to the meaning of Being *(Sinn des Seins)* to the question as to the truth of Being *(Wahrheit des Seins)*. The second *Kehre*, of which there are hints as early as *Zur Seinsfrage* (Frankfurt: Vittorio Klostermann, 1956), would be that of the "erasure of Being" and the recognition that even *aletheia* is inadequate as a stand-in for the classical concept of truth. In speaking of "three" Heideggers rather than "two," there can of course be no construal of this in terms of a chronological-serial development within Heidegger's writings.

logical conception of rationality. Proceeding from such a framework, hermeneutics is reduced to an extension of epistemology and becomes a special method for providing access to the phenomena. When, however, the criteriological conception of rationality is recast in the guise of praxial critique, and the space from which it emerges is seen as communicative rather than epistemological, then the face of hermeneutics becomes transfigured. No longer a neutral, contextless method or strategy, engineered by an abstract epistemological subject, it is understood rather as a *social practice*. Reinscribed as a performance of communal praxial critique, interpretation ceases to be viewed as an isolated mental act. The classificatory schema of mental acts, volitional faculties, affective states, and bodily dispositions is, at best, a Johnny-come-lately, which appears on the scene only after interpretation as an event of communicative praxis has registered its inscriptions.

The understanding of a portion of discourse or an event of social history is an exercise of interpretive comprehension—and one soon finds that discourse and social history cannot be separated all that easily; they are co-features or twin moments of the hermeneutical adventure. John F. Kennedy's immortalized one-liner, "Ask not what your country can do for you, ask rather what you can do for your country," is at once an event of discourse and an event of social history, at once a speech performance and an institutional act. How does interpretation in this amalgamated happening of discourse and institutional imprinting proceed? It proceeds, we submit, not via a matching of mental events in the minds of interpreters with corresponding mental events in the mind of Kennedy, but rather through a discernment and articulation of the communal concerns that have shaped the discourse and social history of American democracy at a crucial juncture in its development. The meaning displayed in Kennedy's utterance and institutional action issues not from isolated and interior mental states but from the tightly interwoven background conditions that have shaped the communal sense of democracy at a particular time and place in the Western world. The interpreted meaning resides in the social practices of the occurrent discursive and institutional engagements.

The consequences of interpretation, thusly conceived, brings us to the threshold of a "radical hermeneutics." In this radical hermeneutics the logocentric nostalgia for a grand truth nestled in the mind of a speaker, author, or actor—behind or underneath the text, somewhere at the bottom of being—is firmly set aside, and a new space for the affirmation of play and becoming is opened up. It is precisely this aspect of the radicalization of hermeneutics that has been highlighted by John D. Caputo in his rather remarkable work, *Radical Hermeneutics: Repetition, Deconstruction and the Hermeneutic Project*.[6] Caputo provides a clear account of the aporias

6. Bloomington: Indiana University Press, 1988.

of logocentrism and carefully details the relevance of flux and becoming for the new hermeneutics. However, in the very design of his project he imposes certain constraints on the subject matter of his investigations, principally because he positions radical hermeneutics within the interstices of a Heideggerian and Derridian overlap, reading Heidegger through Derrida and then reading Derrida through Heidegger. The strictures of such a project reside in a gloss on the resources of praxial critique and the transversal intentionality of communicative praxis. A radical hermeneutics, within the confines of a cross-reading of Heidegger and Derrida, stands in danger of becoming simply textualized on the one hand (Derrida) and poetized on the other hand (Heidegger).

Yet, the contributions of Derrida and Heidegger to a problematization of the grand-truth syndrome in classical hermeneutics need to be acknowledged. It is interesting to observe that the appetition for such an underlying grand truth informed not only the schools of hermeneutics influenced by romanticism and idealism (Schleiermacher and Dilthey), but it was also, somewhat curiously and ironically, present in the "hermeneutics of suspicion" approaches of Marx, Freud, and Nietzsche. Marx's suspicion about the insinuation of bourgeois ideology as a vestige of idealism becomes intelligible only against the backdrop of a presumed grand "truth" of proletarian consciousness. Freud's alleged disclosure of the cover-up operations by the human psyche presupposes the hidden and repressed "truth" of the Oedipal complex. Nietzsche's assault on the stultifying and life- and world-negating norms of the good and bad conscience rests on the alleged "truth" of the will-to-power. All of this should behoove us to become somewhat suspicious of the "hermeneutics of suspicion."

In the radicalization of hermeneutics as an interactional and communicative praxis, the rational requirement for discernment borne by the dialectics of participation and distanciation remains in force. The rationality of interpretation carries on the work of discernment or praxial critique, which, as we attempted to show in the preceding chapter, advances a participatory engagement with the tradition and a reflective distanciation from that which the tradition has delivered. Hermeneutics thus progresses as *both* a hermeneutics of nostalgia and a hermeneutics of affirmation. A radical hermeneut is both nostalgic and affirmative. Admittedly, the nostalgia at issue is not of the logocentric sort, oriented toward a recall of some grand truth enshrined in a lost paradise of untrammeled essences; nor is the affirmation that of a freewheeling self-assertion dislodged from the context of community. There is no good reason why a hermeneut should be frightened by nostalgia. The highly contagious postmodernist phobia about nostalgia needs to be cured rather than facilely accepted as an argument against any project of recollection or recovery. The remembrance of things past can be pruned of its essentialist sedimentations, and one can come to recognize the display of intentionality and the disclosive power of nostalgic reminiscence.

The intentionality and disclosing function of nostalgia is obstructed when it is construed as a disposition for reproduction, a desire to relive the past as it was experienced when it was present. There is a productive and creative quality of nostalgia, activated by the power of an imagination that is never exhausted in the function of simple reproductive recall. Productive nostalgia is a process of meaning-formation that gathers fragments of a remembered past, imaginatively reconstructs them, idealizes their contents, and projects the idealized portrait of the past as a directive for personal and communal actualization.

The liberating and creative power of nostalgia has been given studied attention in the writings of Edward Casey.[7] Casey depicts nostalgia as an ingredient in "ruminescence," which he defines as an intentionality-laden performance, a distinctive posture of mind, that takes place when we remember something. Ruminescence, as Casey develops the notion, is not simply, if at all, an operation of reproduction. It is first and foremost a dynamics of *re*-creation and *re*-vision. When we reminisce, and particularly about past traumatic experiences, "we enter into a ruminescent state; and in turning them over in our minds in this way, we tame them . . . to the point where they become our own *re*-creation."[8] Nostalgia as a distinctive form of ruminescence, according to Casey, refigures our accustomed ways of thinking about memory and the past and opens up a way of appropriating the past that is at once productive and creative. Such an understanding and use of nostalgia has little to do with a metaphysics of presence, and nothing at all with escapism. Indeed, it enables an affirmation of self and society. It is thus that nostalgia and affirmation can remain twin halves of the august event of hermeneutical understanding.

Our sketch of a revised and radicalized version of hermeneutics as a praxis of participation and distanciation, nostalgia and affirmation, does not entail a deletion of the concept of truth from the philosophical vocabulary. Matters of truth will indeed continue to concern us. Admittedly, it may not be all that useful to talk about a single, hegemonic, Grand Truth. But in our conversations and discourses we will continue to speak of the truth of this and that; and we may do well to heed William James's recommendation to speak only of truths in the plural. A radical hermeneutics pluralizes the notion of truth and resituates it within the multiplicity of our language games. Truth is a multiplicity that travels with the varieties of human experience.

The pluralization of truth in a radical hermeneutics immediately raises the specter of relativism and the much discussed "problem of nihilism"— a problem that may be found to be miscast from bottom up. Nihilism supplies an intelligible response only so long as truth is viewed as single,

---

7. See particularly Edward S. Casey, *Remembering: A Phenomenological Study* (Bloomington: Indiana University Press, 1987), and "The World of Nostalgia," *Man and World: An International Philosophical Review*, 20, no. 4, (1987): pp. 361–84.
8. *Remembering*, p. 157. See also pages 275 and 328.

unitary, logocentric, and hegemonic. Nihilism can function as an effective ploy in countering such logocentric and hegemonic claims, as indeed was recognized by Nietzsche. However, Nietzsche also was astute enough to refer to such nihilism as "provisional." In the moment that the plurality of truth, and its association with the varieties of human experience, is acknowledged, the very conditions for nihilism are undercut. Admittedly, the pluralization of truth may engender its own problem—but this problem is not that of nihilism. Indeed it is a quite "opposite" problem. The problem is not that there are no truths, but rather that there appears to be an unmanageable surplus of truths!

It is precisely this problem that a radical hermeneutics needs to address; but to adequately address it requires a recognition of the limitations of its own resources. As we shall learn particularly in the concluding chapter, hermeneutical understanding needs to be delimited by the workings of transversal rationality. The transversal diagonal needs to be grafted onto the hermeneutical circle. Only through this metaphorical shift from the circle of understanding to the diagonal of transversal thinking can the surplus of truths, the polysemy of meanings, and the multiplicity of language games be managed.

From radical hermeneutics we learn that there is no truth at the bottom of being, no final, bedrock, correct interpretation that supplies the *Letztebegrunding*. The search for such is misguided, given the ineradicable contingency of our starting points and the finitude of our conceptual resources. On the other hand, the hurried and facile claim of relativism that every interpretation is as good as every other is equally misguided. As no finite mind is privy to an absolute, strictly univocal, and timeless interpretive truth, so no finite mind can achieve a vision of *all* interpretations, which is required for the judgment that all interpretive claims are relative. In the end, the fashionable re-treading of the absolutism versus relativism debate leads to a conceptual wearisomeness and eventually surfaces as a proverbial red herring. The disputants in the debate unwittingly assume that the abstract logocentric theory of truth is a genuine philosophical *donnée*, either to be accepted or rejected, only to find that no significant redemptions can be secured from purchases on such an abstract philosophical problematic.

In dealing with the multiple truths of interpretation one is always working with concrete situations of consensus or conflict. It is *this* interpretation of a proper reading of a text that is at issue, *this* formulation of a scientific discovery, *this* statement of a moral prescription, *this* installment of a political ideal that needs to be assessed in conjunction with *another* political ideal. Here one can still speak of legitimation and "correctness." However, the correctness is not one that finds its standard in an ethereal realm of pure theory but rather one that proceeds by "correcting" the limitations and misunderstandings of other particular interpretations.

The interpretation of Kant's philosophy by the Marbourg School of neo-Kantianism (which privileged Kant's first *Critique*) is "corrected" by the Heidelberg School (which privileged Kant's second *Critique*), which in turn is "corrected" by postmodernism (which privileges the third *Critique*). Now the correcting that goes on here, in an effort to discern the truth about Kant, is not a matter of finally "getting it right" but rather a process of delimiting the authority of any particular interpretation and discerning the possibilities for the creation of new standpoints through dissent and a revision of perspectives.

It is thus that the grammar of truth, pluralized and polysemic, remains in force in a radical hermeneutics. The consequences of interpretation lead to a profound suspicion about the vocabulary of a univocal, ahistorical, or transcendental truth; but they do not entail a scuttling of the multiple truths articulated in and through our communicative practices. Yet, as we have indicated, hermeneutics needs an empowerment that will expand and enrich its resources, enabling it to manage a communication across the landscape of the conflict of interpretations. This empowerment is supplied by a transversal rationality of praxis, extending over, lying across, and intersecting the changing and developing interpretive practices in such a manner as to achieve a convergence without coincidence. Only with the help of the resources of such a transversal rationality can the essentialism of a *coincidentia oppositorum*, which continued to inform the hermeneutics of modernity, be overcome.

The consequences of such an infusion of transversal rationality into hermeneutics, in the process of radicalizing it, results in a retrenchment of "universal hermeneutics" into a "transversal hermeneutics." A detailed explication of the dynamics of transversal rationality will need to await the concluding chapter of our study. Before moving to it, however, a number of other issues need to be addressed. At this stage it is sufficient to recapitulate our accomplishments in this section of our project, in which we have examined the consequences of interpretation as they lead us to a radical hermeneutics of nostalgia and affirmation, displaying a dialectics of participation and distanciation, that refashions the delivered philosophical concepts of truth and rationality. The point to be underscored at this phase of our investigation is that in this refashioning or refiguration there is no need for a *theory* of truth and a *theory* of knowledge to back up the contingent claims of reason.

DISCOURSE, ARTICULATION, AND TEXTUALITY

The close association of reason and discourse was already recognized by the Greeks. Plato defined the logos as the rendering of an account of the proper objects of knowledge (*logon didōnai*). Aristotle explicated the logos as a discourse (*deloun*) that makes manifest that which is at issue in our thought and action.[9] So already for the Greeks, logos as reason was closely related to discourse, speech, language, and, more generally, articulation.

The discursive feature of logos has received unprecedented attention in contemporary thought. Charles Taylor, in particular, has underscored the role of articulation in rational understanding.

> Rational understanding is linked to articulation . . . we have a rational grasp of something when we can *articulate* it, that means, distinguish and lay out the different features of the matter in perspicuous order. This is involved when we try to formulate things in language, which is why the Greek philosophical vocabulary marks this inner connection between speech and reason, even though at the time not very much was made of language itself as an object of philosophical inquiry.[10]

It soon becomes apparent, however, that the notion of rationality as articulation, discourse, giving an account, making manifest—whether espoused by the ancients or by contemporaries—exhibits a measure of slackness in its varied usages. This slack can be taken up in a number of different ways. Pervading the grammar of articulation there is a vacillation between giving an account by the spoken word and giving an account by the written word. It may indeed be the case that the Greeks exhibited a propensity to take up the slack by privileging speech over writing. Such is the claim of Derrida, for example, who finds in the thought of Plato a rather explicit merger of logocentrism and phonocentrism.[11]

It is questionable, however, whether the Greeks ever worried all that much about the relative merits of *la voix* and *écriture*, speaking and writing. Their principal interest in the doctrine of the logos resided elsewhere. Admittedly, the notion of the logos involved the strategy of giving an account, but it also involved, and more decisively, a metaphysical de-

9. Heidegger has given particular attention to the intercalation of logos and discourse in the thought of Aristotle. Against the backdrop of Aristotle's contribution, Heidegger works out the inner connection of "logos" and "phenomenon" in such a way that phenomenology comes to be understood as a discourse that makes manifest that which shows itself in the manner in which it shows itself. See particularly *Being and Time*, trans. John Macquarrie and Edward Robinson (New York: Harper & Row, 1962), pp. 55–63.
10. Charles Taylor, "Rationality," in *Rationality and Relativism*, ed. Martin Hollis and Steven Lukes (Cambridge, MA: The MIT Press, 1982), p. 90. In another essay, "Overcoming Epistemology," Taylor discusses his notion of rationality as articulation in connection with Heidegger's contribution to the undermining of foundationalist epistemology. Heidegger, according to Taylor, taught us to focus on our engaged dealings with the world and the surrounding background or horizon that provides the holistic context for the comprehension of our everyday dealings and concerns. "These dealings are largely inarticulate, and the project of articulating them fully is an essentially incoherent one, just because any articulative project would itself rely on a background or horizon of nonexplicit engagement with the world. . . . We cannot turn the background from which we think into an object for us. The task of reason has to be conceived quite differently: as that of articulating this background, 'disclosing' what it involves." *After Philosophy: End or Transformation?*, ed. K. Baynes, J. Bohman, and T. McCarthy (Cambridge, MA: The MIT Press, 1987), pp. 476 and 478.
11. Jacques Derrida, *Dissemination*, trans. Barbara Johnson (Chicago: University of Chicago Press, 1981). See particularly Part I, "Plato's Pharmacy," pp. 63–171.

termination of thought. In his *De Interpretatione*, Aristotle is quite unambiguous in his characterization of speech as a symbol of thought; and thought, for Aristotle, is always solicited by its proportionate or connatural object of knowledge (immaterial, real essence). Thus, *de dicto* claims, pertaining to the saying, should not be confused with *de re* claims, which have to do with the contents of that which is said. Indeed, *de re* claims about the proper objects of knowledge govern and ground the myriad *de dicto* expressions. Now we are also informed that as spoken words are symbols of thought, so written words are symbols of spoken words.[12] It would thus appear that writing is placed at a third remove from reality, destined to live with its subordination to speaking, which itself is subordinated to thinking, which in turn remains beholden to real essences as the proper objects of cognition.[13]

The fact remains, however, that the issue of the relative weighting of speaking and writing never emerged as an explicit philosophical concern for the Greek mind, nor was the topic of language more generally marked off as a distinct and autonomous subdiscipline. This all happened somewhat later. The linguistic turn, the semiotic turn, the grammatological turn, the turn to textuality, are all events of more recent date. That hermeneutics elected to respond to these developments in linguistics, semiotics, and textual studies should come as no surprise.

The interest of hermeneutics in matters of discourse and language already became rather firmly entrenched in the late-medieval and early modern periods, during which time scholarship in philology made rather significant strides. It was simply assumed that a hermeneut would be trained in philology; and surely the marriage of philosophy as the "love of wisdom" to philology as the "love of logos" was not an unnatural one. The philologist's province was defined to encompass the study of words, grammar, the history of language, and systems of writing. Yet, the resources of philology for the philosophical tasks at hand were limited because the philological disciplines were unable to deal adequately with the dynamics of understanding. Consequently it was necessary for Dilthey to delimit the role of philology in hermeneutics and focus more directly on

---

12. *De Interpretatione* 16a 3–4, *The Basic Works of Aristotle*, ed. Richard McKeon (New York: Random House, 1941).

13. It would be a mistake, however, to restrict Aristotle's hermeneutical contribution to his *De Interpretatione*. His concern in this work was principally with the consequences of interpretation for an understanding of the claims of "assertions" or "propositions." There is another use and understanding of hermeneutics in Aristotle's philosophy, seldom given specific attention by his commentators. This other use and understanding receives expression in his analysis of rhetorical discourse, where he gives notice of the workings of interpretation in the deliberation, speech, and collaborative action that vitalizes the ongoing life of the *polis*. Heidegger reminds us of the role of interpretation in Aristotle's rhetoric of discourse and action when he refers to the *Rhetorica* as "the first systematic hermeneutic of the everydayness of Being with another." *Being and Time*, p. 178. It is thus important to recognize a double hermeneutical requirement inscribed within the Aristotelian corpus—one issuing from an investigation of propositional claims and the other surfacing in his treatment of persuasive discourse.

the operation of *verstehen* in an interpretive comprehension of the forms of life in our cultural existence.

Somewhat later, linguistics came into its own. Although not precisely datable, the science of linguistics had as one of its most influential progenitors Ferdinand de Saussure. A high-water mark in the development of linguistics as a science was his famous lecture series, later published under the title *Course in General Linguistics*, which he delivered at the University of Geneva between 1906 and 1911. In these very important lectures the content of linguistic science became defined for the first time, and with this definition the future development of linguistics, and more generally semiotics, was effectively charted. The definition centered on the "sign" *(signe)* as the proper object of linguistics, and the sign itself was construed as a coupling of signifier and signified. Working out from his theory of the sign, Saussure set the stage for future linguistic science by differentiating language *(langue)* from speech *(parole)*. Language, conceived as a self-contained system of signs, amenable to objectivizing investigative procedures, was given primacy. This provided the space for a *structural* linguistics that became a paradigm for many of the subsequent inquiries into the nature and function of language.

The role of hermeneutics within structural linguistics (which rather quickly took over the designs of a more comprehensive philosophy of the human sciences) was clearly attenuated. There was little room for the "hermeneutical as" in structuralist methodology. Structuralists set their sights on an algorithm of linguistic behavior and social institutions and proceeded not from an interpretive understanding of discourse and action as events of praxis but rather from an analysis and classification of formal relations. It thus came as no surprise that a response to the structuralist challenge in the guise of a delimitation of linguistics and semiotics, language construed as a system of signs, was initiated. This response took shape, for example, in the form of Derrida's grammatology and Ricoeur's semantics of discourse. Derrida deconstructed the economy of the sign and uncovered an undecidability and indeterminacy in the play of the signifier and the signified.[14] Ricoeur appropriated the structural semiotics of the word (with its scientific analysis of phonemes, morphemes, and lexemes), but then delimited the semiotic enterprise by grafting onto it a semantics of the sentence (which provides the space for the speaking subject and the intentionality of reference).[15]

In these responses to the structuralist challenge by Derrida and Ricoeur, which in no way proceed from identical presuppositions, we observe a delimitation of semiotics that affords an analogy to Dilthey's pre-

14. Jacques Derrida, *Of Grammatology*, trans. G. C. Spivak (Baltimore: Johns Hopkins University Press, 1974), chapter 2, "Linguistics and Grammatology," pp. 27–73.
15. See particularly Paul Ricoeur, *The Rule of Metaphor: Multidisciplinary Studies of the Creation of Meaning in Language*, trans. Robert Czerny (Toronto: University of Toronto Press, 1977), Study 3, "The Debate between Semantics and Semiotics," pp. 66–76.

vious delimitation of philology. However, the critical engagement with the semiotic model led to a more encompassing preoccupation with matters of textuality than was the case in Dilthey's epistemologically oriented hermeneutics. Derrida's much-quoted (and possibly much-misunderstood) one-liner, "There is nothing outside the text,"[16] and Ricoeur's hermeneutics of textuality, in which the strategy of text-interpretation becomes a paradigm for interpretation in the human sciences more generally,[17] evince a turn to textuality, following in the wake of the delimitation of the semiotic model. That the turns effected by Derrida and Ricoeur project different directions is not of primal importance for our present concerns. The principal point is that the motif of textuality provides a new context for the interrogation of the interconnection of interpretation, discourse, and articulation.

The discourse through which our articulations and renderings of accounts advance is a *textualized* discourse. None of the specialized sciences of language (philology, linguistics, semiotics, syntactics, and semantics) can by themselves deliver the dynamic interplay of the articulating and the articulated, the saying and the said, which constitutes discourse as an event of communicative praxis. Philological markings, linguistic forms, semiotic units, syntactical rules, and semantic structures are all sublated into texts in the event of discourse as a praxial accomplishment. The rules of syntactics and the inventions of semantics are always con-*textual*-ized; and the text at issue, it needs be emphasized, can be either spoken or written. Both speaking and writing display a "texture" of interwoven semiotic, syntactic, and semantic arrangements against a background of both the already said and written and the not yet said and written. Although phonocentrist tendencies are discernible in the history of the Western concept of the logos—and such tendencies need to be corrected—there is little to be gained from the rhapsodic phono-bashing that has become fashionable in certain deconstructionist enclaves. The articulative performance of textualized discourse is deployed by both the spoken and the written word, and there seem to be no good reasons for privileging the one over the other.

The consequences of interpretation are rather prominently inscribed in this turn to textualized discourse. Coupled with the integration of the elemental units of linguistic analysis into an event of discursive practice, there is a recognition that interpretation extends all the way across the specialized disciplinary matrices employed in the study of language. Philology makes use of interpretation in tracking the shifts of meaning in the historical development of a language, and particularly in the rendering of meaning as one moves from one language to another. Interpretation traverses the domain of semiotics and brings the sign within the purview of

16. *Of Grammatology*, p. 158.
17. See particularly Paul Ricoeur, "The Model of the Text: Meaningful Action Considered as a Text," in *Paul Ricoeur: Hermeneutics and the Human Sciences*, pp. 197–221.

the "hermeneutical as." We see, for example, interpretation at work in the arrangement and serialization of lexical units. The construction of a dictionary is an interpretive project. Methodological decisions are made to include some words and exclude others. Some lexemes are taken as proper, current usage; others are dubbed as archaic; and still others are considered to be obsolete.

One needs also to reckon with the polysemy in the everyday usage of lexical units, and it is particularly in their usage that the signifying function of words assumes an interpretive stance. In our mundane conversations as well as in our scientific discourse, words are *taken as* meaning such and such, in such and such situations, dictated by the varying circumstances of making statements, asking questions, giving commands, making promises, or uttering prayers. It is in this attentiveness to the role of lexemes in linguistic *usage*, in language as *discourse*, in speaking and writing as events of *communication*, that the interpretive performance of articulation becomes explicit. Our textualized discourse projects an interpretation of the world in the saying of something about something, in articulating configurations of meaning that encircle both the speaking subject and the world as intended referent. It is through a probing of the interpretive deployment of discourse, implicating at once a speaking subject and a referenced world, that the postmodern challenges of the dissolution of the subject, the undecidability of meaning, and the inscrutability of reference can be productively addressed.

It is of some importance to note that the travail of interpretation does not stop on the sentential level. Although it is on this level that the move beyond semiotics and syntactics to semantics becomes decisive, inaugurating the play of meaning, sentences are themselves ensconced within paragraphs and the wider text of the written word, as well as within preceding and anticipated portions of discourse of the spoken word. We are thus brought to a recognition of the context and intertexture that regulates our discourse and that points us to an expanding horizon of background discursive practices, for the most part operating behind our backs, against which our interpretive articulations are oriented.

We are now in position to consolidate the results of our inquiry into the consequences of interpretation as they bear upon the rationality of articulation. The articulative performance of rationality is guided by interpretive practices that bind semiotic units and semantic features within a textualized discourse that encompasses the horizon of the already said and written and the not yet said and written. The logos as articulative and interpretive discourse proceeds as a contextualized gathering of the elements and forces of language, at once spatialized and temporalized. There is a space of discourse, as this discourse proceeds within the parameters of our social practices; and there is a time of discourse, qualified as a becoming that moves from a past into a future. The net effect of such a rendering of the logos of discourse is the divestment of its abstract and

atemporal character, its logocentric determination, which traditional metaphysics and epistemology continued to ascribe to it. The logos becomes
incarnate in textualized and temporalized discourse. This will lead us, in
the succeeding section, to examine the chronotopal matrix of articulative
interpretation.

In concluding this section, however, we need to maneuver an internal
critique that marks out the limits of discourse as articulation. The articulatory performance of the logos extends beyond the realm of language, textuality, and discourse, delimiting the contributions of the spoken and the
written word alike. As there is a time and space of discourse, so there is
a time and space of action, mood, desire, bodily and institutional inscriptions—a vast arena of *nondiscursive* dispositions and practices that also
exhibit an articulatory function.

Although postmodernists appear at times to be excessively preoccu-
pied with matters of discourse, there are some notable exceptions. Certain features of the thought of Lyotard and Deleuze illustrate the point.
We have already discussed Lyotard's assault on the linguistic dialectics of
critical theory because it remains unable to think the proper objects of
investigation, namely work and history, except as language and discourse.[18] Here the delimitation of discourse, specifically of a particular
kind, is unequivocally set forth. We have also seen how the lines of force
in Deleuze's politics of desire move about on the boundaries of language.[19] Here also we seem to be told that language, textuality, and discourse encounter their own limits. However, what is not so easily recog-
nizable in the thought of Lyotard and Deleuze is a discernment of the
articulatory performance of our nondiscursive engagements—principally
because they have discarded the logos in their celebration of paralogy and
the multiplicity of present-becoming.

The task of responding to their challenges on this particular issue is
basically that of reclaiming the articulatory power of our nondiscursive
involvements. The logos as articulation is as much at work in the texture
of our emotions and desires as in the texts of our discourse. The execution of such a task can well make use of the resources of a hermeneutical
phenomenology to elucidate the intentionality of the affects and bodily
comportment. Our actions, desires, emotions, and gestural comportment
are also ways of understanding and articulating ourselves and our world.[20]

18. See chapter one, section 4, "Plurality and Paralogy."
19. See chapter one, section 5, "Power and Desire."
20. The contributions of Sartre and Merleau-Ponty are particularly germane to this point. In
his study on the emotions, Sartre supports, in phenomenological detail, his stated thesis:
"Emotion is a certain way of apprehending the world" (*The Emotions: Outline of a Theory*,
trans. Bernard Frechtman [New York: Philosophical Library, 1948], p. 52). In *Being and Nothingness* (trans. Hazel Barnes [New York: Philosophical Library, 1956]) Sartre provides a phenomenological analysis and description of shame as an occasion of intentionality in which
self and other are simultaneously disclosed. In the experience of shame, in which I am
ashamed in the presence of the Other, I disclose myself to myself as I stand in purview of
the Other's look (pp. 261–63). Merleau-Ponty, pursuing the sense-giving performance in

CHRONOTOPAL INTERPRETATION

In our effort to track the logos as event of articulation, lying across both discursive and nondiscursive configurations, we light upon the relevance and effects of the forms of time and space. In its descent into history and the arena of communicative practices, the logos takes on the determinations of time and space. The claims of reason as events of interpretation and articulation are situated both temporally and spatially. They display retentional and protentional vectors, and they retain a spatial relevance as they move across the sites, localities, and regions of our varied communicative practices and world-engagements. In its most general sense, it is this temporal and spatial conditionedness of interpretive rationality that defines its finitude.

Kant was assuredly on the right course when he sketched the finitude of human reason within the bounds of time and space. Unfortunately, he deviated from this course when he took the transcendental turn, resulting in a construal of time and space as a priori forms of perception, functioning as universal and necessary conditions for possible objects of experience. As logical/transcendental forms, space and time came to be viewed as residing on the hither side of the temporalized and spatialized historical lifeworld, a consequence of Kant's rather rigid decoupling of the transcendental and the empirical. Kant's a priori and transcendental method may well have served the interests of a subject-centered rationality, intent on establishing its purity and autonomy by securing its independence from any attachments to the world. But in the moment that one shifts to a praxis-oriented rationality, concretized in history, social institutions, human embodiment, and language, then a different perspective on time and space is required.

Such a perspective, tailored specifically to the inscriptions of discourse and institutional practices, has been supplied by the Russian philosopher and literary historian, Mikhail Mikhailovich Bakhtin. Bakhtin's vocabulary of the chronotope, heteroglossia, the centrifugal versus the centripetal, and dialogue is particularly helpful in addressing the issues at hand. The "chronotope" is the marker of the intrinsic connectedness of time and space, which are portrayed not as a priori and abstract forms of perception but rather as concrete domiciles of the life of discourse. What is at stake in this Bakhtinian notion of the chronotope is the assimilation of historical time and historical space in the workings of the "dialogic imagination" within the projects of discourse and action. Time and space, within this concrete, praxial spatiotemporal coordinate, become vibrant and vitalized. They are seen as existential dwellings rather than as dead frames

gestures and bodily comportment, provides a similar account of the intentionality of nondiscursive world-involvement. See particularly *Phenomenology of Perception*, trans. Colin Smith (London: Routledge & Kegan Paul, 1962), Part One, chapter six; "The Body as Expression, and Speech."

of reference. "Time, as it were, thickens, takes on flesh, becomes artistically visible; likewise, space becomes charged and responsive to the movements of time, plot and history."[21]

This chronotopal configuration as a time-space assimilation houses a heteroglossia of voices that speak of times and places under varying conditions and varying circumstances. This heteroglossia receives a decisive expression in the literary-artistic chronotope (which defines Bakhtin's principal interest). In the literary-artistic chronotope multiple valences of place (e.g., the place of castles, abbeys, battlefields, and monuments) are assimilated with multiple valences of time (e.g., mythological, idyllic, pastoral, adventure, and biographical). The main point regarding heteroglossia is that there is a plurality of discourses, a multiplicity of language games if you will, that come into play when we attempt to articulate our situatedness in historical time and historical space. Our discourse, which for Bakhtin is always a *dialogic* discourse, is a heteroglot of linguistic functions, moving from one context to another. The texts of our discourse always remain beholden to the *con*-texts—scientific, moral, legal, economic, aesthetic, and religious—from which they emerge.

It is within this chronotopic dwelling of heteroglossic voices that the centripetal and centrifugal functions and forces of discourse play themselves out. The centripetal indicates the centralizing, homogenizing, and hierarchical forces of language and culture. The centrifugal marks the decentralizing, dispersing, and dismantling functions and forces. The novel, according to Bakhtin, is principally a display of centrifugal forces—particularly in its use of carnivalesque and comic genres. This is dramatically illustrated in the move from the epic to the novel. In the discourse of the epic there is a valorization of a particular tradition that binds and centralizes the progression of episodes. In the discourse of the novel the centripetal forces that define the format of the epic are dissolved by irony, laughter, and satire.

We propose the use of Bakhtin's notions of the chronotope, heteroglossia, and the centripetal and the centrifugal for further elucidating the socio-historical matrix of discursive and institutional involvement, from which all interpretation proceeds. It is important to recognize that the time and space at issue for rationality as an articulation of the configurative forms of discourse and action are as constitutive of interpretation as interpretation is constitutive of them. This is to say that time and space are not invariant dimensions that antedate the interpretive response, abstract forms prior to the event of interpretation; they are called into being through the experience of time as *time for* the envisagement and enactment of social practices, and through the experience of space as the proper *place from which* such enactment is to proceed. Time and space are depicted as *lived* time and *lived* space, and their defining features are socio-

21. Mikhail M. Bakhtin, *The Dialogic Imagination*, trans. Caryl Emerson and Michael Holquist (Austin: University of Texas Press, 1981), p. 84.

pragmatic rather than transcendental in character. One might well speak of time and space as "forms of interpretation," analogous to Kant's "forms of intuition"; but the principal difference, and one on which a great deal turns is that time and space in a hermeneutical perspective are always invested with value. They are as much achievements as givens, dynamic and variable, anisotropic rather than isotropic, as much a forming as an already formed. They are features of the world as experienced and articulated, set forth as markings of the time of origin and the time of destruction, the recollection of space lost and the anticipation of space to be regained.

The heteroglossia of voices in the odyssey of interpretation speaks of the constellations of times and places against the backdrop of a moving chronotope—a concrete, lived, historical spatiotemporal assimilation. Within such a scheme of things, the discernment and articulation that is at work in interpretive rationality is to be understood as a praxis rather than as the result of a centripetal, solitary, cognitive act. The theoretico-epistemological matrix, pivoting on a centripetal, insulated consciousness or ego, that provided the supports for a criteriological conception of rationality is effectively dismantled. Rational practices are seen to issue from a discernment and articulation of the configurative patterns concretized in our embodiment, social interaction, and institutional involvement.

The consummate contribution of the Bakhtinian notion of the chronotope is that it highlights the holism of the articulatory performance of textualized discourse. It brings into explicit relief the spatiotemporal background of the interplay of whole and part. Every interpretive practice straddles as it were two constitutive moments—an analytical discernment of parts or elemental units and a synthetical discernment of wholes into which the parts are gathered. These two constitutive moments comprise the binding textuality of discourse. A discursive performance, be it locutionary or illocutionary, is oriented to a saying of something about something, a making manifest in some manner or other. This may involve a description of a state of affairs, an issuing of a command, submitting a question, evoking a mood, or recommending an ethical or an aesthetical perspective.

These particularized portions of discourse, however, resist isolation as self-contained speech acts or atomistic linguistic units. The residual empiricism within "speech act theory" needs to be purged. Speech acts are episodes within the holism of a wider communicative performance. They ride the crest of borrowed meanings from previous portions of discourse, from usages within a public language already spoken. And they are anticipatory of a conversation yet to unfold. It is thus that a temporal horizon regulates all particular instantiations of discourse. Discourse remains irremediably temporalized, moving across a horizon of the already said to that of the not yet said. Correspondingly, discourse is also spatialized. There is always a "place" from which discourse emigrates, an embodied speaker within a social space. Discourse cannot proceed from "nowhere." And the spaces of discoese are as much surrounded by other spaces as the nows of discourse are retentionally and protentionally qualified by past and future times.

The implications of this chronotopal interplay of whole and part for the traditional epistemologically defined problems of understanding and explanation, and meaning and reference, are far reaching. Understanding and explanation, from the perspective of chronotopal interpretation, are refigured as integral moments within a whole/part interplay. We understand a portion of discourse by taking it as an exemplification of a genre or type, however blurred the genre and however open-textured the type might be. The discourse is initially identified as the making of a scientific claim, a moral prescription, an aesthetic evaluation, a panegyric, or a prayer. The determination of genre or type unfolds against the background of a spectrum of social practices and linguistic usages, including social expectancies and institutional forms as well as speakers' intentions.

But such understanding is never complete, always subject to further revision, threatened by ambiguity, and susceptible to breakdown. To assist the understanding in its confrontation with its irremovable finitude and its encounter with the threats of misunderstanding, the services of explanation are required. It is the task of explanation to focus on the distinguishable "parts" of discourse (phonemic and lexical units, grammatical structures, semantical elements) and provide an analytical explication of their functions, always cognizant of the role of these specific functions within the gestalt of discourse as an emergent whole. It is thus that understanding and explanation move to and fro between whole and part, enabling understanding and explanation to work side by side as twin halves of an august discursive event, allowing us to understand as we explain and explain as we understand.[22]

The holistic configuration of the background practices within the chronotopal assimilation of time and space supplies the required sheet anchor against a reification of the parts of discourse as brute facts. Although an analysis of the constituent parts of discourse in the interests of explanation remains an essential feature of the hermeneutical demand, the trick is to keep the analyzed lexical, syntactic, and semantic units from congealing into brute linguistic facts. The notion of a *factum brutum*

22. The efforts of Paul Ricoeur to surmount the unacceptable dichotomy of understanding and explanation are notable. He has sought to demonstrate a strict complementarity between understanding and explanation by locating them "at two different stages of a unique hermeneutical arc." *Interpretation Theory: Discourse and the Surplus of Meaning* (Fort Worth: Texas Christian University Press, 1976), p. 87. He fleshes out his notion of explanation as that which provides the "methodic moment" of hermeneutical comprehension, which proceeds along the lines of an analytical *development;* whereas understanding comprises the "nonmethodic moment," geared to an *envelopment* of the analytical developments within explanation. See "Explanation and Understanding: On Some Remarkable Connections among the Theory of the Text, Theory of Action, and Theory of History," in *The Philosophy of Paul Ricoeur*, ed. Charles E. Reagan and David Stewart (Boston: Beacon Press, 1978), p. 165.

is as much of a conceptual vagary in the domain of discourse as it is in the domains of perception and human action. Linguistic atomism gets us no farther than did the logical atomism of earlier times. Words are not atoms. Neither are sentences molecules, nor are phonemes and morphemes subatomic linguistic units. The construal of words as a species of atomic facts, isolable and quantifiable, divorces them from the text, decontextualizes them, and wrests them from their inherence in the living chronotope of discourse.

Herein resides the error not only of empiricist linguistics but structuralist linguistics as well. The determination of words as signs within a signifier/signified matrix makes purchases on the epistemological model shared by empiricism, albeit the foundational units now become relations rather than sensory qualities. In the shift from epistemology to hermeneutics, from linguistics to communication, words become media of social interaction within a communicative performance. It is in this shift that the Bakhtinian notion of discourse as *dialogic* registers its importance. Discourse is reinscribed into communication, into the dynamics of a speaker/respondent interaction.

It is at this juncture that the post-structuralist phase of postmodernism becomes directly relevant to our project. Derrida is surely to be commended for his contribution of tracking the aporia that results from the play of the signifier and the signified within a structuralist semiotics. But the sad irony in the Derridean project of deconstructing structuralism is that his project unwittingly buys into the structuralist definition of meaning as signification (which in the end is simply a linguistic version of epistemological representationalism). If indeed structuralism properly defined the meaning of meaning, and it is now found that the structuralist project of guaranteeing meaning through signifying representations collapses under its own weight, one may have grounds for abandoning the quest for meaning itself. But the conclusion in no way follows if the premise is problematized. The failure of signification, which Derrida appropriately documents, does not lead us to the conclusion that there is no other possible approach to meaning—and it is precisely this other possible approach that Derrida refuses to consider.

Here one can productively use Bakhtin against Derrida, countering Derridean *écriture* with Bakhtinian discourse as dialogic. As it turns out, both Derrida and Bakhtin make much of play, but whereas Derridean play is non-dialogic and abstract, a play of difference, in which the other is perpetually deferred as an abstract absence within an abstract alterity, Bakhtinian play is dialogic and concrete, insinuated into the density of communicative praxis as a responsive and interactional activity.[23] This

23. For a comprehensive, sustained, and uncommonly perceptive critical comparison of the thought of Bakhtin and Derrida, see Ruth Porritt, *A Textual Dialogue: Bakhtin and Derrida on Meaning in Philosophical and Poetic Texts* (doctoral dissertation, Purdue University, August 1989).

Bakhtinian notion of dialogic discourse as responsive activity opens up a new slant on the issues of meaning and reference—issues that the deconstructionists, for the most part, have consigned to the philosophical archives. In concert with its chronotopal background, dialogic discourse marks out a direction for refiguring the accomplishments of meaning and reference.

This newly won meaning and reference, it should be underscored, is meaning and reference liberated from the strictures of the epistemological paradigm. Meaning is neither the representation of a transparent essence nor a determinate signification; and the refigured reference is not to be confused with a correspondence of word with object. The "what" of dialogic textuality and the "that" of its referential claims are functions of the play of the moving chronotope in living discourse. It is only through a configuring and refiguring of language, borne by a holistic comprehension solicited by the structure and the dynamics of the text, that events of meaning and reference occur.[24] The configurations of meaning at issue here are the work of interpretation, displaying a "taking as" operation, and invoking the claims of the community on what the text means. As a social practice, rather than the adventure of a solitary ego, interpretation remains responsive to a community of interpreters and the claims of the encountered other. The articulation *of* something (meaning) *about* something (reference) always travels with a saying something *to* and *with* the other.

The inscription of meaning and its fulfillment through reference, registered in the discursive practices of humankind, remains within the bounds of a transcendence-within-immanence. This transcendence is both *intra*-textual and *inter*-textual. It follows the route of a dynamics of interpretation that goes all the way down to the constitutive parts of discourse and all the way up to the assemblages of texts and their intertextuality. The laudable gain of this transcendence within immanence is its effective stand against the encroachments of linguistic elementarism and semiotic reductionism. Discourse, praxial and textualized, is seen to play within a holistic, hermeneutical chronotope. This itself, admittedly, is already a rather remarkable achievement. However, it needs to be emphasized that this transcendence remains *within immanence*, limited to the articulations within discourse itself and restricted by the parameters of textuality/intertextuality.

Chronotopal interpretation within such a project remains directly linked

24. Paul Ricoeur has addressed the issue of a possible reformulation of the grammar of meaning and reference in two of his works, *The Rule of Metaphor* and *Time and Narrative*, Volume 3 (trans. Kathleen McLaughlin and David Pellauer [Chicago: University of Chicago Press, 1988]). In *The Rule of Metaphor* Ricoeur assumed the task of refashioning the Fregean epistemological postulate of ostensive reference into a non-objectivating "displayed reference," illustrated principally in metaphorical discourse (pp. 216–56). In *Time and Narrative*, however, Ricoeur abandons the grammars of meaning and reference alike and sets in their place the dyad of configuration/refiguration (pp. 158–59).

to a discursive praxis and a textual exercise. To be sure, it does effect a disclosure of "world," but the world disclosed is essentially the "world of the text." If not delimited, the preoccupation with discourse can slide into a linguistic closure and a pantextualism. But the chronotope, as the assimilated time and space of our socio-historical existence, has wider horizons. It reaches into the worlds of perception, action, desire, and institutional associations—into the domain of *non*discursive practices and engagements. And the rationality that we propose extends into these other worlds as well. The claims of reason that follow in the wake of the consequences of interpretation go beyond the articulatory performances within language, discourse, and textuality. There is indeed something outside the text.

FOUR

Narrative and the Claims
of Reason

THE WORLD OF NARRATIVE

One of the distinguishing marks of postmodernity is its preoccupation with narrative. Jean-François Lyotard defines the projected task of his *Postmodern Condition* to be an examination of the transformations of discourse in science, literature, and the arts "in the context of the crisis of narratives."[1] As a result of the proliferation of discourses, illustrating the heterogeneity of language games, narrativity has gravitated into a situation of crisis. On the most general level, the crisis is that of a discord between metanarratives and local narratives. The grand designs of the metanarratives of modernity have occasioned a crisis of credulity, defining the postmodern reaction, most succinctly stated, as an "incredulity toward metanarratives."[2] A more specific development within the crisis of narratives has to do with the conflict between "narrative knowledge" and "scientific knowledge," fracturing all our efforts to achieve a unity of knowledge and a commonality of discourse.

Given such a rather unpleasant state of affairs in the economy of our narrative discourses, we are challenged to come to terms with the issue of narrativity in its widest ramifications. Our preceding discussion, in which we tracked the consequences of the hermeneutical demand, already set the stage for this coming to terms with narrativity. It was in this discussion that we were able to monitor the play of discourse and textuality within the performance of reason as *articulation.* This articulatory function of reason, we found, operates within a chronotopal horizon of a conjugated time-space frame, from which discourse arises and to which it returns. We thus came to speak of a "chronotopal interpretation" that locates the articulatory posture of rationality within an assimilated time-space manifold and sets forth the "world of the text." The task of the current chapter is to explore the effects of narrativity on the claims of reason by attending to the slide of the "world of the text" into the "world of narrative." The Bakhtinian chronotope, which we found to be so help-

1. Jean-François Lyotard, *The Postmodern Condition: A Report on Knowledge,* trans. Geoff Bennington and Brian Massumi (Minneapolis: University of Minnesota Press, 1984), p. xxiii.
2. *The Postmodern Condition,* p. xxiv.

ful in our explorations of the world of the text, will also be our trust-worthy guide in exploring the world of narrative.

The introduction of the vocabulary of "the world of narrative" at this point is particularly crucial because it advances a fleshing out of the de-limitation of the associated complex of language, textuality, and dis-course. As we shall see, the world of narrative opens up to the "other" of discourse and the "outside" of textuality, forcing an acknowledgment of the alterity of the readers and hearers of written and spoken texts. The world of the text as a world of discourse is always bounded, limited, constrained by readers and hearers who mark out their own integral spaces as they respond to the written and the spoken word. The agency, the effect-producing achievement, of such responsiveness is an intervention, an intrusion of alterity, that delimits the power and the function of the text and opens up a world beyond it.

The responses admittedly assume different forms. They can be re-sponses that devise "another" text, "another" portion of discourse, defin-ing the alterity at issue as one that continues to share the space of lan-guage, textuality, and discourse. But the responses can also entail a more radical rupture with discursive practices, as for example in the responses of silence, which register their own distinctive effects and have their own story to tell.[3] Particularly decisive is the responsive activity across the spectrum of nondiscursive social practices and institutional engagements, which share the plot in the story of our socio-historical existence. The range of the world of narrative includes these nondiscursive and nontex-tualized configurations of behavior, action, and historical events. In such a scheme of things, narrative is understood as an emplotment that in-volves a responsive activity, both discursive and nondiscursive, linguistic as well as extra-linguistic, that defines our socio-historical inherence.

It will be rather quickly noted that our mapping of the world of nar-rative, which extends beyond narrational discourse, inclines us to an *on-tology* of narrative, a notion of emplotment that stands in service of an articulation of our being-in-the-world. Narrative involves not simply the composition of stories, be they literary-fictional constructs or historical-factual accounts; it has to do also with the engaged participants and the panoply of human action that informs, in different ways to be sure, our assemblages of texts.

David Carr's extensive study on narrative is of particular relevance for the ontological turn in narrativity. Carr explicates narrativity as a reflexive structure of temporalized human life and history. One might speak of this as the *strong* sense of narrative (in contrast to the *weak* sense of narrative as a discursive practice), according to which experience and action display an inherent narrative configuration. In developing this strong sense of

---

3. For a discussion of the intentionality and integrity of silence, freed from its subordination as a deficient mode of speech, see Bernard P. Dauenhauer, *Silence: The Phenomenon and Its Ontological Significance* (Bloomington: Indiana University Press, 1980).

narrative, Carr problematizes the vulgar notion of narrative, construed as a *sequel* to experience, a retrospective and after-the-fact imposition. His approach also points out the limitations of the prevailing opinion that narrative is the sole property of literary studies, understood as a textual maneuver in the ordering of the life and action of fictional characters through the construction and implementation of genre, mood, voice, and focalization. "Narrative is not a dress which covers something else but the structure inherent in human experiences and action."[4]

The ontological weight thusly ascribed to narrative as a structure of human experience opens new possibilities for the refiguration of rationality. The logos is resituated within the dynamics of world-historical experience. But it is precisely this perspective of ascribing to narrative the ontological weight of an incarnation of the logos that again elicits the postmodern challenge. Is this not simply a reshuffling of the locus of logocentrism, shifting the locus from the realm of ideas (classical thought), or epistemic foundations (modern thought), to the region of narrative? Are we not now simply asking narrative to do something that neither classical metaphysics nor modern epistemology were able to pull off, namely, provide a principle of unification that binds everything into an unblemished totality?

The worries and fears expressed by postmodernists concerning these matters are not idle fantasies. Indeed, the scenario that frightens them has already developed in the specialized discipline of *narratology*, in which the alleged "logos" of "narrative" appears as a veritable *deus ex machina*. As a semiotic science of narrative structure, narratology inherits all of the problems of structuralist linguistics, inscribing them within the broader parameters of the text itself. Chief among these problems is the violent wrenching of narrative understanding and rationality from its inherence in a moving chronotope of concretely assimilated historical time and space.[5] Narratology comes to rest in an abstract mechanics of narrative form and function and leaves us with a textual cadaver that has neither life nor history, set outside the bounds of lived experience. Summing up, it could indeed be said that narratology congeals into a narratological logocentrism. We are at one with the postmodernists in their worries about this.

The postmodern challenge, however, has another facet. Not only does it problematize the logocentrism of narrativity, it remains skeptical about any rational resources for unifying the diversity of discourses and institutional practices. This facet of the challenge is indeed formidable, but hopefully not unmanageable. We are of the mind that narrative emplot-

---

4. David Carr, *Time, Narrative, and History* (Bloomington: Indiana University Press, 1986), p. 65.

5. Paul Ricoeur articulates this inherent problem of narratology in dealing with narrative understanding when he observes that "narratology constructs an atemporal simulacrum of it." *Time and Narrative*, Volume 2, trans. Kathleen McLaughlin and David Pellauer (Chicago: University of Chicago Press, 1985), p. 14.

ment does indeed bind, integrate, assimilate, synthesize, grasp together, the multiplicity of modes of discourse, the plurality of perspectives, and the diversity of human actions within a chronotopal field. But this binding and grasping together need not congeal into a narratological logocentrism. Narrative thinking articulates patterns and lines of continuity in human experience and transforms stories into cohesive and powerful social instruments. But the logos of such thinking makes no overtures to timeless essences or atemporal transcendental conditions. The logos as a "gathering," which defines its function in narrative rationality, and which is indeed one of the more originative senses of the term, is not to be confused with the metaphysically and epistemologically sedimented conceptions of the logos as a timeless and immutable essence or a privileged locus of representation. Logos as "gathering" respects multiplicity and plurality, flux and becoming. Even Heraclitus, the philosopher of flux (who is one of the few classical philosophers praised by the postmodernists), recognized that flux was gathered by the logos.[6]

The use of narrative to flesh out the gathering function of the logos has some interesting consequences. It expands and enriches, and at the same time delimits, the discursive performance of the logos. The gathering at issue assimilates and binds not only discursive practices but also nondiscursive bodily comportment, emotions and desires, and institutional engagements. Discourse becomes narrative; the logos as "word" is taken up into the logos as "story."

Now there are stories with authors and there are stories without authors. But even in stories that have an explicit or implicit authorship, there is no special privilege to be conferred upon the authorial design. It is not that the author and the attendant authority is displaced. The announcement of the "death of the author" in some of the postmodernist literature, like the before-the-event announcement of the death of Mark Twain, is a gross exaggeration. The point at issue is not that the voice of the author is silenced but rather that the authority of that authorship of narratives is decentralized, redistributed, and resituated within a network of interdependencies. This network involves not only the narrating subject but also the readers and hearers of the narrative; preceding narrators and preceding respondents; and a wider cultural tradition of historical trends and institutions that have left their inscriptions on the body politic of humankind. These are all figures in the emplotment of the stories that

6. One of the more impressive efforts to recover the Heraclitean notion of the logos as "gathering" was undertaken by Martin Heidegger and Eugen Fink in their 1966–67 seminar on Heraclitus at Freiburg University. See *Heraclitus Seminar 1966/67*, trans. Charles H. Seibert (University, AL: University of Alabama Press, 1979). Also, John Sallis has provided extensive coverage of the notion of gathering as the internal working of the logos, particularly as illustrated in the thought of Plato and Kant. See John Sallis, *Being and Logos: The Way of Platonic Dialogue* (Pittsburgh: Duquesne University Press, 1975), and *The Gathering of Reason* (Athens, OH: Ohio University Press, 1980).

are being told, enabling a comprehension of narrative thinking as that which encompasses and gathers the communicative practices of our chronotopal existence.

This move to expand the articulatory performance of reason in the narrational logos, so as to avoid a self-closure of discourse, requires a supplement and complement to Bakhtinian heteroglossia. Heteroglossia needs to be set into complementarity with *heteroprasso*, calling upon the verbal root of praxis, *prassô* (πράσσω), which contains related senses of doing, acting, and accomplishing that are not by necessity discourse-bound. The binding performance of narrative gathers not only a multiplicity of voices but also the variegated activities and engagements of nondiscursive praxis. This move is required to avoid a narratological closure. One must say of narrative what Gary Madison has said of language: "Language does not make sense, is literally meaningless, apart from what phenomenologists call 'lived experience'. There is 'something more' than mere texts and language; there is experience."[7]

The multiple and changing discourses, texts, beliefs, desires, and institutions that make up the panoply of human experience comprise an interwoven web of interdependencies. Sometimes these discourses, beliefs, and practices hang together rather snugly, at other times more loosely, and still at other times they are subject to discontinuity and rupture. The texture of our conglomerate discourse, beliefs, and actions is an *open* texture. The configurations by dint of which they display sense are subject to refiguration or indeed overturned. It is thus that the gathering of the logos at work in their emplotment proceeds not under the guise of preestablished harmonies, invariant rules, or necessary conditions but rather according to a transversality of effects that extend across the multiple lines of communicative responses. In this emplotment there are no overtures to ahistorical universals or seamless totalities. The postmodern injunction to "wage a war on totality" can be appreciated. But the postulates of context-free universals and eidetic totalities are never given a place in our notions of rationality as praxial critique and as articulation. Nor are they given a place in our notion of rationality as narrational emplotment. The task of rationality is to discern and articulate how our discursive and nondiscursive practices hang together, however loosely, within the texture of everyday life. Its business is to track the assemblages of thought and action within the chronotope of our communicative interactions.

Of principal moment in this operation of emplotment and gathering is the determination of beginnings and ends, the inscription of *archē* and *telos*. The chronotope that situates the odyssey of narrative rationality marks out starting points and culminations. The literary narratives of fiction, which have their own special alliance with the moving chronotope that situates narrative as an inherent structure of life and history, have plots

7. Gary B. Madison, *The Hermeneutics of Postmodernity: Figures and Themes* (Bloomington: Indiana University Press, 1988), p. 165.

that begin and come to an end. But these beginnings and ends, in fiction as in life, are charged with contingency. They could have been otherwise. Correspondingly, the places associated with beginnings and ends are variable and contingent. Beginnings begin "somewhere," and endings culminate in both time and space. It is thus that the forces and forms of narrational emplotment suffer both temporal and spatial determinations. The Bakhtinian chronotope remains in play.[8]

In both fictive and historical narrative we are forced to make methodological decisions about where to begin and where to end. On this level one can discern a complementarity of works of fiction and historical accounts. The stories that novelists and historians tell share a matrix of determinations of time and space, although the time and space of fiction assumes different configurations and different reference valences than does that of the narration of historical events. Of greater existential import, however, is that the time and space constituted in both fictive constructions and historical texts is reflexive upon the chronotope of the world of actual experience and history as lived. The narrative structure of everyday life and communicative interaction itself has no absolute beginning and end.[9] It affords neither a stable *archē* nor a stable *telos*. Wherever and whenever we begin, we find that we are always already begun; and designated points of culmination become indicators of another beginning. The autobiographical and communal histories of our lives have already begun when we begin to relate them, and their endings are but overtures to new beginnings.

The location of these histories within the wider story of the sociohistorical tradition of our beliefs and practices does not make the determination of beginnings and ends any easier. Here too the tracking of an *archē* and the projection of a *telos* gravitate into sundry aporias. This intensifies the burdens of a rationality that seeks to bind beginning and end in the story of our communal and historical existence. It also cautions us about the snares in the grammar of "structure," when we speak, for example, of narrative as an inherent *structure* of human life and action. Derrida is surely to be heard when he warns us about the reduction of structure to *structurality*. "The movement of any archaeology, like that of any eschatology, is an accomplice of this reduction of the structurality of structure and always attempts to conceive of structure on the basis of a full presence which is beyond play."[10]

8. It is the marginalizing of the spatiality of narrative that mars Gerard Genette's otherwise illuminating discussion of the "time of the narrating." His claim that "the temporal determinations of the narrating instance are manifestly more important than its spatial determinations" needs to be corrected. Gerard Genette, *Narrative Discourse: An Essay in Method*, trans. Jane E. Lewin (Ithaca, NY: Cornell University Press, 1980), p. 215.
9. For trenchant discussions of some of the problems in the grammar of starting points and beginnings, see Robert Denoon Cumming, *Starting Point: An Introduction to the Dialectic of Existence* (Chicago: University of Chicago Press, 1979), and Edward W. Said, *Beginnings: Intention and Method* (New York: Basic Books, 1975).
10. Jacques Derrida, "Structure, Sign, and Play in the Discourse of the Human Sciences,"

Rationality, as the gathering and binding of the multiplicities of our praxial engagements through the resources of discernment, articulation, and configuration, remains fully cognizant of the play within and across these practices and engagements. These practices exhibit a dynamism of active and reactive forces that remains irreducible to a principle of structure that would bind the forces into an unbroken solidarity. The urge to achieve such a solidarity and impermeability in the domains of human knowledge and action may well have something to do with what Derrida has named "full presence." Such an envisaged full presence might reside in a sphere of transcendent and fixed essences; in a matrix of universal and necessary epistemic conditions; in a structural simulacrum of binary semiotic relations; in an archaeology of an untrammeled beginning; or in an eschatology of a consummatory end. Whichever way one slices the "structurality of structure," so as to accommodate the hope for a full presence, we are dealing in each instance with a fugitive logos on the hither side of history.

The problematization of such a logos outside of history is a recurring project of postmodernity. No proofs for the impossibility of such a logos are offered, as one finds, for example, in Sartre's ontological proof of its nonexistence, which proceeds by way of a demonstration of an internal contradiction within the desire to be God. What we have instead is a joyful paganism of rhapsodic celebration of the "death of God." This Nietzschean aestheticism of affirmation pervades much of the burgeoning postmodern literature and may indeed comprise its dominant formative influence. Simplified to the extreme, postmodernity is a recovery of Nietzschean aestheticism.

This provides us with a more specific way of consolidating the postmodern challenge, enabling a somewhat more direct response to it. The key players in the scenario can now be identified as the absence of full presence and a new historicism that finds all of the action to occur within the historically local and specific. Within such a scheme of things, the full presence of an ahistorical logos remains a conceptual vagary. But there is a "problem" in this problematization of presence and the ahistorical, and it has to do with certain unexamined presuppositions and a slippage in the key notions at issue. The assault on full presence and the ahistorical achieves intelligibility only against the backdrop of a logocentric, theo-metaphysical grand narrative; just as Nietzsche's anti-Platonism only becomes intelligible as a reaction against the Platonism that he purported to deconstruct. In the very positioning of the assault, however, there are unmonitored purchases made on the senses of "presence," "history," and "logos" that pre-define the issues at stake and place undue restrictions on their possible refiguration.

It is presupposed that the only sense of "logos" is the universal logos

in *Writing and Difference*, trans. Alan Bass (Chicago: University of Chicago Press, 1978), p. 279.

of traditional metaphysics and epistemology; the only sense of "presence" is that of a plentitude of being; and the only sense of "history" is that defined through the opposition of the ahistorical and the historically specific. But are these presuppositions themselves unproblematic? It may indeed be the case that the universal logos has become bankrupt, but what compels us to define the logos with the grammar of universality? Is presence somehow by necessity a "full presence," or might one quite meaningfully speak of degrees of presentation, a contingent presence, which in our finite experiencing remains variable, partial, and incomplete—but which is an encountered presence nonetheless? Is the pulverization of historical experience into a random play of the historically specific the only alternative to an ahistorical standpoint, or might one be able to find a place and a time for a *trans*-historical understanding, articulation, and critique that neither voices ahistorical appeals nor settles for the thin historicism of sheer present-becoming?

We have already come a short way in addressing these questions as we respond to the postmodern challenge. Our explication of the dynamics of praxial critique as a performance of discernment, our tracking of the consequences of interpretation for a new perspective on rationality as articulation, and our foray into narrative as an emplotment and gathering of the multiple discourses and actions in our communicative involvements have all shown how the despised logos of the metaphysical and epistemological tradition, which is the bane of all postmodernity, can be refigured and reclaimed. Along the way, the transversal working of the logos, which provides us with an alternative to the universal logos and manages a maneuver "between" the hegemonic, ahistorical claims of the tradition and the rhapsodic play of the new historicism of postmodernity, has already been adumbrated. However, given certain complexities within the notion of transversality, a discussion of its specific relevance for a refigured notion of rationality will have to await a subsequent chapter. In the meantime, additional issues pertaining to the role of narrative, as well as the topic of rhetoric and rationality, need to be addressed.

NARRATIVITY AND KNOWLEDGE

The linkage of narrative and knowledge has been made an explicit theme in the philosophy of Jean-François Lyotard. He pursues this theme against the backdrop of a distinction between metanarratives and local narratives, on the one hand, and a distinction between narrative knowledge and scientific knowledge, on the other hand. The former distinction provides the space for his well-known definition of postmodernity as an incredulity toward metanarratives, in which the term "metanarrative" stands for a discourse of legitimation that makes appeals to some grand story—like that of the dialectics of Spirit, the hermeneutics of meaning, the emancipation of the subject, or the creation of wealth.[11] Metanarratives purport to bind the totality of discourse and action into an overarching or undergirding unity. Local narratives, on the other hand, are always content-specific in their emplotment of human concerns and events. Although Lyotard is not all that generous in providing us with examples of local narratives, it would seem that the story of gender discrimination, the story of the experience of blacks in a racist society, and the story of ethnocentrism in political life would serve quite well as illustrations of local narratives. The chief mark of local narratives is that they are more responsive to the diversity of micro-practices in everyday life and the plurality of language games that pervade our discourse.

More to the point at issue in our present concerns having to do with the intercalation of narrativity and knowledge, however, is Lyotard's distinction between "the pragmatics of scientific knowledge" and "the pragmatics of narrative knowledge." He develops this distinction by way of a strategy of contrastive comparison. Scientific knowledge plays only one language game (denotation) and excludes all others; narrative knowledge embraces a variety of language games (including description, prescription, evaluation, interrogation, injunction, and declaration). Scientific knowledge makes use of statements that do not coalesce into a social bond; narrative knowledge allows the society in which its stories are told to define the criteria of competence and evaluation. The competence required for the legitimation of scientific knowledge concerns the post of the sender alone—no competence is required of the addressee; in narrative knowledge there is a doubling over of the posts of the sender and the addressee. The validity of scientific statements is independent of the fact of their being reported and rests on the success of argumentation and proof; narrative knowledge makes no overtures to argumentation and proof because it does not give priority to the question of its own legitimation. The game of scientific knowledge presupposes a diachronic temporality; the temporality of narrative knowledge is rhythmic.[12]

These distinctions between scientific and narrative knowledge, in which the lines of demarcation appear to be rather rigidly drawn, has led at least one interpreter of Lyotard's thought to see the contrast at issue as "pretty much the traditional positivist contrast between 'applying the scientific method' and 'unscientific' political or religious or common-sensical discourse."[13] This may turn out to be a somewhat hasty conclusion. Although scientific knowledge as defined by Lyotard has built into it the requirement for legitimation, the procedures for such are not of the positivistic, verificationist sort. There may, indeed, be problems in Lyotard's pragmatics of scientific legitimation, but such would not appear to be those

---

11. *The Postmodern Condition*, p. xxiii.
12. *The Postmodern Condition*, pp. 18–27.
13. Richard Rorty, "Habermas and Lyotard on Postmodernity," in *Habermas and Modernity*, ed. Richard J. Bernstein (Cambridge, MA: The MIT Press, 1985), p. 163.

that accompany the positivist's vocabulary of protocol statements and atomic facts. Furthermore, the radical bifurcation of the cognitive and the non-cognitive, legislated by positivism, is absent in Lyotard's contrastive comparison. According to Lyotard, we are to understand both the pragmatics of science and the pragmatics of narrative as forms of *knowledge*. Narrative knowledge displays its own cognitive import and, no less than science, assembles statements within a framework of generally accepted and applicable rules.

> First, drawing a parallel between science and nonscientific (narrative) knowledge helps us understand, or at least sense, that the former's existence is no more—and no less—necessary than the latter's. Both are composed of sets of statements; the statements are 'moves' made by the players within the framework of generally applicable rules; these rules are specific to each particular kind of knowledge, and the 'moves' judged to be 'good' in one cannot be of the same type as those judged 'good' in another, unless it happens that way by chance[14]

Lyotard's concern in contrasting science and narrative is not to set the stage for a reduction of the one to the other; nor is it to isolate the one as honest-to-goodness knowledge and thus cognitively devalue the other. The concern at issue is more of a Wittgensteinian sort, namely that of securing a place for both through an acknowledgment of the diversity of language games. The language game of scientific knowledge plays in a different court than does that of narrative knowledge. The validity of the one cannot be judged by criteria operative in the other.[15]

It is this realignment of scientific and narrative knowledge that is at the base of Lyotard's recoil from the preoccupation with theory and epistemological grounding in the thought of modernity. The diversity of language games prohibits any unification of modernity's celebrated culture-spheres (science, morality, and art) through an appeal to an architectural rationality that binds the spheres in accordance with a theoretical matrix of universal validation and legitimation. The three spheres fall out as diverse spaces of discourse, regulated by heteromorphous language games. The recognition of a heterogeneity of linguistic usage, and the accompanying diversity of criteria, would seem to provide a durable sheet anchor against any freewheeling theoretical constructionism and any urge to consolidate the multifaceted overtures toward knowledge in science, morality, and art into a metanarrative.

Yet, Lyotard's framing of the issues leaves us with some unattended matters. One needs to ask about the ascription of "knowledge" to science and narrative alike, and one needs clarification on the common designa-

14. *The Postmodern Condition*, p. 26.
15. "It is therefore impossible to judge the existence or validity of narrative knowledge on the basis of scientific knowledge and vice versa: the relevant criteria are different." *The Postmodern Condition*, p. 26.

tor, "pragmatics," used in speaking about "the pragmatics of scientific knowledge" and "the pragmatics of narrative knowledge," as the particular discursive situation dictates. In what sense are the two items in Lyotard's contrastive comparison illustrations of knowledge? In what sense do they display the inscriptions of a "pragmatics"? These are questions that need to be addressed, and it is not all that clear how they could be addressed from Lyotard's perspective on the workings of narrativity as it relates, or fails to relate, to the diverse language games in science, morality, and art.

We propose that what is lacking in Lyotard's ruminations on the role of narrative is a recognition of the interpretive moment within both of the alleged forms of knowledge, "narrative" and "scientific" alike. The principal difficulty resides in Lyotard's construal of the task and function of hermeneutics. His opening gambit, in which he identifies "the hermeneutics of meaning" as one of the main exemplifications of the grand narratives of modernity, already gives us a clue that there will be troubles ahead. Admittedly, the mistake of identifying hermeneutics as a grand narrative is understandable. In its somewhat tortuous development, from Aristotle to Gadamer, hermeneutics has at times succumbed to the totalizing urge of metanarrational discourse, to the constructionist designs of a *theory* of interpretation, and to the quest for epistemic grounding. If not presenting itself as a "new epistemology"—and certainly Dilthey's version of hermeneutics came close to that—it often defined its task as that of at least supplementing traditional epistemology, helping epistemology · to do its job, for which it seemed to lack sufficient resources on its own. Given these developments within hermeneutics, and particularly during the modern period, one can appreciate Lyotard's reluctance to invoke yet another appeal to hermeneutical thought. Yet, it is precisely such an appeal that needs to be made—because the hermeneutical requirement is unavoidable, whether one deals with knowledge in science, morality, or art. Caution, however, needs to be exercised so as not to confuse hermeneutics with simply another version of epistemological grounding.

In the preceding chapter we tracked the consequences of the hermeneutical imperative and showed how it can be refigured in such a way as to maneuver an end run, outflanking the modern theoretico-epistemological paradigm. Hermeneutics is neither an extension of nor supplement to nor substitute for the project of an epistemological reconstruction of knowledge. The hermeneutical turn navigates us to another space—the space of communicative praxis, in which the response of interpretation answers not to the request for a *Letztebegrundung* but rather to the requirement for an articulation of the forms of life as they become manifest in a discourse and action positioned against the background of a history of social and institutional practices.

The central point to be made at this stage of our explorations is that interpretation is as much at work in the process of scientific discovery as it is in the emplotment of narrative knowledge. Interpretation goes all the way down and all the way back, whether one is playing the language game of science, morality, art, or religion. One of the more extensive and illuminating discussions of the role of hermeneutics in scientific understanding and explanation has been supplied by Patrick A. Heelan in his recent book, *Space-perception and the Philosophy of Science*. Moving out from a hermeneutic of space-perception and a phenomenology of constitutive profiles within a world-horizon, Heelan shows, almost effortlessly, how this hermeneutic of perception and phenomenology of world-constitution is at the core of scientific observation and research.[16]

To pursue projects of scientific research and discovery one needs to fashion a disciplinary matrix. Lyotard, of course, is quite aware of this and points out that the establishment of such a matrix will involve the selection of an appropriate vocabulary, a determination of the genre of the relevant language game, rules for the combination of sentences, and designated criteria of validation. The point that Lyotard apparently misses is that this constitution of the disciplinary matrix for scientific investigation (which indeed includes all of the things that he mentions) is at once a project and strategy of interpretation.

Interpretation is at work in selecting the vocabulary of science, defining its language game, and demarcating its regions of subject matter. The scientific investigator, in concert with other investigators, constitutes the parameters of inquiry, in which certain data are isolated and pinned down. In this isolating and pinning down, the data in question—be they physical, biological, psychological, or social "facts"—become data only through a hermeneutical performance of *taking something as something*. The "hermeneutical as" is thus already in play when the game of science begins with the constitution of its disciplinary matrix. And on this level of originary constitution, the "as structure" of interpretation is as much in play in the physical as in the social sciences. When the physicist constitutes a disciplinary matrix, data are defined by taking happenings in the physical world as signifying such and such, and by making methodological decisions for the inclusion of one region of happenings and the exclusion of another. In all this, interpretation is already operative. Interpretation rides the crest of all disciplinary constitution, selection and determination of data, and methodological decisions with respect to grammar and procedure.

It is thus the case that in setting the stage for inquiry there is no interesting distinction between the physical and the social sciences. Both respond to the hermeneutical demand in setting up their disciplinary practices. These practices are always informed by a community of investigators and are contextualized within a history of scientific praxis. The constitu-

16. Patrick A. Heelan, *Space-perception and the Philosophy of Science* (Berkeley: University of California Press, 1983). See particularly chapter 1, "Phenomenology, Hermeneutics, and Philosophy of Science," and chapter 13, "Hermeneutics and the History of Science."

tion of a disciplinary matrix, whether in the natural or the social sciences, is a corporate performance by a community of investigators and interpreters. The claims of scientific knowledge, no less than the claims of narrative knowledge, are the claims of community.

Interpretation is thus very much involved with the programmatics of scientific and narrative knowledge alike. Lyotard glosses the play of interpretation across the constituted domains of knowledge. He prejudges "the hermeneutics of meaning" as a metanarrative and then simply includes it among the other metanarratives that he has identified (the dialectics of Spirit, the emancipation of the subject, and the creation of wealth). All of these metanarratives, according to Lyotard, suffer the same fate. They are placed in limbo for want of credulity. Responding to Lyotard's mistake, we have restored the hermeneutical demand within the interstices of the knowledge business as it is transacted in the spheres of science, morality, and art. This restored hermeneutics, however, is not that of a metanarrational variety, guided by a theoretical reconstruction of the foundations of knowledge.

In suppressing the workings of interpretation in the advancement of knowledge, Lyotard also abridges the claims of community upon the scientific enterprise. This follows from his separation of scientific "statements" from what he calls "the social bond." Scientific statements, however, are as much socially bonded as are the language games of narrative discourse. There is no scientific truth decontextualized from the community of scientific investigators and interpreters. Part of the problem in Lyotard's approach to these matters has to do with his restriction of statements in the scientific language game to the denotative or constative type, thus failing to recognize the slide of the denotative into the descriptive and the evaluative, not only in ordinary, everyday discourse but in the annals of expert, scientific knowledge as well. A recognition of this would have mitigated Lyotard's predilection to formulate his contrastive comparison of scientific and narrative knowledge with such a heavy accent on the contrastive features.

The final lesson to be learned from all this is that not only the consequences of interpretation but also the consequences of narrational emplotment are orthogonal to the various culture-spheres of our wider historical existence. Scientists, moralists, and artists are not only interpreters; they are also storytellers. Such is the case even though their interpretations and their stories are about different regions, profiles, and features of the world.

A particularly illuminating illustration of the inmixing of narrative and interpretation across the multiple language games and genres of knowledge is supplied by Michel Foucault in his collection of a variety of accounts of the life of the eighteenth-century French hermaphrodite, Herculine Barbin. After having discovered the diary of Herculine in the archives of the French Department of Public Hygiene, Foucault set Herculine's memoirs alongside the available texts pertaining to the life history of this tragic figure. These texts included chronicles of biographical data, medical records, scientific explanations, press reports, legal documents, and a literary reconstruction ("A Scandal at the Convent" by Oscar Panizza). The consolidated result of Foucault's collecting and editing of these different texts is a multi-narrational collage of stories, overlapping discursive exercises, and blurred genres, accomplishing an emplotment of the world of Herculine Barbin.[17]

NARRATIVE RATIONALITY AND THE LIFEWORLD

Our investigations of the preceding sections into the world of narrative and narrative knowledge have already foreshadowed the relevance of the experience and concept of the lifeworld. The emplotting at work in narrative gathers the figures and scenes of discourse into a world-configuration and articulates the conjunctions and disjunctions of human experience. Narrative knowledge has a hand in the constitution of this world, in its manifold modifications, as a plurality of horizons and profiles open to disciplined explorations. We speak of the "worlds" of science, morality, and art; and in doing so we begin to consolidate our discourse about the culture-spheres that define our historical inherence. But the notion of world suffers further differentiations, both in the everyday speech of the vulgar and the expert discourse of the learned. We speak of the "world of business" and the "world of politics"; the "world of academe" and the "world of sport"; the "world of the adult" and the "world of the child."

There seems to be virtually no end to the proliferation of world-horizons, each of which invites a determination of the contents of knowledge within them. One also notices, pretty much straightaway, that each of these worlds takes on historical predicates. In each there are sub-worlds of predecessors, contemporaries, and successors.[18] The multiplicity of worlds unfolds within a moving chronotope of lived time and lived space. It is this phenomenon of a multiplicity of world-horizons and their chronotopal situatedness that lays upon us the requirement to take up the thematic of the lifeworld, particularly in connection with its bearing upon the resources and limits of rationality.

The vocabulary of "lifeworld" and "world-horizons" has, of course,

17. Michel Foucault, *Herculine Barbin,* trans. Richard McDougall (New York: Random House, 1980).
18. Alfred Schutz and Thomas Luckmann have given specific attention to the temporal and historical features in their analysis of the constitution of the lifeworld. They distinguish four interconnected spatiotemporal world regions: (1) the world of contemporaries that is displayed through face-to-face encounters; (2) the world of contemporaries that consists of those removed from the more intimate we-relation, but that is nonetheless still effectively known; (3) the ancestral world of predecessors; and (4) the world of successors. See *The Structures of the Life-World,* trans. Richard M. Zaner and H. Tristram Engelhardt, Jr. (Evanston: Northwestern University Press, 1973), pp. 84–92.

been with us for some time. Although it would be an exaggeration to say that Husserl invented the concept of the lifeworld, the fact remains that it played an unprecedented philosophical role in his thought, particularly in the thought of his later period. It is common to divide the philosophical contribution of Husserl into two periods, flagged by epigrams selected from his own texts. The thought of the early period was oriented toward a "rigorous science" (strenge Wissenschaft), designed to effect a disciplined and painstaking approach "to the data themselves" (zu den Sachen Selbst). The thought of the later period staged a "return to the lifeworld" (Rückgang auf die Lebenswelt). To what extent these two periods exemplify a basic shift, or even reversal, in the story of Husserl's intellectual development, and to what extent they comprise an unbroken progression, continues to be debated in the literature on Husserl-interpretation. There is, however, agreement on the singular importance of the lifeworld concept in his later reflections.

Husserl's understanding and use of the lifeworld comes into relief against the backdrop of his program of transcendental phenomenology. Whatever modifications may have resulted from the move to Husserl's later period, the transcendental requirement and the search for foundations in a final grounding (Letztebegrundung) remained relatively unaffected. Against this backdrop, the lifeworld emerges as the final constitutive structure of socio-historical experience, culminating the arduous odyssey of a phenomenological reflection as it moves from an objective constitution, to a subjective constitution, to an intersubjective constitution, and then to a constitution of the lifeworld as the encompassing spatiotemporal horizon of life and history.

The legacy of Husserl's concept of the lifeworld is fully visible in the thought of one of the more prominent of his phenomenological successors, Alfred Schutz. However, the concept is put to a different use in Schutz's phenomenology, as a result of his revision of Husserl's original phenomenological program. The most consequential effect of this revision is a defusing of the impelling transcendental/eidetic charge that energized Husserl's phenomenological investigations. "The eidetic domain, i.e., the pure world of essence," says Schutz, "can be left out of account in considering the constitution of the world of experience."[19] According to Schutz, the resources of a "mundane" phenomenology are sufficient to deliver the goods pertaining to the lifeworld. No appeals to transcendental and eidetic constitution are necessary. This alignment of the lifeworld with a mundane rather than a transcendental phenomenology secured its availability for the project of interpretive sociology—and it was in the domain of sociology, and social philosophy more generally, that Schutz's principal interests resided.

Within the context of this revised phenomenological paradigm, the

19. Alfred Schutz, The Phenomenology of the Social World, trans. George Walsh and Frederick Lehnert (Evanston: Northwestern University Press, 1966), p. 79.

lifeworld figures chiefly as the taken-for-granted stock of knowledge that regulates the everyday, intersubjective associations of social agents. This implicit, taken-for-granted knowledge, ensconced within the intersubjective lifeworld of actors and agents, defines the data for the investigations of interpretive sociology. It needs to be noted, however, that in this move from transcendental phenomenology to phenomenological/interpretive sociology, the Husserlian "principle of all principles," the primacy of consciousness, remains intact. The way to the understanding of the lifeworld proceeds by way of "the constitution of meaningful lived experience in the constitutor's own stream of consciousness." [20]

The lifeworld motif was appropriated by other contributors to the philosophical developments of the twentieth century, and here too it underwent significant modifications. In the thought of Heidegger and Gadamer another perspective on the lifeworld is set forth. The backdrop for ruminations on the lifeworld shifts from the designs both of a transcendental phenomenology and a phenomenological sociology to that of an existentially motivated hermeneutical phenomenology, in which the primacy of consciousness and subject-centered reflection are brought into question. In the perspectives of Heidegger and Gadamer alike there is a heavy emphasis on the *pre*-subjective background of the lifeworld, an accentuation of the play of prejudgments *(Vorurteile)* in the understanding of self and world, and a principal importance accorded to language and its role in shaping the contours of the lifeworld.

Of special moment for our current project is the way that another prominent contemporary thinker, the social theorist Jürgen Habermas, appropriates the lifeworld vocabulary. Habermas's implementation of the lifeworld concept is of particular relevance to our concerns because of its role in his design of a theory of communicative rationality, which provides its own distinctive response to the postmodern challenge. The role and function of the lifeworld is quite prominently inscribed in his monumental work, *The Theory of Communicative Action*, and particularly in Volume Two, which is appropriately subtitled "Lifeworld and System: A Critique of Functionalist Reason." [21]

What Habermas offers is basically a *reconstruction* of the lifeworld concept, tailored to fit his general project of devising a broadly gauged social theory, in which the subject-centered rationality of modernity is internally critiqued and supplanted by a communication-based theory of rationality. On the way to this new forum, a number of things happen that rechart the philosophical contribution of the lifeworld thematic. Certain traditional signposts for the terrain of the lifeworld, however, remain—particularly some of those that were erected by Schutz. When, for example, Habermas defines the lifeworld as "a reservoir of taken-for-granteds, of

---

20. *The Phenomenology of the Social World*, p. 45.
21. Jürgen Habermas, *The Theory of Communicative Action*, Volume Two: *Lifeworld and System: A Critique of Functionalist Reason*, trans. Thomas McCarthy (Boston: Beacon Press, 1987).

unshakable convictions that participants in communication draw upon in cooperative processes of interpretation,"[22] we seem to be on rather familiar ground. But the terrain changes when we observe the shift from the "phenomenological concept" to the "communication-theoretic concept" of the lifeworld.[23] Here the old becomes new, and mainly because one has allegedly moved free of the strictures of subject-centered reflection, in which the lifeworld is no more than "the mirror of the isolated actor's subjective experience,"[24] and advanced into the lights of a theoretically based communicative rationality.

This shift to a communication-theoretic concept of the lifeworld transforms the consciousness-imbued intersubjectivity of the classical phenomenological perspective into a discursively oriented lifeworld of "everyday practice" *(Alltagspraxis)*. Such a reconstruction of the lifeworld, Habermas assures us, is eminently better "suited for demarcating an object domain of social science."[25] And it is the supplying of such an object domain by the lifeworld that alone will fulfill the requirements for the theoretical reconstruction of rationality that Habermas proposes.

We are clearly of one mind with Habermas in his dedication to reclaim the resources of reason in the face of intermittent announcements of its demise in certain postmodern neighborhoods. We also agree that the classical phenomenological concept of the lifeworld needs to be reassessed. We harbor our own suspicions about the use of the concept in the interests of a *Letztebegrundung*, and we share Habermas's conviction that the modernist philosophy of consciousness and subject-centered rationality have outworn their usefulness. Yet, we are of the opinion that Habermas's embrace of the protocols of theoretical reconstruction leads to an overdetermination of what rational thought can deliver and glosses the indigenous transversal intentionality of praxial critique, articulation, and disclosure. What we witness as we watch the development of Habermas's theory of communicative action is a progressive slide toward objectification and system-construction, and a tendency to sublate the insight and discernment within a politics of praxis into structures of theoretical cognition. In the process, the lifeworld itself becomes jeopardized, if not disfigured, and the arena of local, sociopolitical praxis, in which the inscriptions of communicative discourse and action make the difference, is abandoned.[26]

22. *The Theory of Communicative Action*, p. 124.
23. *The Theory of Communicative Action*, p. 126.
24. *The Theory of Communicative Action*, p. 130.
25. *The Theory of Communicative Action*, p. 135.
26. For a sustained critique of the particulars in Habermas's construal of the lifeworld, see Fred R. Dallmayr, *Critical Encounters: Between Philosophy and Ethics*, chapter 3, "Life-World and Communicative Action: Habermas" (Notre Dame: University of Notre Dame Press, 1987). Dallmayr is particularly concerned to point out the ambivalence in Habermas's sketched transformation of the lifeworld, as this sketch vacillates among inspirations drawn from

In monitoring this drift of the lifeworld into objectification, congealing into an "object domain of social science," under the aegis of a theoretical imperative, we are interested to learn that the move is facilitated by a somewhat unexpected helpmate—namely, *narrative*.

> In the communicative practice of everyday life, persons do not only encounter one another in the attitude of participants; they also give narrative presentations of events that take place in the context of their lifeworld. *Narration* is a specialized form of constative speech that serves to describe sociocultural events and objects . . . the everyday concept of the lifeworld presupposed in the *perspective of narrators* is already being used for cognitive purposes.[27]

The lifeworld as object domain effectively achieves its status through narration, and the key characteristic of narrative, according to Habermas, is that it is "a specialized form of constative speech," oriented to description, using the lifeworld "for cognitive purposes"—or as Habermas frames it in the portion of text that follows, narrative makes the lifeworld "theoretically fruitful."[28]

The restriction of narration to constative speech, to the language game of description, and to a cognitive/theoretical function, is of course the bugbear in all this. The world of narrative, as we have amply shown, is bounded neither by constative discourse nor theoretical design. It is indeed a world in which a multiplicity of language games play, and at times intersect, and in which the resultant emplotment is a gathering of a combined *heteroglossia* and *heteroprasso*, a mingling and intertexturing of discourse and action that articulate and disclose the conjunctions and disjunctions in the panoply of human experience. That there is a knowledge-moment in this articulation and narration is not denied. But what is contested is the solidification of the range and function of narrative into a structure of "constative speech" and "cognitive purposes." The hegemony of the modern epistemological paradigm resurfaces in Habermas's tailoring of narrative to fit the designs of his social theory, and this in spite of his jettisoning of the primacy of consciousness and the sovereignty of the epistemological subject.

The task that now confronts us is that of collecting the results of our abbreviated sketch of the lifeworld thematic from Husserl to Habermas and arriving at some position statement on the peculiar alliance of the world of narrative with the lifeworld, explicating the role that rationality plays in this alliance. First, it is necessary to consolidate in some manner our understanding and use of the lifeworld as it figures in our wider

Husserlian, Schutzian, Heideggerian, and Gadamerian perspectives, and to show how Habermas fails to bring his theory-based sketch into sync with his earlier discussion of "mythical world-views." See pp. 90–94.
27. *The Theory of Communicative Action*, pp. 136–37.
28. *The Theory of Communicative Action*, p. 137.

project of reclaiming and refiguring the resources of reason. Although there are notable differences in the orchestration of the lifeworld motif from Husserl to Habermas, there does appear to be at least one thread of continuity that persists. This pertains to the play of forces, both active and reactive, in the exigency of *experience*—and herein may reside the distinctive contribution of phenomenological philosophy. Whether one takes as one's measure the directive of Husserl's early period ("to the data themselves") or the directive of his later reflections ("return to the life-world"), what remains is the request for some serious attention to be given to the dynamics of experience as it is *lived through*.

Of singular importance is the recognition that the "experience" at stake in a phenomenological elucidation is not a collection of granular units, isolated sense data, discrete sensations or impressions. The atomistic and reductionist view of experience, the peculiar legacy of classical British empiricism, is effectively undermined by phenomenology, in which experience is portrayed as a field-configuration, positioning the presented contents against a background of the already experienced and a foreground of the yet to be experienced. This chronotopal field encompasses both discursive and nondiscursive determinants, both speech and action, both the personal and the social. It is this global and variegated texture of experience that is indexed by the grammar of the lifeworld.

This expanded and emphatically contextualized notion of experience, vitalizing the figures and lines of force in the concrete lifeworld, was also given expression in the tradition of American pragmatism. William James, for example, in his effort to overcome the pulverization of experience into discrete and disconnected sense impressions by traditional empiricism, made much of the need to recover what he called "the world experienced."[29] He came to understand such a recovery as comprising the central task of his *radical* empiricism. What James called "the world experienced" looks very much indeed like the phenomenological "lifeworld," and an understanding of the issues at hand could be greatly advanced by a reading of the one through the other.[30]

The specific contribution that a pragmatist reading of the lifeworld could supply is an explicit orientation of the notion in the direction of praxial engagements and social practices, providing a corrective not only to the transcendental turn of classical phenomenology but also to the use of the lifeworld concept in the service of theoretical reconstruction. As James was intent on showing that radical empiricism had no need for a tran-

29. William James, *Essays in Radical Empiricism* (New York: Longmans, Green and Co., 1942), p. 170.
30. The main lines and directions for such a cross-reading of the philosophy of James and phenomenology have already been marked out by Bruce Wilshire in his book *William James and Phenomenology: A Study of "The Principles of Psychology"* (Bloomington: Indiana University Press, 1968). Also see Charlene Haddock Seigfried, *William James's Radical Reconstruction of Philosophy* (Albany: SUNY Press, 1990).

scendental ego to swoop down from on high to provide the connections within experience, so one might generalize the target of James's criticism to include theoretical construction in all of its guises.

This translates into an admonition to take praxis seriously and lay to rest the dreadfully dreary exercise of restating the old theory/practice dichotomy. Let us suppose that the pragmatist principle that all distinctions arise from experience merits consideration. Let us further suppose that the experience at issue here is that of an expanded and contextualized world-experiencing life. Let us further suppose that the lines of force in this experiencing lead to engaged participation and distanciating critique, to articulations through the spoken word and the enacted deed, to a gathering and configuration of beliefs and practices through the emplotment of the conversation and deeds of humankind. Consequent to these suppositions we have no need for a grand theory to back up praxial critique, articulation, and narrational configuration, all of which are quite capable of accomplishing their designs within the dynamics of experience itself.

In this alliance of the world of narrative with a refigured praxis-oriented lifeworld, narrative rationality takes on a peculiar posture and role. The definition of narration as a form of constative speech designed to facilitate description places undue restrictions on the range and resources of narrative. In the preceding sections of this chapter we have delineated the world of narrative in such a manner as to make visible an emplotment of figures and events across a landscape of multiple language games and a variety of discourses. In this emplotment, rationality is at work in the guise of configuring and gathering the details of the story being told. But we also were led to recognize the limits of narrative as a discursive accomplishment, thus invoking a retrenchment of narrative as a patterning of life and history itself, within a chronotopal matrix of lived time and lived space. We distinguished between the weak and the strong sense of narrative. The weak sense pertains to narrative under the patronage of discursivity and textuality; the strong sense is indicative of the functioning of narrative in the life of perception, action, desire, and human institutions. Understood in the strong sense narrative is a chronotopal structure of life and history as lived.

We are now in position to see how this distinction between the weak and the strong sense of narrative is essentially the effect of the slide of the "world of narrative" into the "lifeworld," occasioning a delimitation of narrative as a discursive and textual accomplishment. The peculiar status and function of narrative is that it completes rationality as articulation in its progression from the lexeme, to the sentence, to the text, to the story. But in this function of completing rationality as articulation, narrative still labors under certain constraints, due to its close fraternization with discourse and textuality. It thus becomes a candidate for its own delimitation, forced to acknowledge that just as there is something outside the text, so there is also something outside discursive narration. This delimitation is announced most profoundly in the slide of the world of narrative into the lifeworld.

To track the dynamics of rationality one needs to give particular attention to what transpires *between* the world of narrative and the lifeworld. This will bring to prominence rationality as a performance of *disclosure*. Admittedly, the disclosive function of rationality is closely allied with its articulative function. Indeed, according to Charles Taylor, they are so intimately connected that he sees the one as collapsing into the other. The "task of reason" in dealing with the background of nonexplicit engagements with the world, says Taylor, is "that of articulating this background, 'disclosing' what it involves."[31] We, however, wish to maintain a distinction between articulation and disclosure, not for the sake of proliferating distinctions that make little difference, but rather to seize the opportunity to readdress concerns about meaning and reference without relying on the presuppositions and postulates of the criteriological rationality of epistemology, and in doing so supply another response to the postmodern challenge of undecidable meaning and inscrutable reference.

We propose to reframe and refigure the problem of meaning and reference against the backdrop of the close association, indeed entwinement, of articulation and disclosure. Articulation answers the call for meaning; disclosure responds to the requirement for reference. The interplay of articulation and disclosure will need to be kept in view as reason responds to the double demand for meaning and reference. Rationality as disclosure does not displace rationality as articulation. It works hand in glove with it. The logos as articulation of the world of narrative remains in harmony with the logos as disclosure of the wider lifeworld of perception, desire, action, and lived-through historical experience. Logos as disclosure is geared to the globally situated "phenomena" of lived experience. Logos thus eventuates as the "logos of the phenomena" in a refigured phenomenology of the lifeworld.

The disclosure at issue houses the related senses of uncovering, making manifest, bringing out of closure, opening up, letting something be seen, facilitating a showing of that which shows itself. It is important to note that disclosure, phenomenologically and hermeneutically understood, is not a facile making transparent, laying bare, representing, or somehow mirroring the recessed structures of everyday life. On this point we do well to take seriously the lesson that can be learned from Heidegger's radicalization of phenomenology, in which "phenomenon" is explicated not simply as that which "shows itself" (*das Sichzeigende*) but as a somewhat more ambiguous state of affairs in which the showing always has an underbelly of not-showing, of remaining hidden or concealed. A

31. Charles Taylor, "Overcoming Epistemology," in *After Philosophy: End or Transformation?*, ed. Kenneth Baynes, James Bohman, and Thomas McCarthy (Cambridge, MA: The MIT Press, 1987), pp. 477–78.

phenomenon thus displays the paradoxical feature of both showing and not showing, unconcealing and concealing, making manifest and remaining latent, becoming present with insinuations of absence.[32] There is no making manifest that is not accompanied by a covering up or concealing. There is no presence without an admixture of absence. There is no transparency of phenomena and no lucidity of disclosure. This effectively places disclosure outside the matrix of epistemology, either of a realist or idealist sort, and frees it from the aporia of a representational theory of truth. The realism/idealism controversy itself, and the associated debates on representationalism and constructivism, are diffused by the radicalization of phenomenology as a hermeneutical rather than an epistemological undertaking.

Within such a scheme of things, phenomena take on the character of perceived objects, forces of desire, habits, and social practices that appear against the background of an ever-receding chronotopal horizon that offers only partial and changing perspectives, constrained by an irremovable finitude. Ontologically expressed, this defines the intrusion of nonbeing into the realm of being, the insinuation of absence into every instance of presence. This was the principal truth of Hegel's doctrine of negativity, which taught that nonbeing as negativity is ensconced within the life of Spirit itself. Hegel's mistake, his wrong turn, as it were, was the construction of a metanarrative of totalizing rationality in which every negativity is sublated into a higher positivity.

The event of disclosure, in this struggle with negativity and the constraints of finitude, reckons with the obtrusiveness, alterity, incursivity, of the phenomena-as-encountered. Disclosure is thus a *responsiveness*, a "responsibility" in the sense of being able to respond to that which is "other." This responsiveness, reckoning with the otherness of the phenomena as encountered within the interstices of the lifeworld—whether in the realm of perception, social interaction, or institutional intervention—takes on a Janus-faced posture. There is the "face" of the encountered other that presents itself for description, evaluation, understanding, and explanation; but there is also the "face" that remains hidden, with its profile not shown, a *facies absconditus* that escapes presence and determination but yet figures in the encounter as a penumbral horizon that intrudes upon every configuration of sense.

The effects of this alterity and incursivity are what supply the referential context in the odyssey of disclosive rationality. Rationality as disclosure or making manifest involves a response to the otherness of the phenomena, a referring that is occasioned by an impingement from the outside. Our refigured performance of reference is thus initiated not from the side of a sovereign epistemic subject, caught up in quandaries about the determinability or indeterminability of independently existing objects or sense

32. Martin Heidegger, *Being and Time*, trans. John Macquarrie and Edward Robinson (New York: Harper & Row, 1962), pp. 51–55.

data, but rather from the side of the alterity and incursivity of the phenomena in their Janus-faced posture of showing and not showing, presence and absence. This is the decisive juncture where both the epistemological and the semiotic routes to reference encounter an impasse. The epistemologist works with a theory of mind that enjoins a centripetal cognitive act to represent reality via a concept of ostensive reference. The semiotician appeals not to a theory of mind but to a theory of the sign, which is burdened with the requirement to pin down the veridically signified, be it either of a transcendental or an empirical sort. To point out, as postmodernists of a deconstructionist persuasion are inclined to do, that these projects of reference end up in failure is clearly a contribution of some consequence. But this may simply be to give notice that the issue of reference is too important to leave to epistemology or semiology.

The claims of deconstruction in its assault on reference, however, are more encompassing, issuing an indictment of all strategies of decidability. But in issuing such an indictment deconstruction falls victim to a peculiar version of the *petitio principii* fallacy. The deconstructionist case against reference, bringing to the witness stand evidence for undecidability on the side of the signifier and indeterminacy on the side of the signified, will muster litigative force only if the premises of a sign-systems approach to reference, and to discourse more generally, are taken as valid. If discourse is construed as operating within the matrix of a theory of the sign, then the route to reference will remain effectively blocked—or will need to be posted with interminable "detour" signs. However, to point out the aporia into which a semiotic, sign-systems approach to reference gravitates is not yet to mount a compelling argument or reasoned claim against all figurations/refigurations of reference. A deconstruction of the semiotic model for reference does not entail a jettisoning of reference in every sense you please.

The limitations of the epistemologically defined concept of ostensive reference, and the failure of reference within a semiotic model, have already been addressed by Paul Ricoeur and ourselves; and they have been countermanded by our respective refigurations of "metaphorical reference" and "hermeneutical reference."[33] However, the profound importance of alterity has not been sufficiently acknowledged in the elaboration of these notions. We suggest that this lacuna can now be filled through a reclamation and refiguration of the phenomenological concept of the lifeworld and a radicalization of "phenomenon" as the insinuation of alterity in the life of perception, discourse, and action. Against the background of such refiguration and radicalization, the disclosive function of rationality sorts itself out as an *incursive* disclosure.[34]

33. See Paul Ricoeur, *The Rule of Metaphor*, trans. Robert Czerny (Toronto: University of Toronto Press, 1977), pp. 216–56, and Calvin O. Schrag, *Communicative Praxis and the Space of Subjectivity* (Bloomington: Indiana University Press, 1986), pp. 69–71 and 180–84.
34. For a helpful discussion of the rather profound impact of the thematic of alterity upon contemporary thought, see the collected essays in *The Question of the Other*, ed. Arleen B. Dallery and Charles E. Scott (Albany: State University of New York Press, 1989).

The multiple postures of otherness that play in the disclosure of the intertexturing of our perception, social practices, and institutional involvements testify of unexpungeable referents in the concrete lifeworld. We need to take note that our grammar leads us to speak of "reference" in the plural. There is no foundationalist given—in the guise either of an object or a subject, a concept, a property, or a substratum—that answers to the question about the referents of our discourse and action. The reference that is displayed through the incursivity of the lifeworld is multiplied. At times the multiple references are peculiarly conjunctive; at other times they remain heteromorphous. Reference, in either case, is destined to a life of polysemy. As William James has urged us always to think about "truth" in the plural, so we recommend that in our vocabulary of reference we also accommodate its pluralistic usages. The referent that is at issue in the perception of a tree on the mall is not cut from the same cloth as is the referent in the encounter with an enraged political dissident who is about to blow up the plane. The multiplication of referents, however, does not displace their reality-function in our life of discourse and action.

Now it is precisely this reality-function that is the critical ingredient in the move from the world of narrative to the lifeworld, from the narrational claim of rationality to its explicit phenomenological claim. We have already discussed how the narrative structure of discourse slides into an emplotment of our everyday life and history. Narrativity enables us to comprehend configurations of experience within a vibrant assimilation of time and space. And this is made possible by narrative because our life and history itself exhibits an emplotment of events. But there is also, as we noted, a tension between the world of narrative and the lifeworld, arising from the discursive and textual weight of narrative, courting a suspension of the dynamic of disclosure as it is oriented toward the referents in lifeworld experience. It is because of this that a phenomenological account of disclosure is required to keep open the space between the world of narrative and the lifeworld, between fictive narration and everyday experience, as well as between historical narration and the events of historical actors as they live through them.

As Husserl's phenomenology of the lifeworld undermined the epistemological constructivism of an abstract empiricism and reinscribed the full-bodied intentionality of lived experience, so our refiguration of the lifeworld as a field of praxial engagement projects a recovery of experience in response to postmodern-inspired predilections to turn everything into grammatology, textuality, or narrational discourse. There is indeed something outside the effects of textuality and narrativity. There is perception and there is human action. When Derrida, for example, announces "I don't believe that anything like perception exists,"[35] one is

---

35. Derrida's reply to Doubrovsky in *The Languages of Criticism and the Sciences of Man*, ed. Richard Macksey and Eugenio Donato (Baltimore: Johns Hopkins University Press, 1970), p. 272.

naturally inclined to request further clarification. Admittedly, he does offer some. "Perception," he says, "is precisely a concept, a concept of an intuition or a given originating from the thing itself, present itself in its meaning, independently from language, from the system of reference."[36] Now one may indeed be somewhat bewildered as to what such a conceptual construal of perception might mean—to say nothing of asserting its "existence"! But surely such a conceptualization has little to do with the perceptual experiences of everyday life, occurring within an envelopment of lived time and lived space. Through language, discourse, and narrative we do indeed emplot our perceptual experiences of the world. But the alterity and incursivity at work in perception often contravene the stories that we tell. To account for the phenomena of perception as they are experienced we need to recognize a continuing interplay between the world of narrative and the lifeworld.

The slide of the world of narration into the lifeworld, it should be underscored once more, does not displace the unique contribution of narrational discourse to an understanding of the unifying and integrating power of reason. We have spoken of a productive alliance of these two worlds, by virtue of which narrative and life conspire to chart a fresh approach to the old problem of meaning and reference by refiguring the problem as one of articulation and disclosure. Our concern is to monitor this alliance and keep narrative from being suffocated in an all-devouring discursivity and textuality. And on this point one needs to be reminded that narrative discourse itself opens a path to the "outside" of discourse through its *implication* of the "world of the reader." Here there is an opening to a space beyond that of the text and the narrative itself. Even though we are here still within the intermediary space of the "implied reader," who does not occupy existential space, the aperture to a world of *actual* readers, situated within a lifeworld of perception, action, and political practices, has been marked out. Thus one is able to maintain a relative autonomy of emplotment within narrational discourse and still recognize the relevance of narrativity for the actual context of lived experience.

Paul Ricoeur, as is well known, has addressed many of our concerns in his monumental three-volume work, *Time and Narrative*. He sets the problematic in terms of the consequences of a narrative refiguration of time for addressing the aporia resulting from the clash of cosmological and existential-phenomenological time. Working with the Augustinian view of time and the Aristotelian definition of plot, Ricoeur is particularly interested in the convergences and ruptures that come to the fore in a comparison of fictive and historical narration, the world of the text and the world of the reader, literary praxis and the reality of human action and suffering. It is quite significant that he concludes his three-volume study with a discussion titled "The Aporia of the Inscrutability of Time and the

36. *The Languages of Criticism and the Sciences of Man*, p. 272.

Limits of Narrative."[37] Admittedly, he does place considerable weight on the congruence of interests that travel with concerns about time and narrative. "There can be no thought about time without narrated time," he says; and, again, there is no "experience that is not already the fruit of narrative activity."[38] At this point in Ricoeur's explorations one may begin to fear an upcoming move toward a species of narratological closure. However, he quickly allays our anxieties with a full recognition that "not even narrative exhausts the power of speaking that refigures time,"[39] and with a consummatory "confession of the limits of narrative in the face of the mystery of time that envelops us."[40] Narrativity cannot surmount the aporia of the inscrutability of time. The "fragility of life" and the "power of time that destroys"[41] falls outside the emplotment strategies of narrative. Translated into our vocabulary, this is to say that the limits of the world of narrative are defined by the peregrinations of speakers and actors as they make their way about in a concrete lifeworld of discourse, perception, and action.

37. Paul Ricoeur, *Time and Narrative*, Volume 3, trans. Kathleen Blamey and David Pellauer (Chicago: University of Chicago Press, 1988), pp. 261–74.
38. *Time and Narrative*, pp. 241 and 248.
39. *Time and Narrative*, p. 261.
40. *Time and Narrative*, p. 274.
41. *Time and Narrative*, p. 273.

FIVE

Reason and Rhetoric

THE SITUATION OF RHETORIC

Our investigations of the texture and dynamics of praxial rationality as illustrated in critical discernment, hermeneutical articulation, and narrational disclosure lead us to a consideration of rhetoric. Allusions to the role of rhetoric were already made in our explications of the workings of discernment and assessment in praxial critique, in our examination of the claims of reason as they are operative in the articulating performance of interpretation, and in our investigations of the rationality of narrational disclosure. The task now before us is that of situating more explicitly the role of rhetoric as it pertains to the demands of reason.

The relevance of rhetoric can be detected at a number of crucial junctures in our general project of addressing the resources of rationality. Rhetoric is in position to preside over the disputes between speaking and writing. As there is a rhetoric of speech, so there is a rhetoric of composition. These two modalities of discourse, the spoken and the written word, are acknowledged as partners in the rhetorical enterprise. Not only, however, does rhetoric lie across these two modalities or forms of discourse; it also binds discourse with action. As there is a rhetoric of discourse, of the spoken and the written word, so also there is a rhetoric of action or a rhetoric of the deed.[1] Here too rhetoric is situated in such a wise as to enable it to function as a mediator, mediating discourse and action.

The relevance of rhetoric is also evident in the wider scenario of bridging discourse and action with the solicitations of community and the requirement for communication. Persuasive discourse and action are directed to the "other"—to the hearer and to the reader. One's audience and one's readership are not incidental features of the rhetorical performance. It is of the very design of rhetoric to elicit a hearer or a reader response. Aristotle had already made this abundantly clear when he de-

---

1. The rhetoric of action has been given one of its more precise expressions in Kenneth Burke's notion of "administrative rhetoric," a nondiscursive performance of persuasion that articulates a configuration of sense through actional deployment. "The concept of Administrative Rhetoric involves a theory of persuasive devices which have a directly rhetorical aspect, yet include operations not confined to sheerly verbal persuasion." *Language as Symbolic Action* (Berkeley: University of California Press, 1968), p. 301. Burke's well-known example of administrative rhetoric is that of Theodore Roosevelt's "goodwill mission" to Germany, ostensibly a friendly visit, yet displaying military force as a means of persuasion.

scribed the rhetorical art as that in which we take pains "not to annoy our hearers" and concentrate on "whatever it is we have to expound to others."[2] Rhetoric is the interweaving of discernment, deliberation, and action, oriented to the actualization of that which is deemed to be good for the polis.

The situation of rhetoric in our exploration of the various facets of rationality has a yet more direct pertinence. In its effecting of discernment and deliberation, always attendant to the claims of community, it illustrates the rationality of praxial critique. In its display of meaning through the figuration of discourse and action, it illustrates the rationality of articulation, making manifest, giving an account. In its emplotment of figurations of meaning against the backdrop of the history of public concerns, it takes on the lineaments of narrative and exhibits a narrative rationality of disclosure that opens up a lifeworld of everyday praxis.[3] It is thus that rhetoric appears to assume a posture of ubiquity, extending across the three principal moments of the rationality of praxis that we have identified—critique, articulation, and disclosure. As such, the situation of rhetoric within our wider design provides an integrating force and function, binding the economy of reason across a topography of community-informed and communication-oriented discourse and action.

Before attending to some of the particulars in this situation of rhetoric as a ubiquitous binding force, moving across the multiple expressions of rationality, there is another feature of the situation of rhetoric, somewhat more encompassing in its range, that needs to be considered. This has to do with the historical situatedness of rhetoric as a disciplinary matrix and project.

The establishment of rhetoric as a special discipline, entrusted with the art of persuasion, reaches far back into the heritage of Occidental thought and has left in its wake a troubled history of disagreements and disputes regarding its proper definition and function. The marginalization, and at times outright denunciation, of rhetoric as a special discipline is now a cultural fact in any sociology of knowledge of the Western world. Much of the contention pertaining to the role of rhetoric has had its locus in exchanges between practitioners in the disciplines of philosophy and rhetoric.

As the proverbial every schoolboy knows, Plato was unable to conceal

2. Aristotle, *Rhetorica* 1404a 4–10, in *The Basic Works of Aristotle*, ed. Richard McKeon (New York: Random House, 1941).
3. One of the more extensive discussions of narrative deployment in rhetorical praxis is supplied by Walter R. Fisher in his book *Human Communication as Narration: Towards a Philosophy of Reason, Value and Action* (Columbia: University of South Carolina Press, 1987). Fisher develops what he calls "the narrative paradigm," in which the portrait of the rhetor is that of *homo narrans*, a storyteller, who makes his or her way about in the polis by appealing to a narrative logic of "good reasons," which is contrasted with the scientifically inspired logic of rigid designators, epistemological demonstration, and ironclad proofs. The narrative paradigm thus carves out a space for a new perspective on the claims of reason, that of a "narrative rationality."

his disdain for the ancient Sophists, who were the veritable founders of the rhetorical art. Perpetrators of sham wisdom is what he called them, and he never missed the opportunity to indict them for playing the game of deception, making the weaker argument appear to be the stronger. Aristotle secured a more sheltered space for the rhetorical exercise and conferred upon it a legitimacy and a degree of autonomy—but speaking and writing as a philosopher, he of course kept the advantage! And everyone familiar with the pedagogy of philosophy knows that Artistotle's *Ars Rhetorica* seldom makes its way into the required reading list of the Occidental philosophical canon.

The marginalization and devaluation of rhetoric by philosophy has assumed a variety of forms. Rhetoric has been marginalized as a method of disputation and polemics, inviting a reduction of rhetoric to eristics. In a related move it has been defined as a technique of argumentative discourse, couched in the format of a debate, marginalizing rhetoric by reducing it to a forensic exercise. It has also at times suffered the fate of being identified with its epideictic function, which itself is devalued as nothing more than a display of ornamentation and ceremonial stylistics. Again, it has been construed as the construction of literary devices designed to create effects through the use of "figures of speech" (metaphors, metonymies, ironies, hyperboles, and synecdoches), and thus identified with tropology.

Through these varied reductions rhetoric is granted a degree of autonomy and a measure of legitimacy. As a method of disputation, or a technique of debating, or an embellishment of style, or a study of tropes, it is recognized as having a localized autonomy within quite specifically defined parameters. In less generous moments, however, both the vulgar and the learned have taken on more jaundiced perspectives and have viewed the rhetorical art as *"mere* rhetoric." With the proper intonation, it is the adjective that tells the story, making it clear to everyone in the academic neighborhood that rhetoric is outside the purview of anything that might resemble knowledge or truth. Here the urge to devalue rhetoric is no longer concealed. Even the cosmopolitan and usually restrained Immanuel Kant could not curb his disdain for the discipline of rhetoric, which he concluded could "be recommended neither for the bar nor the pulpit"—to say nothing of its place in philosophical discourse! According to Kant, rhetoric translates into "the art of deluding by means of a fair semblance," designed "to win over men's minds to the side of the speaker before they have weighed the matter, and to rob their verdict of its freedom."[4]

The long-standing controversy over the function and proper placement of rhetoric has been activated by certain assumptions regarding the roles of reason, knowledge, and truth. Even those who grant rhetoric a

4. Immanuel Kant, *The Critique of Judgment*, trans. James Creed Meredith (Oxford: The Clarendon Press, 1952), "First Part: Critique of Aesthetic Judgment," 53, p. 192.

degree of local autonomy find its function to be at best ancillary to the achievement of knowledge and truth. It is not deemed to be a resident within the domicile of reason. In defining this received view on rhetoric, it must be said of rhetoric generally what Derrida finds in the traditional bias toward metaphor, namely that "metaphor, when well trained, must work in the service of truth, but the master is not to content himself with this, and must prefer the discourse of full truth to metaphor."[5] Admittedly, according to this rather negative received assessment, rhetoric might become quite proficient in developing eristic and forensic techniques, and it may excel in the study of tropes, but if it wishes to have something to do with the claims of reason, it will need to import these claims from another discursive regime.

This peculiarly jaundiced view of rhetoric, coupled, one should add, with an equally jaundiced view of philosophy as the guardian of reason, produced a noticeably fragile alliance between the two disciplines, balancing their respective economies along the lines of import and export transactions. To transact its business, philosophy may find it profitable to import techniques of persuasion from the manufacturers of rhetoric. In exchange, it will agree to export its principles of reason. The enterprise of rhetoric, in turn, will handle its economy by exporting forensic techniques, ceremonial style, and figures of speech, intent upon achieving that ineluctable balance of trade—two tropes for the principle of sufficient reason!

The general design of our current chapter is that of resituating rhetoric by restructuring the two economies in such a way that neither will be dependent on the supply-and-demand indicators regulating the academic import and export business. This will result in a reformulation of the relation between philosophy and rhetoric within a matrix of transversality, enabling a complementarity in place of the old polar opposition, which in turn will make manifest the indigenous rationality of rhetoric and the intrinsic features of style, metaphor, and persuasion within philosophical discourse. Rationality, it will be argued, is transversal to the discourse of the two disciplines.

The situation of rhetoric as an autonomous disciplinary regime was beset with problems from the very beginning. The Aristotelian corpus of the collected treatises on rhetoric, ethics, poetics, and politics already problematized any clean categorial cuts dividing the discourses on these related subject matters. An intricate warp and woof stitches the tapestry that extends across the specified concerns in these treatises. The autonomy of rhetoric was again problematized in the design of the medieval trivium, which linked rhetoric, logic, and grammar under the aegis of an interdisciplinary network of concerns and practices. The situation of rhetoric in modernity took a more decisive turn, principally as a result of the

5. Jacques Derrida, "White Mythology: Metaphor in the Text of Philosophy," in *Margins of Philosophy*, trans. Alan Bass (Chicago: University of Chicago Press, 1982), p. 238.

bifurcation of logic and rhetoric and the emergence of grammar as a highly specialized science of linguistics. The modern mind, with the help of its formal epistemological paradigm, using mathematics and the natural sciences as its touchstone, construed logic as a regimen of rules that govern abstract and technical reasoning and marginalized what was left of the ancient and medieval discipline of rhetoric, divesting it of all resources of rationality. The postmodern predicament of rhetoric, consequent to the deconstruction of the epistemological paradigm of modernity, suffers its own peculiar problems, occasioned by the postmodern celebration of a seemingly unmanageable heterogeneity of discursive practices.

Given our task of fashioning a response to the postmodern challenge, specific attention to the situation of rhetoric in postmodernity is required. Not surprisingly, the situation of rhetoric in postmodernity falls out as an array of curiously diversified portraits. Nietzsche's contribution to postmodern thought on this matter remains quite singular. His reduction of truth to a "movable host of metaphors, metonymies, and anthropomorphisms" and his elevation of the rhetorical art to a sovereign status informed much of what current-day postmodernists have to say about the role of rhetoric.[6] Heidegger picked up on the topic of rhetoric but did not do all that much with it. In his early treatise, *Being and Time,* Heidegger praised Aristotle's *Rhetoric* as "the first systematic hermeneutic of the everydayness of Being with one another."[7] He found in the second book of Aristotle's *Rhetoric* a systematic interpretation of the affects ($\pi\alpha\delta\eta$) as they play in the self-understanding of the rhetor and the interlocutor alike. But there are few references to rhetoric in Heidegger's subsequent works—although in his later works he does indeed have much to say about poetics, developed along the lines of a Hölderlinian "poetical dwelling."

It was Heidegger's left-wing successor, Jacques Derrida, who seized the opportunity to fill the lacunae of rhetoric in Heidegger's legacy with an unblushing embrace of the rhetorical. Derrida's deconstruction of metaphysical discourse, with it logocentric principle, proceeds basically through an appeal to the rhetorical power of the text. This rhetorical power, activated through a free play of signification, spreads its mantle over all genres of discourse and effects a subversion of logic and philosophical discourse more generally. Admittedly, there is an acknowledgment of a play with the distinction between rhetoric and philosophy, the metaphorical and the literal, the fictive and the factual, narrative and history. In the end, however, we are enjoined to recognize that it is the rhetorical

6. "What then is truth? A movable host of metaphors, metonymies, and anthropomorphisms: in short, a sum of human relations which have been poetically and rhetorically intensified, transferred, and embellished, and which, after long usage, seem to a people to be fixed, canonical, and binding." "On Truth and Lies in a Nonmoral Sense," in *Philosophy and Truth: Selections from Nietzsche's Notebooks of the Early 1870's,* ed. Daniel Breazeale (Atlantic Highlands: The Humanities Press, 1979), p. 84.
7. Martin Heidegger, *Being and Time,* trans. John Macquarrie and Edward Robinson (New York: Harper & Row, 1962), p. 178.

power of the text that governs these distinctions and that any substantive contents referenced in these distinctions are indefinitely deferred. All discourse unfolds within a joyful and free play of signifiers, rhetorically feeding upon each other—and there is nothing outside the rhetorical text.

Derrida's situating of rhetoric moves out from a deconstruction of the tropology of classical rhetoric, at once liberating metaphor and rendering rhetoric ubiquitous. Indeed, "the flowers of rhetoric" are seen to bloom across the expansive fields of our variegated discourse.[8] Metaphoricity is found to be all pervading, residing as much in our philosophical discourse as in our literary inventions. As such, it never congeals into stable points of reference and determinable contents of knowledge but instead gravitates toward an "abyss of metaphor," within a perpetual flux of a Nietzschean-like becoming.[9] In this accentuation and universalization of metaphor, the left-wing Heideggerianism of Derrida becomes explicit. Here the teacher and the student diverge. For Heidegger the metaphorical resides in the metaphysical.[10] Derrida unties the Gordian knot that laces metaphor to metaphysics and grants to rhetoric the freedom to roam the expansive terrain of discourse.

Another contemporary voice addressing the situation of rhetoric in our time is that of Hans-Georg Gadamer. Although Gadamer is clearly more restrained in his universalization of rhetoric than is Derrida, he does, nonetheless, inform us that "the ubiquity of rhetoric, indeed, is unlimited."[11] But we are told this not in support of a Derridean project of erasing all distinctions between the literal and the metaphorical and leveling the genres of discourse, but rather to make us aware of the indissoluble linkage of rhetoric with universal hermeneutics.

And so we see that the rhetorical and the hermeneutical aspects of human linguisticality completely interpenetrate each other. There would be no speaker and no art of speaking if understanding and consent were not in question, were not underlying elements; there would be no hermeneutical task if there were no mutual understanding that has been disturbed and that those involved in a conversation must search for and find again together.[12]

Rhetoric and hermeneutics are thus seen to be incommiscibly yoked, complementary and mutually reinforcing—distinct perhaps, but yet indissoluable. They travel with each other, and they travel together all the way

8. See particularly the section titled "The Flowers of Rhetoric" in Derrida's essay "White Mythology," in *Margins of Philosophy*, pp. 246–57.
9. ". . . this abyss of metaphor will never cease to stratify itself, simultaneously widening and consolidating itself: the (artificial) light and (displaced) habitat of classical rhetoric." *Margins of Philosophy*, p. 253.
10. Martin Heidegger, *Der Satz vom Grund* (Tübingen: Verlag Gunter Neske Pfullingen, 1957), p. 89.
11. Hans-Georg Gadamer, *Philosophical Hermeneutics*, trans. David E. Linge (Berkeley: University of California Press, 1976), p. 24.
12. *Philosophical Hermeneutics*, p. 25.

down and all the way back. They are both oriented toward an articulation of meaning and an achievement of self-understanding against the backdrop of public concerns. The rhetorician and the hermeneut alike are trained to recognize misunderstanding as it issues both from the infelicities of grammar and from deviations in the body politic.[13] A peculiarly advantageous spin-off from this Gadamerian bonding of rhetoric and hermeneutics is the opportunity for a reclamation and refiguration of the medieval trivium. The logic of the tradition would be refigured by the logos of hermeneutical understanding, and traditional grammar would become the "linguisticality *(Sprachlichkeit)* of being"; and both would be seen to inform the rhetorical posture.

Paul Ricoeur's perspective on the situation of rhetoric displays certain similarities to that of Gadamer. Ricoeur, like Gadamer, is interested in highlighting the hermeneutical moment in the rhetorical art, and he voices similar concerns about the danger in the technologization of rhetoric as a compendium of techniques geared toward calculation and control.[14] However, Ricoeur is more aggressive in his effort to salvage the referential function of rhetoric. By installing a new postulate of reference at the heart of rhetoric, Ricoeur is able to extract from the rhetorical performance a claim upon reality and an implicatory concept of truth. The reference at work in rhetoric is named, interchangeably, "metaphorical" and "displayed" reference, which we are given to understand is a reformulated notion of reference that no longer finds its touchstone in the ostensive and denotative referring of scientific statements. Reference construed as the picking out of isolable and descriptive features of objects and events is suspended, and a new notion of reference as a display of the world (and here we can read "lifeworld") takes the place of the old.[15] It is particularly at this juncture that the ontological weight of metaphor in the performances of philosophical discourse becomes evident, and we are invited to witness the interplay of rhetoric and rationality. Rhetoric joins

13. Giving particular attention to the contribution of Gadamer to the integration of rhetoric and hermeneutics, Gary Madison has worked out a fresh approach to the philosophical status and hermeneutical significance of rhetoric, showing how *effective* rhetoric, as an orientation toward communication, cultivates insights and strategies of self- and societal understanding. See "The New Philosophy of Rhetoric," in *Texte: La rhétorique du texte* (Toronto: Les Editions Trintexte, 1989). Also, on the same topic, see Michael Hyde and Craig Smith, "Hermeneutics and Rhetoric: A Seen but Unobserved Relationship," *The Quarterly Journal of Speech* 65 (1979): pp. 347–48.

14. "Rhetoric cannot become an empty and formal technique." *The Rule of Metaphor: Multidisciplinary Studies of the Creaton of Meaning in Language,* trans. Robert Czerny (Toronto: University of Toronto Press, 1977), p. 29.

15. "My whole aim is to do away with this restriction of reference to scientific statements. Therefore, a distinct discussion appropriate to the literary work is required, and a second formulation of the postulate of reference, more complex than the first, which simply mirrored the general postulate that every sense calls for reference or denotation. The second formulation is stated as follows: the literary work through the structure proper to it displays a world only under the condition that the reference of descriptive discourse is suspended." *The Rule of Metaphor,* p. 221.

forces with philosophy in making claims upon reality and employing a concept of truth.

Now it is precisely the notion of reference that intensifies the turbulence occasioned by the postmodernist perspective on rhetoric. One of the principal spokespersons for high postmodernity, Jean-François Lyotard, views the rhetorical situation as determined by a "rhetorical agonistics," in which the *différend* (defined as the irremediable conflict between two parties that resists resolution for want of a common rule of judgment) separates the "partisans of agonistics" from the "partisans of dialogue."[16] Given such a state of affairs, not only is the hermeneutics of meaning and its appetition for consensus through dialogue displaced, the function of reference is dispersed within a heterogeneity of language games. The referent of ostensive phrases, for example, "this is white," remains incommensurable with the referent of nominative phrases, such as "Napoleon is a strategist."[17] The function of naming operates within a different cognitive sphere than does the function of showing, and both naming and showing need to be differentiated from signifying. The referents of scientific statements, imperative commands, normative prescriptions, interrogations, and exclamations all testify of an unmanageable inflation of senses infecting our economy of discourse. Within this economy no stable network of addressors, addressees, and referents can be determined. Sense remains indeterminate, reference inscrutable, and the situation of the rhetor and the interlocutor alike indefinable.

> The addressor of an exclamative is not situated with regard to the sense in the same way as the addressor of a descriptive. The addressee of a command is not situated with regard to the addressor and to the referent in the same way as the addressee of an invitation or of a bit of information is.[18]

The situation of rhetoric in our time is a confluence of forces that mark out a field of blurred genres and overlapping disciplinary regimes. Rhetoric remains an art, a *technē*, but the resources of this venerable art of persuasion have become problematized. The very telos of persuasive discourse has been called into question. The limitations of dialogue and communication have been highlighted, and the effects of the intrusion of power into the disciplinary regimes of discourse have been accentuated. Rhetorical criteria of meaning and strategies of reference have become threatened by deconstruction and displacement. Rhetoric indeed appears to be adrift. To advise the rhetorician to look to the sister discipline of philosophy to provide either an anchor or a safe port at which to disembark

16. Jean-François Lyotard, *The Differend: Phrases in Dispute*, trans. Georges Van Den Abbeele (Minneapolis: University of Minnesota Press, 1988), p. 26.
17. *The Differend*, p. 51.
18. *The Differend*, p. 49.

may only further confound the predicament. The ship of philosophy appears to be as much adrift as is the ship of rhetoric, and it is not all that evident in a situation such as this who is to be the helpmate of whom.[19] The only remaining viable task would appear to be that of making an effort to repair the respective ships at sea.

We have attempted in this section to provide a portrait of the "situation of rhetoric," caught up in the cross currents of disciplinary constitutions and fragile alliances, unclear about the claims of reason upon it, and uncertain about its distinctive vocation. Throughout our discussion the attentive reader may well have been asking questions about the bearing of our sketch of the situation of rhetoric upon the grammatically similar construct of "the rhetorical situation," which has achieved a degree of institutionalization in the writings of some practicing rhetoricians. Lloyd F. Bitzer, for example, has described the "rhetorical situation" as being comprised of three principal constituents: exigence, audience, and constraints. These constituents function as markers and directions for a rhetorical deployment.[20] Kenneth Burke has also supplied three situational characteristics—congregation, segregation, and identification—which, according to him, comprise the "essential attributes" of the rhetorical situation.[21]

The definitions constructed by Bitzer and Burke provide answers to the question "What comprises the nature of the rhetorical discipline?" Rhetoric is defined through a consolidation of the attributes or properties that make up the rhetorical enterprise. Although such a search for "essential attributes" and defining properties may indeed have its own rewards, our interrogation of the situation of rhetoric has shifted the inquiry away from the vocabulary of attributes (be they essential or accidental attributes), designed to provide answers to a "what" question, to concerns having to do with the background conditions that contextualize the "how" of rhetoric as an ongoing praxial engagement. In this shift the disciplinary matrix of rhetoric, defined as a field of inquiry with a distinctive nature or essence, is itself problematized. It is problematized on the level of disciplinary genres and on the level of aporias of reference, requiring a refiguration of our figures of discourse, rhetorical and philosophical alike.

THE BINDING TOPOS OF RHETORIC

Our explorations of the situation of rhetoric have left us with a map of uneven contours, elevations and depressions, plateaus and quicksands.

19. See the author's essay "Rhetoric Resituated at the End of Philosophy," *The Quarterly Journal of Speech* 71 (1985): pp. 164–74.
20. Lloyd F. Bitzer, "The Rhetorical Situation," in *Philosophy and Rhetoric* 1, no. 1 (1968): pp. 1–14.
21. Kenneth Burke, "The Rhetorical Situation," in *Communication: Ethical and Moral Issues*, ed. Lee Thayer (New York: Gordon and Breach Science Publishers, 1973), p. 263.

In its long history, rhetoric has been both accorded eminence and subjected to disparagement; at times it has occupied a position of centrality, and at other times it has been moved to the periphery. We have noted proposed alliances of rhetoric with hermeneutics and with narrativity, and we have reviewed the rhetoric of postmodernity that sets the "partisans of agonistics" against the "partisans of dialogue." The task of our present section is to inquire whether in the midst of this melange of perspectives, both historical and contemporary, one might still land upon a "binding topos" of rhetorical praxis.

Exploring the topography of rhetoric, we will look for assemblages of discursive practices that achieve integration without totalization, that effect combinations without coincidence, that produce solidarity without homogeneity. Our thesis will be that such a binding topos can indeed be found within the interstices of our amalgamated speech and action, writing and reading, textual inventions and institutional involvements, narrative and history. This is to say, simplified to the extreme, that the binding topos of rhetoric is supplied by the expansive terrain of communicative praxis. Rhetoric within such a scheme of things announces itself as *communicative rhetoric*.

Such a thesis, proposing a refiguration of rhetoric as *communicative* rhetoric, would seem to encounter insuperable obstacles in the initial stages of its development. Have not the notions of community and communication become so problematized by the postmodern turn that their resources for the venerable art of persuasion are effectively depleted? Does not Lyotard's "rhetorical agonistics" block any and all paths to a communicative rhetoric, in which the "partisans of dialogue" would have at least an equal voice with the "partisans of agonistics"? It would seem that the very grammar of a "binding topos" would be denied any accommodations within the assorted vocabulary of agonistic rhetoric, with its celebration of heterogeneity, paralogy, and dissensus. If the regimes of discourse, "phrase regimens" in the idiolect of Lyotard, are condemned to incommensurability for want of a common principle of judgment, and if the end of discourse is indeed paralogy rather than consensus, then our thesis would appear to be undermined even before our story gets under way.[22]

Clearly, the postmodern challenge will have a rather profound effect on the way that our story of communicative rhetoric, within the folds of communicative praxis, is told. The realities of plurality and heterogeneity, the play of difference, and the ruptures of communication through an insinuation of the reactive force of power, will need to be acknowledged.

---

22. "Incommensurability, in the sense of heterogeneity of phrase regimens and of the impossibility of subjecting them to a single law (except by neutralizing them), also marks the relation between either cognitives or prescriptives and interrogatives, performatives, exclamatives. . . . For each of these regimens, there corresponds a mode of presenting a universe, and one mode is not translatable into another." *The Differend*, p. 128.

At the same time, however, we are motivated to question the unmonitored slide of plurality into heterogeneity and paralogy, as well as the isolation of the various forms of locutionary and illocutionary discourse into autonomous and self-contained phrase regimens. The configurations of communicative praxis in the concrete lifeworld disclose patterns of *mixed* discourse, in which descriptive, normative, prescriptive, imperative, exclamatory, and poetic functions of discourse mix and mingle.

When my wife tells me that the garbage smells, she is at once providing a description of the condition of the garbage and uttering an imperative that it be taken out. When I exclaim "Fire!" in a crowded theatre, I am making a statement about an existing state of affairs and submitting a strong recommendation, if not a command, to exit the building. When a nuclear physicist makes an assertion about the dangers of nuclear armaments, she or he is performing a speech act that is at once constative and evaluative. When the poet enunciates that "poetically man dwells," he is offering both an aesthetic judgment and an existential claim. The alleged purity of our various locutionary and illocutionary speech acts needs to be brought under scrutiny. The discourse of our praxial engagements is a mixed discourse.

In a similar vein, the appeal to rule-governedness as the regulator in the multiplicity of our forms of discourse requires delimitation. The distinction between consensus and dissensus, to say nothing of the distinction between sense and nonsense, does not rest on a simple applicability/ non-applicability of a rule, but rather on an acknowledgment of the contingency of rules and an understanding of the history of their effects on our efforts to make sense together. The binary oppositions of rule-determined and rule-free, the logical and the paralogical, the commensurable and the incommensurable, require reflective reassessment.

Of equal pertinence for coming to terms with the binding topos of rhetoric is a review of the play of power in our discourse and action. Foucault is surely to be credited for having discerned and detailed the effects of power in the constitution of the discourses of the human sciences and in the disciplinary practices that have generated forms of knowledge in the history of the asylum and the prison. One wishes, however, that he would have given more attention to the ambiguity of the normative factors that are in play in the power/knowledge nexus, showing both its negative and positive expression in the institutional life of humankind. This is why the consummate assessment by Michael Calvin McGee and John R. Lyne on the insinuation of power into the situation of rhetoric is so squarely on target:

> In sum, rhetoric must operate in the context of persuasive power structures, normative commitments, and practical needs; and the rhetoric of the human sciences should take note of that as its starting point. The problem is not finding with Michel Foucault that power/knowledge is a unity, and hoping

that unmasking this connection is a liberation from power and passion. Rather, the human sciences should be seeking ways of managing the inevitable integration of power/knowledge within discourses that give life direction. This is what it must mean to treat knowledge claims rhetorically, if rhetoric is not to slide into sophistry, on the one hand, or become a new mode of academic self-perpetuation on the other.[23]

There is a power that ruptures, violates, and alienates—a reactive and negative expression of power. But there is also a power that creates and produces, an active and positive power of affirmation of self and other. Certainly Nietzsche recognized this in his celebrated doctrine of the will-to-power. However, Nietzsche's insistence on locating the will-to-power "beyond good and evil," so as to cut aesthetics free from morality, invited a severance of aesthetic creativity from moral commitment. Power beyond good and evil makes possible the living of life above the oppressive norms of herd morality; but it also supplies the license to live below the moral constraints of justice and communal responsibility. Herein reside the dangers of aestheticism, privileging one of the culture-spheres over the others and transvaluing morality into the power of aesthetic self-affirmation. When power is redistributed across the rhetorical space of discernment and deliberation, affecting the life of the community, then its ambiguous texture is revealed. It can indeed function as an agent of rupture and dissensus, but it also functions as an agent of social cohesion and solidarity.

Our effort to locate the binding topos of rhetoric against the backdrop of community, within the texture of communicative praxis, accommodating the multiple aims of discourse and the play of power, involves a reformulation of the disciplinary designs of classical rhetoric. It is not that classical rhetoric had no binding topos; the relevant point is that it construed the topos of rhetoric against the backdrop of a particular conceptual scheme. Aristotle was unequivocal in assigning rhetoric a place within the *polis*. The polis provided at once the *archē* and the *telos* of classical rhetoric. The collaborative deliberation and the strategies of persuasion that inform the rhetorical enterprise were designed for an actualization of that which is good for the polis. The Greek concept of the polis, however, was not yet either the modern concept of the state or the postmodern notion of the political. The Greek polis was defined by a substance-attribute categorial scheme and was viewed as falling under the aegis of determinate ends, fixed orders, necessity, and destiny. It was seen as having its origin in the cosmic order of things, understood as an extension of nature, subject to the determinations of its universal laws—which were deemed to be quite readily accessible.

23. Michael Calvin McGee and John R. Lyne, "What Are Nice Folks Like You Doing in a Place Like This?", in *The Rhetoric of the Human Sciences: Language and Argument in Scholarship and Public Affairs*, ed. John S. Nelson, Allan Megill, and Donald N. McCloskey (Madison: The University of Wisconsin Press, 1987), p. 400.

It was to this polis that the rhetor, particularly as she or he stood in the services of a political-deliberative rhetoric, remained beholden. The address of the rhetor was directed to the public as the proper addressee, and the public was defined as a congregation of auditors set to receive the persuasive discourse that would lead to an enhancement of virtue in the wider body politic. It was thus that Aristotle could seize the opportunity to emphasize the role of the audience in the rhetorical situation and set the telic aim of persuasive discourse in the direction of the hearers of the discourse. The discourse of rhetoric was *to* and *for* others. However, this did not displace the rather unique function and considerable responsibility of the rhetor, whose task it was to select the appropriate figures of speech and accurately read the mood of his hearers. Yet, the rhetor and the audience alike did not have the freedom to move outside the structural determinants of the polis, which came equipped with the fixed orders and ends that provided the binding topos of the rhetorical situation.

The modern concept of the state displaced the determinants of universality, necessity, and destiny as defining features of the body politic. Modernity effected a transubstantiation of the ancient cosmological categories of Greek thought, drawn from a reading of the book of nature, into the more humanistically oriented and subject-centered categories of particularity, individuality, and freedom. The epistemological expression of this became evident in the turn to an insular cogito as the source and foundation of knowledge; the ethical expression was illustrated in modernity's preoccupation with personal and subjective freedom; and the political ramifications were registered in a notion of the state as a collection of atomistically defined individuals. Within such a scheme of things, the state is no longer seen as regulated by natural law and teleological design but is viewed rather as the result of human contrivance, contractual agreement, and the achievement of consensus.

The social concern of modernity to maximize personal freedom and individuality invited on the one hand an absolutization of the autonomy of the individual subject and installed a reaction against any congealing of the collective will of the individuals into a hegemony of herd morality and a tyranny of public opinion. On the other hand, the contractual imperative courted overtures toward more collectivist designs. The modern state, as a collection of individuals, was caught up in the ambiguity of affirming the personal freedom of the individual while tending toward a collectivism that totalizes and dictates.

The social thought of postmodernism, to a significant degree, can be understood as the effort to manage this conflict of the autonomous individual with the hegemonic tendencies of statism, with what Deleuze has suggestively named "the state apparatus." Postmodernism offers no "social philosophy," no "theory of society"; instead we are initiated into a "new politics." This new politics takes on the lineaments of a politics of desire, conceived as rhizomatic societal assemblages of lines of force (Deleuze); a politics of power, bearing the inscriptions of assorted micro-practices (Foucault); a politics of opinion that issues from the phrase regimens of our local narratives (Lyotard); and a politics of the simulacrum of hyper-realities (Baudrillard). The initiation into this new politics involves a commitment to the historically specific and to the present-becoming of our social practices. In this new politics there are accommodations neither for a stable subject and a self-constituting individuality nor for the unifying functions of the state. Both the classical matrix of fitting the citizen into the designs of the polis and the modern dialectic of the individual and the state are dismantled.

Thus, the shift to the new politics of postmodernity problematizes at once the binding topos of classical, polis-oriented deliberative rhetoric and the modern constructs of a science of society. Although modernity jettisoned the stabilizing categories of substance that secured the foundations of the Greek polis, it could still appeal to the desideratum of consensus, the resources of dialogue, the good faith of negotiation, and the solidarity achieved through social critique. All of this is effectively swept away in the radically deconstructive move of postmodernism. The consequences for rhetoric that fall out from such a move are quite far-reaching. Rhetoric becomes, in effect, an agonistic intervention. War, it would appear, continues to be the father of us all.

We thus find ourselves at another stage in addressing the postmodern challenge, responding to the new politics of postmodernity and its agonistic rhetoric, sans binding topos, and sans consensual discourse. Again, our strategy is one of thinking *with* the postmoderns whilst thinking *against* them, and in our very strategy we hope to be able to show how postmodern thought can be used against itself. So long as one thinks with someone, manages some species of a dialogue, keeping the conversation going, one remains in that delicate situation of the "between." One is "between" affirmation and denial, acceptance and rejection, agreement and disagreement, consent and disavowal.

It is precisely this space of the "between" that identifies the landscape of communicative praxis, on which are located the performatives of communicative rhetoric. Within this "between," bearing the traces of our discursive and institutional practices, there is no room for the constructs of pure theory, be they of a classical metaphysical or a modern epistemological sort. Here we *agree with* and *consent to* the claims of postmodernity. In so doing we reach a dialogic consensus—provisional, to be sure, but certainly not without its rather profound effects. The remarkable achievement in this is that we are able to say "we." And this "we" remains operative whether one agrees or disagrees, consents or disavows. Even in the most adamant disagreeing and disputing, I *address the other* as the one *with whom* I am in disagreement.

The occlusion of the ability to say "we" may turn out to be the principal chink in the political armor of the new politics of postmodernism. Richard Rorty needs to be credited with having helped to sensitize our concerns on this particular issue. He singles out the "dryness" of Foucault's dispassionate observation of disciplinary practices, and suggests that such dryness is characteristic of the wider postmodern contingent. Commenting on the discourse of Foucault, Rorty remarks:

> It is a dryness produced by a lack of identification with any social context, any communication. Foucault once said that he would like to write "so as to have no face." He forbids himself the tone of the liberal sort of thinker who says to his fellow-citizens: "*We* know that there must be a better way to do things than this; let us look for it together." There is no "we" to be found in Foucault's writings, nor in those of many of his French contemporaries.[24]

The absence of any explicit acknowledgment of we-relationships and we-experiences in the annals of postmodernity testifies of a glaring lacuna in its new politics. And if there is no we-experience there can be no I-experience, because as we have known for some time the recognition of oneself as "I" is enabled only through an acknowledgment by the other within a community of we-relationships. In occluding the we-experience, postmodernism obstructs, in the same move as it were, the path to self-knowledge via the I-experience.

Our recovery of the space of communicative praxis restores the dense network of we-relationships that supplies the binding topos of rhetoric. This restoration, however, is not a simple return to the rhetor/interlocutor alignment of classical rhetoric. Although classical rhetoric made much of persuasive discourse as an intentionality *to* and *for* the other, it was unable to appreciate the rhetorical situation as that of a being-*with*-the-other. Because of its substantializing of both the rhetor and the polis, it held the dynamics and the dialogue of the concrete we-relationship at a distance. Thus, the classical notion of rhetoric requires at least an amendment if not a more radical reformulation. Classical rhetoric situated the rhetor as the agent, the active voice, in the mode of causal efficacy, acting upon the hearer as patient and recipient, defined as the *terminus ad quem* of the force of persuasion. Within such a constitutive framework, the rhetor functions in the mode of being-*to*-and-*for*-the-other. The mosaic of we-relationships that limns our communicative rhetoric refigures this relationship as a collaborative deliberation and action *with* the other. Dialogical interaction and the reciprocity of proposal and response replace the seriality of rhetorical speech directed to the interlocutor.

One of the more direct consequences of our refashioning of the ancient polis into a community of we-relationships is the decentering of the rhetor within the rhetorical situation. Communicative rhetoric no longer

---

24. Richard Rorty, "Habermas and Lyotard on Postmodernity," in *Habermas and Modernity*, ed. Richard J. Bernstein (Cambridge, MA: The MIT Press, 1985), p. 172.

accords a privileged authorization and voice of sovereignty to the rhetor. The developing reciprocity of question and answer, challenge and response, is strictly a communal affair. Communicative rhetoric replaces subject-centered rhetoric, in which the rhetor as knowing and speaking subject is invested with a panoptic vision and a controlling knowledge— a controlling knowledge that is always on the edge of coercive force and manipulation.

There are also consequences for the other side of the rhetorical coin— the audience. Communicative rhetoric desubstantializes both the rhetor and the audience. Neither function as prime causal agents in the rhetorical exercise. The dialogical play in communicative rhetoric circumvents control both by the rhetor and by the audience. The dynamics of communicative rhetoric is one of responsive activity rather than centripetal force. The discourse of rhetoric is indeed a display of power. Foucault is right about that. But the power of communicative rhetoric does not reside in a hegemonic center. It is illustrated by the reciprocity of social interaction. Communicative rhetoric continues to make appeals to authority, but the authorship of such is disseminated within a network of interdependencies, involving the rhetor, the audience, and the ethos of the tradition in which both stand.

Neither the rhetor nor the audience can be defined prior to the rhetorical situation. The binding topos of our intertextured communicative praxis first calls the rhetor and the audience into being. Neither stable and perduring substance nor monadic and centered sovereign subject, the rhetor is an *implicate of* and an *emergent from* the history of praxis. Correspondingly, the audience is announced not as a brute given of collected monadic subjects and atomistic individuals but is itself a contingent constellation of social practices. This refigures the rhetorical performance in such a wise that neither the rhetor nor the audience function as originating, generative, and quasi-causal principles. The essentializing of rhetor and audience alike needs to be problematized, as does the attributive grammar that confers upon them properties of causal efficacy.

The decentering of the rhetor as sovereign subject and the dismantling of the audience as a conglomerate group substance or collective does not, however, entail a pulverization of rhetor and audience into an indeterminate flux of becoming, a *Walpurgisnacht* of chaotic indeterminacy. The engaged rhetor and audience deploy their own inscriptions of sense and reference, and maneuver their own interventions, albeit not from the vantage point of founding and originating principles but rather from the perspective of involvement and responsiveness across a landscape of we-relationships. The self and other, rhetor and interlocutor, as citizens of this landscape, are twin halves of an achieved intersubjectivity that is constituted institutionally instead of self-reflexively. Such an institutional constitution does not displace the autonomy and integrity of self and other. Rhetor and interlocutor retain their power of responsivity. This power, however, is exercised only within the network of interdependencies that textures the space of being-with-others.

Our response to the postmodern challenge concerning matters of rhetoric has taken the route of reclaiming a sense of community, in the guise of a mosaic of we-relationships that remains in force during times of disavowal as well as times of consensus, shared alike by the "partisans of agnostics" and the "partisans of dialogue." It is this sense of community and orientation toward communication that answers to the question of the binding topos of rhetoric. Yet, our response to the postmodern challenge is mindful of that which is "challenging," and that which is most decisively challenging in regard to the issues at hand has to do with finding a place for the agonistic posture, ruptures of discourse, intrusions of incommensurability, or indeed the very *breakdown* of communication, within our binding topos. This is indeed a formidable challenge. If there is an irremediable negativity, a recalcitrant *différend*, that invades our communicative practices, what peculiar sense of community can remain intact?

Our line of argument, our proffered response, will be that a recognition of the play of negativity, the encroachment of the differend, does indeed delimit the positive resources of conversation and dialogue, but it does not entail a jettisoning of the background of communicative praxis itself. The sirens of postmodernism should make us wary of an *overdetermination* of the solidarity that can be achieved through conversation and dialogue. This is a danger that has already been voiced by practicing rhetoricans. Michael McGee and John Lyne, for example, caution us about the overweighting of "the metaphor of conversation," which would not allow for the possibility to "simply withdraw from talk that fails to meet one's expectations of it."[25] There is no necessity for keeping the conversation going. Dialogue can suffer rupture, one can elect not to respond, and communication can simply break down. How does one then account for these radical ruptures, intrusions of negativity, within the republic of communicative rhetoric?

It may be profitable to begin by sorting out a distinction that plays within the grammar of negativity itself, namely, the "negativity of alterity" as distinct from the "negativity of alienation." The negativity of alterity has to do with the intrusion of that which is "other" into our life of perception, discourse, and action; and as such it functions as a decisive mark of human finitude. This is the negativity that is at issue when I encounter a portion of text that I have not written, a style of behavior that I have not produced, an institution of which I am not a part, a self that is other than the self that I am. These instances of alterity or otherness point to that which is not of my own doing, not the result of my inventions. The *other* text, the *other* institution, the *other* self, are illustrations of

25. *The Rhetoric of the Human Sciences*, p. 400.

a condition of facticity, in which one simply encounters that which stands over against one's existential space.

This negativity of alterity, as a general condition of human finitude that already delimits the range and power of communication, should be distinguished from the negativity of alienation, exemplified by the emergence of a contradiction within a belief structure, a conflictual social practice, a clash of political ideals, a disruption of a friendship. Whereas the negativity of alterity is an index of human finitude, the negativity of alienation is the mark of human finitude under the conditions of estrangement—which introduces additional strains and stresses on the communicative practices of humankind. One could speak of the negativity of alienation as a modality of the negativity of alterity, as an index of human finitude somehow gone wrong.

The emplotment of the concept of negativity in the story of Occidental thought from Plato to Augustine to Hegel, articulated as the problem of non-being, took several turns and twists. In the thought of Plato, negativity as non-being maintains a liaison with the structures of being, figuring in the very constitution of being itself, insofar as every instance of being suffers finite determinations of what it is and infinite determinations of what it is not. Augustine, accepting the classical doctrine that being and good are convertible, defined evil as the intrusion of the negativity of non-being into the realm of being. Hegel's proposed resolution is assuredly the boldest of all. The negativities determining human finitude and alienation alike are sublated, taken up into a higher unity, into a coincidence of thought and reality, essence and existence. For Hegel every breakdown in the travail of the human spirit is but a moment, albeit a necessary one, leading to an eventual synthesis. To achieve this synthesis and unification, at once a teleology and a theodicy, the services of speculative universal reason had to be enlisted. That Hegel's metanarrative of speculative reason provided a systematic place for negativity within the binding topos of discourse and action can hardly be denied. Indeed, the topos was bound in such a way that not only the discontinuities of alienation but also the very constraints of finitude were putatively overcome.

It was principally the anti-Hegelians, Marx and Kierkegaard, who discerned, from different perspectives to be sure (that of concrete socioeconomic existence on the one hand, and that of concrete ethico-religious existence on the other hand), the comic feature of Hegel's proclaimed synthesis. Granted, Hegel delivered a grand synthesis and unity; but this synthesis and unity, claimed Marx and Kierkegaard, resided only in Hegel's head, in the realm of pure thought, and had not yet made its way into the praxial engagements of everyday socioeconomic and ethico-religious existence. Hegel could bind the topos of our communal existence only by placing himself at the end of history.

Searching for the binding topos among the moving figurations of our historical inherence does not allow us the luxury of a metanarrational vantage point of speculative reason. Yet, the jettisoning of such a vantage point does not abandon us to a flux of incommensurable discourse, heterogeneous language games, and irretrievable ruptures in our public life. One needs to attend to the historically situated speech acts, local narratives, micro-practices, and particularized forms of life in such a way as to allow them to "show themselves," become present as *phenomena* in the originative sense of the term. Such an imperative and procedure, we submit, occasions a recognition of the binding topos of communicative rhetoric as it shows itself in the dynamics of praxial engagements.

In the daily conversations of everyday life, in our talking about and talking with, we are already able to discern the impact of negativities upon our communicative projects. In our face-to-face exchanges and in our conversations over the telephone, there is both that which is *not*-understood and that which is *mis*-understood. Often we mis-speak, become guilty of grammatical infelicities, or articulate cumbersomely and confusedly that which we intend to say. So we backtrack, reformulate, revise, repair our syntax and semantics, reorder our thought, so that we can move on. But we never achieve an untrammeled, perfect, or ideal manner of speaking or mode of communication. The best that we can do is land upon that which is fitting for the occasion. That which is not-understood and that which is mis-understood can never be expunged from the speech situation. As there is no translucent cogito, so there is no translucent speech act. Discourse cannot outstrip the opacity and distortions that accompany the intrusions of the negativities of alterity and alienation. The marvel and wonder of our everyday speech performances is that we are able to communicate and be understood *in spite of* the negativities that pervade our discourse.

In the achievement of that which is fitting for our discourse *in spite of* the accompanying misdirections, the negativities of alterity and alienation are in some fashion "taken up," accommodated within the ongoing conversation and dialogue. Even the allegedly extreme cases of incommensurability, rupture of paradigms, abrogation of rules, and disproportionality of figures of speech remain within the folds of discursivity. The very recognition of that which is incommensurable, outside the normal rule-governed strategy of measurement, testifies of its being "understood" in some sense—understood as being different. Talk about the incommensurable or the differend in a situation of disagreement and dissent belies a discernment of their effects on our conversational engagements. The fringe of the incommensurable registers its effects in our commensurate discourse. Dissensus figures in every occasion of consensus, as does consensus remain in the background of all dissensus. The myths of pure consensus and pure dissensus, translucent commensurability and sheer incommensurability, require demythologization. There are no undivided, solidified, hermetically sealed chunks of either commensurable or incommensurable discourse, of either consensus or dissensus. The vocabulary of "either/or" remains peculiarly impoverished for dealing with the mixed discourse that is at issue here. Both the effort to privilege consensus as the proper end of discourse (Habermas) and the effort to secure this privilege for paralogy (Lyotard) can only lead to a conceptual wearisomeness; and Rorty's project of "splitting the difference" between Habermas and Lyotard on this issue may be one of the more sensible of its kind in the neighborhood.[26]

In accommodating the negativities of communication within a dynamical praxis that is able to make do in spite of their incursions, we have secured a place for their effects in the binding topos of rhetorical discourse. Rhetoric, even in its agonistic turns, continues to display the claims of communication upon it.

AN ECONOMY OF REASONS

The network of we-relationships and communicative interactions comprises the topos of rhetoric. The claims of community upon rhetoric mark out its topography. This topography, we have observed in the preceding section, is inhabited by rhetors and interlocutors, speakers and audiences, who share an ethos, a historical dwelling. We have already alluded to the dynamics of rationality that stimulates the economy of rhetoric thusly situated. Community makes up the topography of rhetoric; rationality energizes its economy. The task now before us is that of discerning and articulating the intersecting and interweaving of the topographic and the economic in the comportment of rhetoric.

The contributions of Hans Blumenberg to the performance of the task that we have set for us provides a convenient starting point. Blumenberg places us on a promising path when he invites us to approach rhetoric with an eye to "seeing in it a form of rationality itself—a rational way of coming to terms with the provisionality of reason."[27] The qualification of reason as "provisional" is of some consequence. What is at issue for Blumenberg is no longer the logocentric principle of sufficient reason, but rather a doxastic deployment of "insufficient reason," based on an anthropological doctrine of the human being as a "creature of deficiencies" (*Mangelwesen*). "The axiom of all rhetoric is the principle of insufficient reason (*principium rationis insufficientis*). It is a correlative of the anthropology of a creature who is deficient in essential respects."[28] This principle of insufficient reason, pruned of all a priori rules and antecedent criteria, subject to inescapable limitations and fractures, is able to supply

26. *Habermas and Modernity*, p. 173.
27. Hans Blumenberg, "An Anthropological Approach to the Contemporary Significance of Rhetoric," in *After Philosophy: End or Transformation?*, ed. Kenneth Baynes, James Bohman, and Thomas McCarthy (Cambridge, MA: The MIT Press, 1987), p. 452.
28. *After Philosophy: End or Transformation?*, p. 447.

only provisional claims. It can only provide "good reasons" for thought and action within the changing circumstances of the times. It cannot yield criteria of universality and necessity that would be applicable to all situations at all times and places. But this provisional reason is reason nonetheless, and it leaves its inscriptions on our variegated thought and action. It is this radically finite reason that Blumenberg finds to be peculiarly exemplified in the rhetorical art.

Accepting Blumenberg's challenge to see rationality as an indigenous feature of rhetoric, we will chart an exploration of the workings of reason across the topos of our communicative practices. The economy of reason transacts its business across the communal topography without invoking either invariant structures or necessary conditions for the patterning of discourse and action. There are no ahistorical, metaphysical guarantees. There is no subject-centered rationality, privy to preestablished criteria that might insure certainty. Reason remains "insufficient" for such lofty designs and is forced to make do with the contingent and the probable. This insufficiency, contingency, and probability, it should be underscored, is the result not of isolable methodological limitations that with some additional effort might be overcome; it is the consequence of reason being situated within the exigencies of historical and communal existence.

The historico-communal situationality of reason disallows any separation of the act of knowledge and the achievement of truth from the context of community. It was such a separation that informed the modern epistemological paradigm and accounted for its eventual demise. Descartes took it quite for granted that the achievement of knowledge and the discovery of truth comprised events separate from their being communicated. To have knowledge is one thing; to communicate it is another. Our new paradigm of communicative rhetoric as an economy of reasons undermines this most basic of all presuppositions of modernity. Communication is not an event ancillary to the conquest of knowledge and truth. Knowing and articulating, truth and communicability, are twin halves of an undivided occasioning. This intercalation of knowledge and truth with the articulatory and disclosive functions of rhetoric becomes evident when we understand, with Henry W. Johnstone, that "truth in philosophy is equivalent with the itinerary leading to it, and this itinerary is in principle an exercise in communication."[29]

Knowledge and truth are the effects of the practices engaged in by a community of investigators and interpreters, and they become part of the text of discourse only through the dynamics of consent and disavowal, agreement and disagreement, acceptance and rejection, that textures the forces of communicative praxis. It is not that one first knows, by tapping the resources of a silent cogito, and at some later date communicates what one has learned. Communication is constitutive of the act of knowledge

29. Henry W. Johnstone, Jr., *Validity and Rhetoric in Philosophical Argument* (University Park: The Dialogue Press of Man and World, 1978), p. 74.

and the quest for truth. The consequences of this for rhetoric are considerable. When rhetoric becomes *communicative* rhetoric it establishes a new fraternity with the rationality that envelopes knowledge and truth, and it instructs us about knowledge without epistemology and about truth without theory.[30]

To properly identify the rationality intrinsic to rhetoric, the rhetoric of knowledge and truth, one needs to attend to the structure and dynamics. of rhetorical reference, to that which rhetoric is about, to that which is at issue in the doing of rhetoric, to that which calls rhetors and audiences into being. If the goal of rhetorical discourse is persuasion, then the subject matter at issue needs to be persuasive. Attention needs to be given to the conditions and contents of being persuaded.

Michael McGee has chided his colleagues in the field of rhetoric precisely for their failure to give due consideration to such conditions and contents. "Rhetoricians have invested so heavily in the *technē* of persuasion that we rarely ask what it means to exist in a condition of having been persuaded."[31] It is an investigation of these existential conditions of being persuaded, of the persuasiveness of rhetorical discourse as an orientation toward shared understanding and collaborative action, that brings us directly to the issue of the relevance of reason for the rhetorical art. And it is only through a specification of such conditions and contents that one will be able to distinguish rhetoric from propaganda, manipulative practices, and coercion. Persuasiveness, the condition of being persuaded, requires the giving and receiving of *good reasons*, the evocation of new perspectives of belief and new patterns of action. Rhetoric becomes effective by providing good reasons through the evocation of fitting responses in our collaborative thought and action.[32]

It is at this juncture that our discussions in the previous chapters concerning the intercalated moments of praxial rationality as critique, articulation, and disclosure bear directly on our project of exploring the lines that intersect the topography and economy of rhetoric. The good reasons that inform the economy of rhetoric become effectual through praxial critique, articulation, and disclosure of the changing scene of configurations of thought and action. Rhetoric persuades by critiquing, articulating, and disclosing.

As a critical performance, rhetoric displays a mosaic of discernment,

---

30. The contribution of Karl Jaspers to a clarification of the interlacing of truth and communication has surprisingly remained unacknowledged in the burgeoning literature on rationality and rhetoric. See particularly his essay "Truth as Communicability," in *Reason and Existenz*, trans. William Earle (New York: The Noonday Press, 1955), pp. 77–106.

31. Michael Calvin McGee, "On Feminized Power," *The Van Zelst Lecture in Communication* (Evanston: Northwestern University School of Speech, 1985), p. 14.

32. Henry Johnstone has suggested a revitalizing of the economy of rhetoric by delimiting its received mission as "the art of persuasion" through a refiguration of rhetoric as "the art of evocation." Whereas persuasion tends to be basically a unilateral act, evocation simultaneously issues a call for authentic existence to the rhetor and the interlocutor. See *Validity and Rhetoric in Philosophical Argument*, p. 76.

assessment, and judgment. The resources of praxial critique, as we have seen, reside not in the theoretical constructs of a subject-centered rationality, projected from the center of an epistemological space, but issue rather from the discernment and assessment of the concrete forms of discourse and action as they play off against each other. Operative within the space of communicative praxis, on the hither side of the modern theoretico-epistemological network of a priori rules and antecedently specified criteria, praxial critique in the economy of rhetoric moves with the flow of our concrete discursive and nondiscursive practices as these practices at times enjoy continuity and at other times suffer discord. Praxial critique exercises discernment through contrastive comparisons, noting how the various forms of life play off against one another, monitoring the transgression of accepted beliefs and sedimented perspectives. All of this occurs within the space of praxis and its solicitations of thought and action. The discernment within praxial critique does not have to wait upon a glassy essence in which our lifeworld engagements are mirrored or for a set of transcendental conditions to provide the standpoint of critique with intelligibility. Communicative rhetoric supplies its own resources for discernment, assessment, and understanding. It can proceed quite well without a theoretical backup coming either from epistemology or social theory.

Our project of finding a place for praxial critique in the economy of rhetoric has certain family resemblances to J. Robert Cox's effort to locate the "critical principle"of rhetoric in the "temporal horizon of *doxa*."[33] Cox is concerned, as are we, to keep the function of critique alive in the rhetorical enterprise; and, like us, he situates the performance of this critique within the horizon of doxa instead of against the backdrop of theory. He explains the dynamic of his critical principle as a "dialectic of repetition and disavowal."[34] In working out the dialectic that provides the dynamics of the critical principle, Cox acknowledges his indebtedness to Heidegger's vocabulary of repetition (*Wiederholung*) and disavowal (*Widerruf*), which Heidegger had used in his hermeneutics of historical understanding.[35]

That which particularly interests us in Cox's program of critical rhetoric is his illustration of the applicability of the notions of repetition and disavowal to the rhetorical situation. Rhetoric displays a dynamics of repetition, through which the variegated social practices and forms of life of the tradition are taken over through a participatory appropriation. This taking over, however, remains a *critical* appropriation, thanks to the distanciating moment of disavowal, whereby the contents of the tradition are questioned, reappraised, transvalued, or simply overturned. Cox's understanding and use of "the dialectic of repetition and disavowal" should

33. J. Robert Cox, "Cultural Memory and Public Moral Argument," *The Van Zelst Lecture in Communication* (Evanston: Northwestern University School of Speech, 1987), pp. 7 and 10.
34. *The Van Zelst Lecture in Communication*, 1987, p. 10.
35. *Being and Time*, pp. 437–38.

remind the reader of our discussion in chapter one, where we landed on a dialectic of participation and distanciation as the contextual background of praxial critique, a background that subsequently proved to be useful for articulating the play of nostalgia and affirmation in the hermeneutical imperative. We are now in position to see how this general background, so decisive for a tracking of the dynamics of rationality, achieves a relevance for comprehending rhetoric as an economy of reasons.

Of central importance in all this is the recognition that the economy of rhetoric as praxial critique transacts its business on the topography of a historically and temporally qualified community. Critique remains embedded within the interstices of a remembrance of things past and an anticipation of things to come, preserving that which has been and inventing that which is not yet. Rhetorical critique is never traditionless; but neither is it tradition-bound. It uses the tradition to temper invention, and it uses invention to restrain the tradition. It is at once recollective and revolutionary, always proceeding from the language and the institutions of the tradition, but never simply subordinated to their delivered contents. Rhetoric, particularly in its political-deliberative form, illustrates this posture of critique in its deliberations about the fitting responses in the collaborative discourse and action of the community.

In salvaging the moment of critique in the economy of rhetoric we are making possible a revisitation and a refiguration of the linkage of logic and rhetoric in the medieval trivium. The revisitation is a refiguration in that the metaphysically grounded logic that became normative for the trivium is recast into a pragmatically oriented logic of good reasons. This refiguration of classical logic has its counterpart in the refiguration of the logic of modernity, which tended to reduce logic to a *mathesis universalis*. The logic at work in rhetorical critique is a logic of good reasons, comported by a discernment of that which is fitting for the occurrent historical circumstances, a logic of probability rather than certainty, contingency rather than necessity. Rhetoric convinces but it does not demonstrate. It persuades but it does not offer rule-governed proofs.[36]

Rhetoric as an economy of reasons displays yet another feature and function, closely allied with praxial critique. This is the function of articulating, rendering an account, making manifest, enunciating a perspective, letting something be seen and heard. As we noted in chapter three,

36. Although our sympathies with the recent "rhetoric of inquiry" school of thought are broad and deep, we have certain concerns about the intermittent tendencies within this school to set a "rhetoric of inquiry" in simple opposition to a "logic of inquiry." Although it is clear enough that what the proponents of this school understand by logic is a strictly formal set of rules and criteria, which admittedly does not play all that well on the court of rhetoric, what is not so clear is why we need to give logic over to the rule technicians. A rhetoric of inquiry has its own logic, the logic of good reasons, the logic of the fitting response, which does not jettison the *logos*, but instead vitalizes and expands it to incorporate the rationality of communicative interaction and public affairs. For some representative statements on the "rhetoric of inquiry" approach, see the collected essays in *The Rhetoric of the Human Sciences*.

the notion of rationality as articulation can be traced back to the ancient Greek concept of the logos, depicted by Plato as the giving of an account and by Aristotle as the making manifest of that which is at issue in one's discourse. Here rationality is linked more directly with speech, discourse, and language. That rhetoric might ally itself with this feature of rationality should come as no surprise. Rhetoric is very much a matter of discourse, even though it is not restricted to it, as there is also a rather explicit rhetoric of action. More specifically, the discourse of rhetoric is a collaborative discourse about the proper beliefs and actions required to maintain the virtuous life of the community.

Again, one is presented with an opportunity to revisit the medieval trivium. As our recollection of the interconnection of "the logic" and "the rhetoric" of the trivium led us to a refiguration of rationality as praxial critique, so our return to the interface of "the grammar" and "the rhetoric" in the trivium opens new perspectives on rationality as articulation. It is important, however, that in maneuvering this return we remain squarely on the terrain of communicative praxis. It is this terrain that provides the peculiarly propitious site for a reformulation of the interface of grammar and rhetoric in accord with the articulative function of reason and for an amalgamation of this function with that of praxial critique. With this accomplished, rhetorical rationality will come to stand as at once an articulation and a critique of the variegated facets of public life.

However, as our reclamation of the logic component of the trivium involved a deconstruction of its classical metaphysical and its modern mathematical foundations, so our recollection of the rhetoric/grammar liaison broaches a refiguration of medieval and modern grammar alike. Grammar is not simply elocution and composition, speechcraft and rules of inscription; neither is it reducible to a branch of the science of linguistics. Grammar is inseparable from discourse, the production of texts, the history of language, and the intertextuality of stories. This broadens the work of grammar and makes explicit its role in the articulatory function of reason.

It is in the articulative function of rhetorical rationality that the consequences of interpretation become prominent. Gadamer's insistence on the interdependence of rhetoric and hermeneutics becomes particularly decisive at this point. The hermeneutical task of articulating and making manifest the configurations of meaning in our social interaction is seen as an intrinsic component of the task of rhetoric. Rhetorical discourse arises because understanding and consent have been placed into question. Mutual understanding has been disrupted by the insinuation of misunderstanding, and the task of hermeneutical rhetoric is to strive for a rectification of this misunderstanding through a collaborative project of making sense together.[37]

37. *Philosophical Hermeneutics*, p. 25. See also Michael Hyde and Craig Smith, "Hermeneutics and Rhetoric: A Seen but Unobserved Relationship," *The Quarterly Journal of Speech*. It is interesting to note that I. A. Richards, coming to the topic of rhetoric from a quite different

The expansion of grammar through an analysis of it into discourse and textuality, soliciting the hermeneutical task, opens up the terrain of narrativity. We have sketched the broad impact of narrativity in the previous chapter, tracking the narrational claims upon reason. We are now in position to see how this narrative rationality plays in the economy of rhetoric. The rhetorician, by trade and function, is a story-telling animal, assigned to the task of invoking her or his hearers to become participants in the stories about the discursive and institutional practices of humankind. Rhetoric effects its own strategies of emplotment, articulating the ethos of the community, delineating possibilities for thought and action, marking out alternatives for social change, by telling stories about the actors and events that make history. The rhetorician Walter Fisher has given concentrated attention to the uses of narrative rationality in rhetoric by developing a "narrative paradigm of human communication." Fisher's narrative paradigm is designed to replace the "rational-world paradigm," which is wedded to self-evident propositions, demonstrations, and proofs. The narrative paradigm provides the space for "public moral argument," whose rationality is determined by *narrative probability* (the coherence of the story being told) and *narrative fidelity* (the story's fittingness with lived experience).[38]

The third component of the economy of rhetorical rationality has to do with the effecting of a disclosure, a bringing to presence of that which is to be seen and heard, a referring to the varied contents that obtrude upon our lived experience. This component travels side by side with the articulatory function of rationality. One might speak of disclosure as the fulfillment of articulation. Articulation is a search for meaning; disclosure is an event of reference. Disclosure comprises the referential moment of rationality, the move to the outside of the text and the outside of the narrative as a discursive form. It transports articulation beyond the threats of closure, beyond a ceaseless circling of discourse back upon itself, beyond the self-cannibalizing process of textual production and textual re-reading, beyond the aporias of textual and narrational closure.

Disclosure exercises a claim upon the lifeworld, which unfolds as a mosaic of patterns of perception, intentionalities of desire, configurations of action, institutional forms, and existential involvements. It determines the stories that we tell and hear as being *about* something. It comports a structure and a dynamics of reference, albeit not a subject-centered intentionality of reference in quest of the objectively determinable, nor a reference of signification caught up in the aporia of a system of signifiers and signifieds, but rather a reference elicited by the intrusion of alterity, a reference borne by an incursive disclosure effected by the lifeworld.

In following the lines and forces of disclosure, rhetoric is in an advan-

perspective, also recognizes clearly enough its hermeneutical requirement. "Rhetoric," he writes, "I shall urge, should be a study of misunderstanding and its remedies." *The Philosophy of Rhetoric* (New York: Oxford University Press, 1965), p. 3.
38. *Human Communication as Narration*, pp. 47–49 and 105–21.

tageous position for monitoring the move to the lifeworld. Because of its communicative orientation, which is always a matter of discourse and action, rhetoric exercises a peculiar hold on the lifeworld. Its incursive disclosure antedates the projects of ostensive and self-reference. It privileges neither epistemic objects nor interiorized subjects. It is a responsive activity, attending to the incursion of that which is other.

RATIONALITY ACROSS THE GENRES

Our explanation of the economy of rhetoric as an economy of reasons has enabled us to draw upon the discussions in the preceding chapters, in which rationality has been elucidated as a praxial intercalation of critique, articulation, and disclosure. We have tried to show how these interwoven workings of reason structure the economy of rhetorical dynamics as it moves about within its communal topography. We have thus been able to address the claims of reason on the rhetorical art and assist Blumenberg in finding resources of rationality in rhetoric itself.

A new perplexity and a new set of challenges, however, have been generated by our sketch of the topography and economy of the rhetorical enterprise. These challenges have to do with what Jürgen Habermas has catalogued as the leveling of genre distinctions among philosophy, rhetoric, and literature. He is of the mind that this is an acute problem for postmodern thought generally and for Derridean deconstruction more specifically.[39] The wider backdrop of these emergent complexities and challenges is the claim of modernity for an autonomy of reason and a separation of the culture-spheres, and the postmodern reaction to this claim by disseminating reason and collapsing the genres of discourse that have traditionally defined the parameters of science, morality, and art. Clearly, in such a state of affairs, the specific roles traditionally assigned to philosophy, rhetoric, and literature become acutely problematized.

Are the topographies and economies of these disciplines basically similar or do they consist of distinct genres? To what extent are the discourses in each autonomous and to what extent do they overlap or indeed blur and blend into each other? How do philosophy, rhetoric, and literature fit into the differentiated culture-spheres of modernity? Do they belong to the sphere of science, morality, or art? Do they share a common responsibility for the care and nurturing of reason? Is the rationality of each different in kind from the other two? Or is perhaps rationality the property of one and denied to the others? The perplexities occasioned by the above interrogations would seem to be rather tremendous.

In some sectors of the postmodern world there is a profound proclivity to subvert all distinctions between culture-spheres and all differentia-

39. See particularly Habermas's essay "Excursus on Leveling the Genre Distinction between Philosophy and Literature," in *The Philosophical Discourse of Modernity*, trans. Frederick Lawrence (Cambridge, MA: The MIT Press, 1987), pp. 185–210.

tions of genre. Derrida calls upon us to witness the collapse of all assemblages of signifiers and all genres of discourse into each other. As we have already noted, he is unable to locate any interesting distinction between philosophy and literature, and he has the "flowers of rhetoric" bloom across the wider expanse of human knowledge. All expectations for distinguishing the metaphorical and the literal, the fictive and the allegedly factual, are destined to be upended. There is nothing outside the text of metaphor. A somewhat curious fallout from the deconstructionist collapse of genre distinctions is that the textuality of metaphor in the rhetorical exercise assumes a certain primacy and hegemony. The rhetorical text becomes not only pervasive but also foundational.

Although one might resist going all the way with Derrida in his rhetorical underwriting of all modes of discourse, there is much that he teaches us about the permeation of both everyday discourse and the specialized vocabularies of science and philosophy with rhetorical strategies, fictive inventions, and metaphorical usage. Metaphors indeed pervade the paradigmatic constructs of science and mix quite freely with conceptual models. Giambattista Vico, in his provocative *Novum Szientia,* had already alerted us to this state of affairs in his criticism of the divorce between science and rhetoric as a consequence of the Cartesian devaluation of the rhetorical art.

More recently, philosophers and historians of science have called our attention to the positive contribution of rhetoric and metaphor to the scientific enterprise. One is reminded, for example, of the writings of Mary Hesse, Thomas Kuhn, Ian Barbour, George Lakoff, and Mark Johnson.[40] Of particular interest and relevance to our project is Donald N. McClosky's recent exploration of the rhetoric of inquiry in the highly quantified fields of micro- and macroeconomics, whose vocabularies are saturated with matrix algebra and four-quadrant diagrammatics. McCloskey has shown, with remarkable lucidity, how economics, this most highly quantified of all the social sciences, continues to draw its life blood from the employment of metaphor and the display of rhetorical means of persuasion.

Economics uses mathematical models and statistical tests and market arguments, all of which look alien to the literary eye. But looked at closely they are not so alien. They may be seen as figures of speech—metaphors, analogies, and appeals to authority.[41]

40. Mary Hesse, *Models and Analogies in Science* (Notre Dame: University of Notre Dame Press, 1966); Thomas Kuhn, *The Structure of Scientific Revolutions* (Chicago: University of Chicago Press, 1962); Ian Barbour, *Myths, Models and Paradigms* (New York: Harper & Row, 1974); and George Lakoff and Mark Johnson, *Metaphors We Live By* (Chicago: University of Chicago Press, 1980).
41. Donald N. McCloskey, *The Rhetoric of Economics* (Madison: The University of Wisconsin Press, 1985), p. xvii.

The invasion of rhetoric, metaphor, and literary invention into philosophical discourse has also become well documented. Although Derrida's *White Mythology: Metaphor in the Text of Philosophy* is probably the most frequently cited work on the topic, there are numerous other works in which the philosophical importance of metaphor and the interface of rhetoric and philosophy are addressed.[42] Among these works, Ricoeur's *Rule of Metaphor*, which we have already had occasion to cite in some of our preceeding discussions, is of particular relevance to our concerns because in it he maps out a new notion of reference on the terrain of metaphorical discourse. This new notion of reference—"metaphorical reference" is what Ricoeur has named it—no longer finds its touchstone in the objectivating procedures of ostensive, empirical reference, designed to pick out isolable and determinable sensory objects and physical properties. Instead, it is a reference that displays a lifeworld of labor, enjoyment, suffering, and human associations.

Ricoeur articulates his new notion of reference against the backdrop of the Fregean distinction between "sense" and "reference," enabling him to characterize the odyssey of reference as a passage from "the structure of the work" (sense) to "the world of work" (reference).[43] In thus displaying a world through the dynamics of metaphorical deployment, rhetoric makes a claim upon reality and implies a concept of truth. Rhetoric and philosophy are hence viewed as joining forces in the pursuit of common tasks. Rhetoric calls upon an analysis and interpretation of concepts of reality and truth, and philosophy requires the resources of metaphor and the rhetorical art more generally.

The lesson to be learned from the recent sundry discussions of rhetoric and metaphor is that they are indeed operative across an expansive spectrum of modes of discourse and disciplinary practices. From this evident overlapping of discourses and disciplines effected by the uses of rhetoric and metaphor, at times resulting in blurred genres, it does not, however, follow that genres can be simply collapsed or leveled. Admittedly, one could say of metaphor what one says of interpretation, namely, that it goes all the way down and all the way back. But for metaphor and interpretation to go all the way down and all the way back does not mean that *everything* is metaphor and interpretation. A recognition that there is no discourse without metaphor does not entail that discourse and metaphor comprise the last horizon in which all communicative practices are

---

42. Some of the more prominent philosophical contributions to the topic are found in Gaston Bachelard, *The Poetics of Space*, trans. Maria Jolas (Boston: Beacon Press, 1969); Max Black, *Models and Metaphors* (Ithaca: Cornell University Press, 1962); Ernst Cassirer, *The Philosophy of Symbolic Forms*, trans. Ralph Mannheim (New Haven: Yale University Press, 1953); Nelson Goodman, *Languages of Art: An Approach to a Theory of Symbols* (Indianapolis: Bobbs-Merrill, 1968); Paul Ricoeur, *The Rule of Metaphor*, trans. Robert Czerny (Toronto: University of Toronto Press, 1977); Colin Murray Turbayne, *The Myth of Metaphor* (New Haven: Yale University Press, 1962); and Philip Wheelwright, *Metaphor and Reality* (Bloomington: Indiana University Press, 1968).
43. *The Rule of Metaphor*, pp. 216–56.

somehow anchored. An acknowledgment that there is no life without textuality and narrative does not legitimate the inference that textuality and narrative constitute the world. Discourse, textuality, narrative, and language more generally are delimited by the incursion of nondiscursive lifeworld praxis.

One of the most ardent contemporary spokespersons against the collapse of all genres of discourse, and the obliteration of distinguishable culture-spheres, is Jürgen Habermas. Habermas's specific target on this issue is Jacques Derrida, although the ramifications of Habermas's critique for an assault on postmodern thought more generally are patently evident. Habermas chides Derrida for glossing the genre distinctions among the discourses of literature, rhetoric, science, philosophy, law, and morality and for his failure to acknowledge the polar tension between expert knowledge and the taken-for-granted opinions in the everyday lifeworld. "Derrida holistically levels these complicated relationships in order to equate philosophy with literature and criticism. He fails to recognize the special status that both philosophy and literary criticism, each in its own way, assume as mediators between expert culture and the everyday world."[44] Specifically addressing the role of rhetoric in Derrida's standoff battle with logocentric rationality, Habermas concludes: "Derrida wants to expand the sovereignty of rhetoric over the realm of the logical to solve the problem confronting the totalizing critique of reason."[45]

Habermas's rejoinder to Derrida's elevation of rhetoric, poetics, and literature to a status of primacy rests on the claim that the two domains, the rhetorical/poetical/literary on the one hand and the philosophical/logical on the other hand, retain their relative autonomy. The kicker in Habermas's argument is his distinction between "capacities for world-disclosure" and "problem-solving capacities." Although the polar tension between these two capacities "is held together within the functional matrix of ordinary language," the specialized forms of discourse and modes of knowledge that move out from this functional matrix are "shaped and worked out within the compass of *one* linguistic function and *one* dimension of validity at a time."[46] The problem-solving domain, the domain of prosaic, innerworldly communication, in which the everyday business of the world is carried on, installs its distinctive locutionary and illocutionary functions and legitimates its claims with distinctive criteria of validation. Although the domain of rhetorical/poetical/literary world-disclosure also has its integrity and autonomy, its constitution involves a suspension of the illocutionary forces that bind ordinary discourse and a bracketing of the structural constraints of the communicative functions of everyday life.

Habermas's distinction between problem-solving capacities and capac-

44. *The Philosophical Discourse of Modernity*, p. 207.
45. *The Philosophical Discourse of Modernity*, p. 188.
46. *The Philosophical Discourse of Modernity*, p. 207.

ities for world-disclosure has a certain utility, and it provides at least a measure of leverage for responding not only to Derrida's all-devouring textualization and universalization of the metaphorical but also to Heidegger's privileging of poetical dwelling. Heidegger's existential appropriation of Hölderlin's vision of poetical dwelling admittedly has its merit for countering the hegemony of the modern, scientific-technological paradigm of human behavior. However, the space of communicative praxis is not reducible to a habitat for poetic thinking and understanding. Its topography includes also the terrain of prosaic dwelling, interests and concerns of everyday life as they pertain to the material conditions of our socio-historical existence, requiring the activation of pragmatically oriented problem-solving strategies.

The distinctions between the prosaic and the poetical, between ethico-political involvement and fictive text production, between social uses of knowledge and literary elucidations, are clearly distinctions that make a difference. Yet, the central issue of rhetorical rationality, which comprises the general topic of our current chapter, slides through the cracks in Habermas's rejoinder to Derrida, and this is the result of Habermas himself glossing a distinction that is of some consequence. Habermas simply permits the rhetorical and the poetical to move into one another in too facile a manner, leading to an engulfment of the grammar of rhetoric by the grammars of fiction and poetic disclosure. "The rhetorical element," concludes Habermas, "occurs in its *pure form* only in the self-referentiality of the poetic expression, that is, in the language of fiction specialized for world-disclosure."[47]

This facile collapse of rhetoric, poetics, fiction, and world-disclosure mixes much that needs sorting out. That the rhetorical and the poetical at times mingle and fraternize cannot be denied, but the topography and economy of rhetoric cannot be so easily equated with the poetical sphere. This is particularly the case when one is dealing with political-deliberative rhetoric, where the carrying on of the practical affairs of the everyday lifeworld is very much at issue.[48]

Our principal intention in pursuing the rationality of rhetoric has been to show how the economy of rhetoric is stimulated by the dynamics of praxial critique, articulation, and disclosure, as this dynamics operates within the binding topos of communicative praxis. In concert with Blumenberg's project, we have found a rationality within the folds of rhetoric itself, a rationality that comports its distinctive moments of critique, articulation, and disclosure. Hence, contra Habermas, we have been able to locate a rhetoric of lifeworld disclosure that extends beyond the delimited

47. *The Philosophical Discourse of Modernity*, p. 209.
48. Michael Hyde has addressed the delimitation of Heidegger's privileging of poetical dwelling by grafting onto it a complement of "rhetorical dwelling," thus expanding the space of dwelling for *homo humanus* to include the praxis-oriented engagements of public discourse and action. See Michael Hyde, "Rhetorically Man Dwells: On the Making-known Function of Discourse," *Communication* 7 (1983): pp. 201–20.

disclosure of fictive and poetical worlds. World-disclosure cannot be confined to literary production and the poetic imagination.

Thus, although we can profitably use Habermas against Derrida's pantextualism and Heidegger's proclivity to privilege poetic dwelling, we must in the end use Habermas against himself by pursuing further his own request for differentiation. Already from Aristotle we learned that the *ars rhetorica* and the *ars poetica* comprise different forms of *technē* and are not to be fused. Habermas's collapse of the one into the other occludes the distinction between the lifeworld-disclosing function of rhetoric and the fictive world-disclosure of literary invention. The fact of the matter appears to be that Habermas, at least at this stage of his consummate philosophical contribution, has been unable to address the rhetorical claims of reason on their own terms.

In this chapter we have sought to locate the claims of reason within the rhetorical situation by rendering it as a topographical nexus of communal practices and an economy of good reasons for thought and action. We have again landed on a praxial rationality, illustrated by the performances of critique, articulation, and disclosure. This rationality is not housed within any specific genre of discourse and form of knowledge. It is operative *between* genres and *between* forms of knowledge, transversal to the differentiated culture-spheres, lying across their disciplinary constitutions.

In particular, we have been concerned to explicate the dynamics of rationality between rhetoric and philosophy, with an effort to get a bead on the rationality of rhetoric without devaluing the rhetoric of rationality. As a consequence, the traditional portrait of philosophy as "the guardian of reason" has indeed been deconstructed, but not in such a manner that the disciplines of philosophy and rhetoric come off as being identical. Gary Madison, reflecting and writing in the spirit of Vico, states the matter rather well when he tells us that the proper approach is one that "does not simply seek to substitute 'rhetoric' for 'philosophy'; it seeks rather to emphasize the rhetorical nature of philosophy and the philosophical status of rhetoric."[49] One cannot step outside the history of the two disciplines, philosophy and rhetoric. They each display their own genres of discourse, knowledge regimes, and peculiar constellations of disciplinary practices. The task is to fathom the claims of reason that are transversally operative between them.

49. Gary B. Madison, *The Hermeneutics of Postmodernity: Figures and Themes* (Bloomington: Indiana University Press, 1988), p. 164.

Transversal Rationality

TRANSVERSALITY ACROSS THE DISCIPLINES

The relevance of the concept of transversality has already been registered, albeit somewhat obliquely, in the preceding chapters. Our discussions of the dynamics of praxial rationality as a deployment of critique, articulation, and disclosure, as this deployment develops in hermeneutical understanding, narrational emplotment, and rhetorical engagement, have already pointed in the direction of a transversal performance of reason. The specific task of our concluding chapter is that of making this transversal play of rationality explicit, and in doing so consolidate the resources of reason as a praxial accomplishment.

Transversality has appeared on the scene as a recurring figuration of thought across the disciplines for some time. The notion has achieved a rather wide currency among the various disciplinary matrices that make up the academy of the arts and sciences. Mathematicians define transversality as a generalization of orthogonality, enabling a line to intersect two or more lines or surfaces without achieving coincidence. Physiology employs the grammar of transversality in describing the networking of bands of fibers. In anatomy the term is used to define the lateral movements of vertebra. Physicists make use of the concept of transverse mass in working out the ratio of accelerating forces. In philosophy the concept of transversality has been used to describe the dynamics of consciousness and the interplay of social practices.

Surveying the polysemic figuration of transversality across the disciplines, one is confronted with a plethora of senses that seem to shift as one moves from one discipline to the next. Proceeding in awareness that the meaning of a term resides in its use, one is nonetheless tempted to search for family resemblances that might become visible in its multidisciplinary usages. Any such search, however, needs to proceed with a high degree of caution. The particularities of the disciplinary practices that guide the sense of transversality should not be glossed. Yet, it is surely of some consequence that we are here dealing with a grammatical figure and concept that enables us to approach a variety of subject matters, including the topology of lines and surfaces, forces of acceleration, the interweaving of fibers, movements of vertebra, the dynamics of consciousness, and the interplay of social practices. The use of the concept/ metaphor of transversality in all of these approaches exhibits interrelated senses of lying across, extending over, intersecting, meeting and converging without achieving coincidence. By way of complex maneuvers of borrowing and conjugation, metaphorical play and refiguration, the various disciplines make use of these interrelated senses ensconced within transversality to understand and explain geometrical space, events of nature, anatomical structures, physiological processes, human behavior, and cultural and historical configurations. It is thus that transversality, most generally construed, provides a window to the wider world of thought and action.

However, as is the case with all such windows, one is afforded only perspectives on a changing scene. It is thus that certain tendencies in the employment of the vocabulary of transversality need to be resisted. Chief among these tendencies is the rationalistic impulse to sublate the several usages in the various disciplines into a higher concept that totalizes the different faculties of knowledge into a seamless unity viewed from above, as well as the positivistic impulse to determine a usage that is somehow paradigmatic and normative for all the rest, inviting a hegemonic "unity of the sciences" seen from below. A vigilance over the imperialism of a concept or a metaphor, be it that of transversality or some other, needs to be strictly maintained. The task is to discern how the use of each concept or metaphor plays in its own court, without sublation and without reduction. Only then will genuine communication across the disciplines become possible.

Our principal concern is with the use of transversality in the discipline of philosophy, and particularly with regard to its utility for advancing an understanding of the dynamics of reason. In probing its philosophical capital, we of course do not stand at the beginning. Transversality as a figure of philosophical discourse has already made its debut. So we pick up on a story that has already been told; however, we propose to retell this story in such a manner that its pivotal character, its leading figure, undergoes a refiguration.

The story of transversality as a philosophical concept in modernity is an account that links transversality with a subject-centered philosophy of consciousness. The plot of this story has been prominently illustrated in Sartre's appropriation of transversality in his effort to solve the problem of the unity of consciousness. The problem is one that he inherits from Husserl. He proposes to solve it, however, without Husserl's appeal to a transcendental ego wherewith to ground the unity of consciousness. Sartre's position contra Husserl on this issue is well known. The unity of consciousness, according to Sartre, is secured not by way of anchoring it in a transcendental and identical pole of consciousness, residing in the depths of the cogito, but is seen rather as the result of a constituting act of consciousness. A result rather than a given, a product *of* consciousness rather than a necessary condition *within* consciousness, unity is an achievement of a performative intentionality. Consciousness, which for Sartre is from bottom up intentional, unifies itself through its own resources by dint of transversal relays that bind present consciousness with its past. Thus, Sartre is able to speak of a "consciousness which unifies itself, concretely, by a play of 'transversal' intentionalities which are concrete and real retentions of past consciousness."[1] Through a species of self-reflexivity, consciousness achieves a bonding with itself by reclaiming the consciousness that it has been through a remembrance of things past. Consciousness comes to a stand, as it were, through an interweaving of the lines of psychic forces that lie across its retentional span.

The philosophical use of the grammar of transversality by Sartre to account for the unification of consciousness may indeed have its own rewards within the limitations of his project, namely that of providing an internal critique of Husserl's theory of consciousness. But it is precisely the limitations of Sartre's project that require attention, for it is these limitations that have certain consequences for an employment of the concept of transversality. Sartre engineers an internal critique of Husserl's egological concept of consciousness, demonstrating, in a rather imaginative manner to be sure, that the transcendental ego has no clothes. But he stays with the Husserlian project of designing a philosophy of subjectivity that moves out from the primacy of consciousness. In this regard both Sartre and Husserl remain with the programmatics of modernity. They proceed from the postulate of an originating consciousness and seek to render an account of its dealings and contents. In the case of Husserl, this account follows the route of a transcendental and egological turn. Sartre maneuvers his way about sans the services either of transcendental reductions or egological postulates. He sketches instead an "existentialist theory of consciousness." Nonetheless, both Sartre and Husserl proceed from the primacy of consciousness as center and origin. This defines their shared phenomenological prejudice.

In the preceding chapters we have already voiced our criticisms of the philosophies of subjectivity and consciousness that became part of the mind-set of modernity, be they epistemological/transcendental or existentialist. We have recognized the contribution of postmodern thought in problematizing such ventures, and on this particular point we are disposed to align ourselves with the postmodern challenge to the philosophical world. It should, however, also be made clear for the record that although we have jettisoned a subject-centered approach to the claims of

1. Jean-Paul Sartre, *The Transcendence of the Ego: An Existentialist Theory of Consciousness*, trans. Forrest Williams and Robert Kirkpatrick (New York: The Noonday Press, 1957), p. 39. Sartre mounts two specific arguments against Husserl's doctrine of the transcendental ego. It is superfluous; it remains an abstraction that performs no utility in accounting for the unity and individuality of consciousness. And it is a hindrance; it severs consciousness from itself, functioning as an "opaque blade" that separates present consciousness from its retentional qualification (pp. 39–40).

reason, we are not lobbying for a deletion of the vocabulary of subject and consciousness. A displacement of the sovereignty of the subject, and its consciousness-centered rationality, does not entail a dissolution of the subject and consciousness in every manner conceivable. Although it may be problematic to begin with the subject, either as an epistemological and self-reflecting subject or as an existentially isolated self, one still has to end with the subject, duly decentered and refigured. Our topography of communicative praxis enables us to effect such a decentering without loss of either the speaking or the acting subject. The subject finds a new space as an emergent within the dynamics of discursive and institutional practices. Although we are sympathetic with the postmodern problematization of subject-centered philosophy, we are concerned about the failure of nerve in postmodernism to acknowledge the weight of tradition and the background of communicative practices against which the subject assumes a new posture.[2]

There is a further limitation in Sartre's use of transversality, a limitation that travels with his commitments to the sovereignty of the existential subject. This limitation arises from his peculiar stance on temporality, in which a primacy is conferred upon the present at the expense of devaluing the efficacy of the future. Sartre's appeal to transversal intentionality is motivated by a desire to account for the retention of past consciousness within the interstices of present consciousness. It is clear enough that the dynamics of transversal intentionality moves backwards; what is not clear from Sartre's account is how it moves forward. The protentional vector of transversality remains underdetermined. Consciousness extends across its past occasions, perpetually defining the present as retentionally qualified. But there is no explicit acknowledgment of a protentional qualification of the workings of transversal intentionality—as there is, for example, in the thought of Heidegger and Merleau-Ponty.

Given these limitations pertaining to the figuration of transversality within a subject-centered philosophy of presence, a refiguration is required. This refiguration is governed by a shift away from a phenomenological description of consciousness as a given datum to an interpretation of the configurations of discourse and action as communicative achievements. Consequent to this shift, the principal focus is no longer on a present event of consciousness, and much less upon a belief structure that accompanies such an event, but rather upon the assemblages and patterns of discourse and action as progeny of communicative praxis. We are no longer dealing with a serial succession of moments of consciousness but rather with societal assemblages and gestalts of praxis.

The transversality of these gestalts of praxis, lying across varying forms of discourse, modes of thought, and institutional configurations, exhibits

2. For a sustained discussion of the recovery of the subject in the aftermath of its deconstruction as a metaphysical substrate and an epistemological residuum, see Calvin O. Schrag, *Communicative Praxis and the Space of Subjectivity* (Bloomington: Indiana University Press, 1986).

conjunctions and disjunctions, accommodations and alterations, solidifications and ruptures. Some constellations of thought and action slide into one another, occasioning mutual acknowledgment and consensus; others follow the lines of deviation and difference, occasioning agonistics and dissensus. The transverse mass of our social practices indeed comprises a multiplex phenomenon of converging and diverging gestalts. To be sure, the subject and moments of consciousness are at play in this transversal dynamics. The point, however, is that these emerge as implicates of communicative praxis and never enjoy the metaphysical and epistemological security of originating principles. The sense of transversality that is at issue for our concerns is that of a transversality socially and historically contextualized.

The social contextualization of transversality has received particular attention in Félix Guattari's explication of the workings of "transversality in the group."[3] Guattari, a practicing psychiatrist, details the performance of transversality in the institutional setting of a psychiatric hospital, providing us with a concrete illustration of the effect of the figuration of transversality across the disciplines. He employs the term to help explain the networking of the different constellations of power and seats of decision making that are involved in the psychiatric practice. The institutional setting is structured by a peculiar network of groups and subgroups, types of expertise, lines of authority, and concerned parties. There are the administrators, the doctors, the nurses, the assistants to the doctors and nurses, the patients, and the families of the patients. All of these groups play some role in the program and process of psychiatric healing. The exercise of decision making, with its multiple rationales, is transversal to the different groups and various social roles that make up the institutional complex.

The degree of transversality in operation depends upon the effectiveness of a dialogue across the various groups and sectors of concern, fostering a recognition of the otherness of each of the groups involved and leading to a "dialectical enrichment."[4] Transversality thus at once heightens the self-understanding in each of the involved groups through a mutual acknowledgment and sets the requirement for adjustments and accommodations in recognition of the contributions by the several groups. In developing self-understanding among the several groups and encouraging shared responsibility, transversality avoids both the hegemony of a decision-making process that proceeds vertically from top down and the impasse of horizontally dispersed groups warring with each other.

Guattari summarizes this transversal networking of groups as follows: "Transversality is a dimension that tries to overcome both the impasse of pure verticality and that of mere horizontality; it tends to be achieved

3. Félix Guattari, *Molecular Revolution: Psychiatry and Politics*, trans. Rosemary Sheed (New York: Penguin Books, 1984), p. 22.
4. *Molecular Revolution*, p. 22.

when there is a maximum communication among the different levels and, above all, in different meanings."[5] Guattari's location of the dynamics of transversality within the heart of a praxis that informs the management of a psychiatric hospital provides us with a concrete and local exemplification of its workings. What interests us in particular about this appropriation of the figure of transversality is its alignment with the intentionality of social practices as this intentionality operates without appeals to the protocols and postulates of pure theory. Transversality falls out as a praxial accomplishment in which understanding, mutual acknowledgment, dialogic interaction, decision making, and various vectors of concern remain in play. These ingredients of communicative praxis display an indigenous intentionality of an economy of discernment, understanding, articulation, and assessment on the hither side of a priori principles, antecedently specified criteria, and predetermined methodologies. In short, it is an intentionality that operates in advance of any purchases on the holdings of the modern theoretico-epistemological paradigm and its subject-centered concept of rationality.

It is this aggressive move to transversality as an achievement of communicative praxis that places into sharp relief the limitations in Sartre's construal of transversal intentionality as a determinant of a sovereign and subject-centered consciousness. Sartre's "existentialist theory of consciousness," in spite of its warranted assault on the transcendental postulates of modern rationalism, remains at best a late-modern reaction that is unable to dispel the ghosts of a centripetal, originating consciousness.

The grammar of transversality has made its way into the various texts of postmodernity, but only sporadically and quite obliquely. For the most part, it has been called upon in the making of local and isolated observations. No consolidation of its usage has been offered, and much less has a systematic account of it been given. Lyotard invokes the term in discussing the quandaries of translation. "Translation," he submits, "requires pertinences that are 'transversal' to languages."[6] In translating from one language into another one needs to land upon phrase regimens and genres of discourse in the one language that have their analogue in the other. This requires the discernment of pertinences that lie across the two languages, which are somehow analogous, exhibiting a sameness-within-difference. Although Lyotard is markedly pessimistic about the possibility of translations, given the recalcitrance of the *différend* that determines the life of phrase regimens, he does recognize the role that transversality would need to play in a translation project.

Foucault has generalized transversal praxis to encompass the play of power relations that congeal into a variety of social forms, such as the "opposition to the power of men over women, of parents over children,

---

5. *Molecular Revolution*, p. 18.
6. Jean-François Lyotard, *The Differend: Phrases in Dispute*, trans. Georges Van Den Abbeele (Minneapolis: University of Minnesota Press, 1988), p. 49.

of psychiatry over the mentally ill, of medicine over the population, of administration over the ways people live."[7] The specific forms of these power relations vary from political situation to political situation, but the struggles through which the forms are defined display common concerns and motivations. Foucault speaks of them as "transversal struggles":

> They are "transversal" struggles; that is, they are not limited to one country. Of course, they develop more easily and to a greater extent in certain countries, but they are not confined to a particular political or economic form of government.[8]

A more explicit and somewhat more concentrated use of the figure of transversality occurs in Deleuze's interpretation of Proust. Indeed, according to Deleuze, transversality supplies the "formal structure" on which Proust's entire *Remembrance of Things Past* rests.

> It is transversality which permits us, in the train, not to unify the viewpoints of a landscape, but to bring them into communication according to the landscape's own dimension, in its own dimension, whereas they remain non-communicating according to their own dimension. It is transversality which constitutes the singular unity and totality of the Méséglise Way and of the Guermantes Way, without suppressing their difference or distance. . . . It is transversality which assures the transmission of a ray, from one universe to another as different as astronomical worlds. The new linguistic convention, the formal structure of the work, is therefore transversality, which passes through the entire sentence, which proceeds from one sentence to another in the entire book.[9]

Deleuze's use of transversality to disentangle the formal structure of Proust's masterpiece supplies another example of the utility of the concept across the disciplines, highlighting its relevance for the agenda of literary studies. The principal lesson to be learned from Deleuze's application of transversality within the literary domain is that it affords a thinking about the unity and structure of a work that is not superimposed, is not introjected from the outside, but is rather seen to develop within the work itself. Transversality effects a unification and integration, a communication across differences, that does not congeal into a seamless solidarity or locus of coincidence. It brings the various viewpoints lying across the landscape of the remembered past into a communicative situation that recognizes the integrity of particularity and the play of diversity.

It is the postmodern use of transversality, particularly by Deleuze in

7. Michel Foucault, "The Subject and Power," in Hubert L. Dreyfus and Paul Rabinow, *Michel Foucault: Beyond Structuralism and Hermeneutics* (Chicago: University of Chicago Press, 1982), p. 211.
8. "The Subject and Power," p. 211.
9. Gilles Deleuze, *Proust and Signs*, trans. Richard Howard (New York: George Braziller, 1972), pp. 149–50.

the arena of literary studies and by Guattari in the field of psychiatry, that raises the intensity level of the postmodern challenge. They have brought the concept to the forefront and have made us aware of its utility for problematizing the traditional and modern appeals to predetermined unities and fixed universals. It is this that comprises for Deleuze the "anti-logos" of the "literary machine," a reactive stance against traditional and modern uses of reason. But it is precisely at this dramatic juncture that the postmodern challenge becomes attenuated and requires supplementation, if not a more radical reformulation.

The limitations of the postmodern use of transversality reside principally in the tendency to define its workings from the perspective of an "anti-logos" reactive stance. This enables postmodernism to undermine the pretentious claims that traveled with the logos doctrine in classical and modern thought, but postmodernism comes up short in addressing the less pretentious claims of reason that continue to be operative in transversal communication. The philosophical stance of postmodernity is principally that of a reaction, an assault on the vagaries of logocentrism, a preoccupation with the motif of "the despised logos," all of which tends to congeal into a battle against the claims of reason itself. Its contribution toward dispelling the ghosts of a subject-centered and theory-grounded universalizing rationality needs to be recognized, and herein may well reside its most durable legacy. But its troublesome presupposition that a subject-centered and theory-based rationality is the only candidate for the office of reason has eluded careful scrutiny. The fact of the matter is that postmodernism has been unable to come to terms with the issue of rationality from a more positive perspective. It has landed on the figure of transversality as a promising resource, but it has failed to capitalize on its potential for a transformed portrait of reason.

Throughout our study our attention has been directed precisely to such a transformed portrait of reason, which we have come to call "praxial rationality." This praxial rationality does not entail a jettisoning of the logos but rather a refiguration of it within an economy of communicative praxis in which the claims of reason become effective by dint of praxis-oriented critique, articulation, and disclosure. We have followed the descent of the logos into the interstices of communicative praxis and have tracked its inscriptions as they play in the configurations of our discourse and action. An effort has been made to meet the challenge of postmodernism by providing a portrait of the life of reason after the demise of logocentric principles. The logos is refigured and reformed, pruned of its pretentious claims for pure theory, and reinstalled in the life of our praxial engagements.

Our explorations have led us to an acknowledgment of the role of transversality in the economy of reason as it operates within the polis of our practical affairs. This enables us to speak of a *transversal rationality* after the holdings of the universal logos of traditional metaphysics and epistemology have gone into foreclosure. What is now demanded of us is an explication of this transversal rationality relative to its temporal and spatial determinations, its liberation from the strictures of universalization, and its transhistorical relevance.

THE CHRONOTOPAL FIELD OF TRANSVERSALITY

The figure of transversality, inscribed across the disciplines as an extending over and intersecting of lines, forces, velocities, fibers, moments of consciousness, and social practices, displays both temporal and spatial determinations. One might be disposed to speak of transversality as "presupposing" a spatiotemporal field, whether one is dealing with the transverse mass of subatomic particles in motion or whether one attends to the transverse configurations of social practices and their peculiar constellations of power. Caution, however, should be exercised in the appropriation of the vocabulary of "presuppositions" so as not to abstract time and space from the moving particles and the living practices. Caution also should be used in visiting the various disciplines with a univocal sense of time and space. The time and space of material particles is not that of the time and space of consciousness. The time of historical narratives is not that of fictive inventions. Admittedly, an inevitable borrowing and accommodation of senses occurs in the passage from region to region and discourse to discourse, but one will need to be aware of certain aporias that emerge in the course of this passage.

Paul Ricoeur has given concentrated attention to the aporetic of temporality in his *Time and Narrative*, in which he details the paradoxes and quandaries that follow the separation of objectively measured cosmic time from subjectively lived existential time. He approaches this aporia, resulting from the clash of cosmic and lived time, by consulting the resources of narrativity, suggesting that we first look for the "connectors" between cosmic and lived time in the strategies of emplotment within historical narration. Historical narration bridges the chasm separating these two regions of time by joining measured time with historical events. This involves harmonizing seasons and years with festivals, biological processes with the sequence of generations, and delivered documents with a participatory understanding of the past. Now there is, according to Ricoeur, a complementing response to the disproportion of cosmic and lived time on the part of fictive narration, which in turn occasions an aporia on another level, that of a split between historical fact and fictive invention. This requires a refiguration of the time of narrativity, leading to an acknowledgment of a "third time" that borrows figures from both history and fiction, and which articulates through the resources of a productive imagination an intersection of the actual world of lived experience and fictive invention.

The boldness of Ricoeur's project is unparalleled in the philosophical literature dealing with the problematic of temporality. The problematic, most generally stated, is one that results from an inability to forge an immediate access to time, whether one is dealing with cosmic or with lived time, with historical time or with the time of fiction. One thus seems to be left with an unmanageable polysemy of temporality, with a multiplicity of senses, that appears forever to preclude any consolidation of the meaning of time as a unified phenomenon. In the face of this, Ricoeur's bold venture in marking out a "third time" that intersects the complexes of cosmic and lived time, historical and fictive time, is at once provocative and challenging. Indeed, Ricoeur's venture helps to inspire our own, as we experiment with the figure of transversality in addressing the economy of reason. The transversal play in the understanding and communication of our praxial engagements is a play that is peculiarly temporalized in its lying across a spectrum of intertextured senses of time.

We thus project a *weiterdenken* with Ricoeur on the aporetic of temporality, exploring its relevance for the dynamics of a transversal rationality. As we shall see, this will require an interpretive understanding and reflection that simultaneously moves through the aporetic of spatiality. The dynamics of reason not only envelops configurations of temporality, it also traverses various regions of spatiality. Our social practices are informed by boundaries as well as durations, places as well as moments, passages across space as well as movements through time.

It is at this juncture that a revisit to our previous discussion of the Bakhtinian notion of the chronotope is in order. The claims of reason move about in a chronotopal field of value-imbued times and places. Praxial rationality, as a composite of strategies of critique, interpretive articulations, and incursive disclosures, suffers the qualifications of both time and space. Bakhtin's understanding and use of the chronotope can be of some help in marking out certain directions for our own explorations. However, his interest resided principally in showing how the chronotope, as an intertextured assimilation of time and space, is illustrated by the dialogic imagination in its fictive inventiveness—and, more specifically, within the discourse of the novel. Ricoeur's contribution resides primarily in his isolation of a "third time" that folds over the narratives of historical events and those of fictive invention, providing a new way for dealing with the aporia of the clash of cosmic with lived time. We suggest that what is required in a *weiterdenken* with both Bakhtin and Ricoeur on the issues at hand is the grafting of a supplementary exploration of "space and narrative" onto Ricoeur's "time and narrative," and an extension of Bakhtin's chronotope beyond the realm of fictive discourse, broadening the assimilative space-time matrix to include the play of intentionality across the lifeworld of human emotions and human action.

To the extent that one would be successful in such collaborative reflection on the issues with Bakhtin and Ricoeur, one would open up a spatiotemporal field that spans the regions of discourse, perception, human emotions and actions, and institutional involvements. The spatial and temporal determinants within each of these regions retain their praxial orientations. They announce valences of value-imbued and socially defined times and places instead of abstracted instants and points. The chronotope of discourse marks out times and places for assent and disavowal, negotiation and intervention, in response to the claims and activities of the encountered other. The chronotope of perception opens up a perceptual field that assimilates the oriented space of the embodied perceiver with experiences of before and after.[10] The human emotions are qualified by durations of joy and elation, pain and suffering, that are coordinated with places and regions to be visited or avoided. Human action proceeds from places invested with value, enacting projects at the right or opportune moment. The institution of festivals and social events involve a commemoration and anticipation of both times and places. It is thus that temporality and spatiality, in their multiple valences and expressions, invade the expansive terrain of human endeavor and qualify our comprehension of the world.

This comprehension, we have urged, follows the route of an intertextured critique, articulation, and disclosure, which comprise our three moments or phases of the rationality of praxis. In this chapter our concern is to explicate the transversal dynamics of this rationality, exploring how reason is transversal to the multiple configurations of discourse, perception, human emotions and actions, and institutional complexes. As transversal, reason neither simply transcends the panoply of human experience nor is it simply immanent within it. The metaphysical/epistemological matrix of transcendence versus immanence is more of a conceptual liability than a hermeneutical resource for an understanding of the spatiality and temporality of human reason.

Reason remains transversal to the various forms of our personal and social forms of life. It lies across them diagonally; it is neither vertically transcendent to them nor horizontally immanent within them. It operates "between" them in such a manner that it is able to critique, articulate, and disclose them without achieving a coincidence with any particular form of discourse, thought, or action. The integrity of otherness—other forms of thought and other social practices—is maintained, accomplishing at once a better understanding of that which is one's own and a recognition of the need to make accommodations and adjustments in the response to the presence of that which is other. Within such a scheme of things, the dynamics of transversal rationality falls out as a convergence

10. M. Merleau-Ponty has given particular attention to the role of time and space in the phenomenon of perception. He speaks of "the phenomenal field" of perception as a figure-background configuration in which perceiving is an event of embodied consciousness that integrates the determinations of a lived time and a lived space. See particularly *Phenomenology of Perception*, trans. Colin Smith (New York: The Humanities Press, 1962).

without coincidence, an interplay without synthesis, an appropriation without totalization, and a unification that allows for difference. Such is the transversal dynamics that motivates rationality as a concernful struggle within communicative praxis.

The effect of time and space on the potentialities of human reason has already received considerable attention in the history of modern philosophy, and particularly in the philosophy of Kant and later in the philosophy of Husserl. Insofar as one is condemned to think with the tradition, even when one thinks against it, a critical dialogue with Kant and Husserl on the role of time and space within the economy of human reason may well be unavoidable.

Kant's doctrine of the unity of apperception, framed as a synthesis of perception, imagination, and conception, places considerations of time and space very much in the foreground. Time and space, defined by Kant as a priori "forms of intuition" (*Anschauungsformen*), provide the elemental structures of the world as experienced. All experience, from which knowledge begins but does not arise, occurs within a manifold of appearances that are temporalized by virtue of being either simultaneous or successive and spatialized by dint of their separateness from each other. Although time and space are themselves not experienced—there is no direct experiential access to either time or space—they are necessary conditions for experience to occur. On the level of perceptual phenomena, space (as the outer sense) is given equal billing with time (as the inner sense). However, as one moves from perception to conception, via the mediating work of the imagination, the role of temporality is increasingly accentuated. The schematizing operation of the imagination, Kant informs us, finds its grounding in "the transcendental determinations of time."[11] It is thus that the whole range of presentative acts of consciousness (sensation, perception, imagination, conception, and judgment) have some dealings with time.

The accentuation of the role of temporality in the knowledge-bearing odyssey of consciousness reaches a further stage of intensification in Edmund Husserl's *Phenomenology of Internal Time-Consciousness*.[12] In this work Husserl undertakes the task of demonstrating how temporality supplies the immanental unity of consciousness as it moves from a primal present to a past that is perpetually reclaimed as a horizon of retentional modifications of the streaming present. The passing present continues to "sink off" below the surface of the flux of consciousness, becomes sedimented, and requires for its accessibility a performance of retrieval, via both a passive and an active synthesis. The passive synthesis of retentional uni-

11. "Thus an application of the category to appearances becomes possible by means of the transcendental determination of time, which, as the schema of the concepts of understanding, mediates the subsumption of the appearances under the category." *Critique of Pure Reason*, trans. Norman Kemp Smith (London: Macmillan and Company, 1953), p. 181.
12. Edmund Husserl, *The Phenomenology of Internal Time-Consciousness*, trans. James S. Churchill (Bloomington: Indiana University Press, 1964).

fication courts an active synthesis of a constituting, recollective act of consciousness. The unity of consciousness is thus the achievement of the workings of a passive synthesis of retentional moments and the active synthesis of an explicit, objectifying, recollective act. Through these syntheses the lost primal present is, as it were, perpetually restored. In the more fully elaborated phenomenological program of his subsequent reflections, and particularly during the phase of the transcendental phenomenological idealism of the *Cartesian Meditations*, Husserl secured a theoretico-epistemological guarantee for the unity of the temporal flux of consciousness by installing a timeless transcendental ego.[13]

Husserl's discussion of temporality in his *Phenomenology of Internal Time-Consciousness* can be particularly instructive, as Sartre had already clearly seen. This early work of Husserl offers a veritable object lesson in the performance of detailed and painstaking phenomenological analysis and description. His project is that of articulating the "immanent unities" of internal time-consciousness as they "are constituted in the flux of multiplicities of temporal shading." The diverse and multiple contents of this temporal shading are suspended over the past and take their place as "retentional modifications of the primal content in the now-character."[14] This primal content is a vehicle or carrier of first-order apprehensions that constitute a temporal unity as consciousness moves back into its past. The phenomenological importance of the primal content of the now-character resides principally in providing an "identical materiality" in the "exhibition of the same" within the "continuing succession" of consciousness.[15]

There is thus a unification that is built into the primal, streaming present itself, as it is surrounded by a horizon of retentional modifications. Admittedly, the primal present sinks off below the surface, but in so doing it is not dispersed into a random succession of multiplicities on the longitudinal axis, but instead becomes sedimented into a vertical coincidence, a "coincidence of identity."[16] This coincidence of identity ensures a continuity and sameness, enabling one to remain conscious of that which endures as being identical with itself. Herein resides the phenomenological constitution of time, exhibiting at once a passive and an active constitution. It is the latter, the active constitution, that makes possible the objectification of time, and through a move of generalization is seen to be operative in the constitution of other objectivities.

This early analysis and description of internal time-consciousness was developed later, against the backdrop of Husserl's mature phenomenological and transcendental idealism, in conjunction with an explicit egol-

---

13. Edmund Husserl, *Cartesian Meditations: An Introduction to Phenomenology*, trans. Dorion Cairns (The Hague: Martinus Nijhoff, 1960). See particularly "Fourth Meditation: Development of the Constitutional Problems Pertaining to the Transcendental Ego Himself," pp. 65–88.
14. *The Phenomenology of Internal Time-Consciousness*, p. 119.
15. *The Phenomenology of Internal Time-Consciousness*, p. 120.
16. *The Phenomenology of Internal Time-Consciousness*, p. 121.

ogy. This egology enabled Husserl to explain the achievement of a primal constitution that yields at once coincidence and identity as the effects of the immanental agency of a transcendental ego, the originating source and condition for all identification, objectification, and constitution.

We have undertaken this brief excursus into Kant's and Husserl's understanding and use of temporality because there are certain lessons to be learned from a critical engagement with their reflections on the issues at stake. One of these lessons instructs us on the limits of a subject-centered and consciousness-based approach to temporality. The success of Kant and Husserl in explicating the structure and dynamics of the faculties and presentative acts of consciousness needs to be noted. Indeed, within the requirements of the modern epistemological paradigm, their contributions may well stand as unparalleled. They have shown, with both clarity and detail, how the knowing subject with its epistemic consciousness needs to come to terms with temporality. One might even be inclined to say that modern epistemology comes to its fulfillment in Husserl's phenomenology as a rigorous science.

However, the delimitation of the resources of an epistemological, subject-centered approach has already been prominently inscribed on the preceding pages of our current project—as well as in a previous work.[17] In our move beyond epistemology, from philosophy as a subject-centered system of beliefs to philosophy as an elucidation of human discourse and action, the historically conditioned background practices of our world engagements have moved into prominence. Knowledge itself is viewed as being inseparable from its social sources. The determinations of praxis extend even to the epistemic domain. Within such a scheme of things the contributions of Kant and Husserl suffer a consequential delimitation.

In Kant's perspective on temporality, both vis-à-vis its role as a form of intuition in the life of perception and its workings in the schema of the imagination as a transcendental determination of time, as well as in Husserl's doctrine of internal time-consciousness, the socio-historical and politico-institutional constitution of temporality remains abridged. The temporalizing that occurs between the subjective time of consciousness and objectively measured cosmic time is occluded. It is precisely this "third time" (as Ricoeur has suggestively named it), moving between subjective and objective time without becoming coincident with either, that our praxially imbued temporality of transversality exemplifies. The delimitation of the subjective time of consciousness and cognition becomes explicit in this appeal to the transversality of our social practices and their historical inherence.

A second lesson to be learned from a critical engagement with Kant and Husserl on temporality involves an awareness of the pitfalls in over-estimating the continuity of memory. Husserl's theory of retentional con-

---

17. *Communicative Praxis and the Space of Subjectivity*. See particularly chapter five, "The Illusion of Foundationalism," pp. 94–111.

sciousness, as well as Sartre's existentialized version of it, gives insufficient attention to the fragility of memory. In defining their projects within the conceptual parameters of modernity, as an explanation of the unity of consciousness, they suppress the discontinuities of remembering and the ruptures of recollection. In the case of Husserl, this suppression is principally the result of his purchases on the concept of representation to solidify the retentional continuum. The past is perpetually reclaimed through a process of re-presenting *(Vergegenwartigung)*, presenting again the past nows of consciousness as they sink off below the surface and achieve an identity with the primal, streaming present. This heavy investment in the resources of representation to deliver the translucency of the past ensconced within the present occludes both the fugitive nows that escape presence and those that undergo transformation in the process of being recalled.

Husserl and Sartre recognize clearly enough that some species of repetition is operative in all forms of remembering. But in their penchant for the founding of sameness they fail to recognize that repetition generates difference. The memory span, both that of personal consciousness and social history, suffers ruptures and refigurations. The past as remembered is never a representation of it as it once occurred. Gary Madison supplies the needed corrective to the epistemological concept of representation when he adduces: "To understand an experience, to reconstruct the past is not to 'represent' it to ourselves; it is to *transform it.*"[18]

The third lesson to be learned from our problematizing of the epistemological paradigm of temporality (specifically as employed in the transcendental tradition of Kant and Husserl) involves a more explicit recognition of the relevance of spatiality. The more that temporality becomes recessed in the depths of subjectivity, the less attention is paid to the spatial determinants. This ascendancy of time over space disturbs the effects of the chronotopal assimilation of forms of discourse and action and tends to restrict memory to a reckoning with time. The subordination of space to time became an increasingly distinctive feature of modernity from Kant to Hegel and from Hegel to Husserl. Even in the philosophy of Heidegger, which is commonly documented as a chief formative influence in the development of postmodernism, temporalization is given a preeminent emphasis. Spatiality somehow follows in its wake, a kind of supplement to the temporalization of human existence.[19]

18. Gary B. Madison, *The Hermeneutics of Postmodernity: Figures and Themes* (Bloomington: Indiana University Press, 1988), pp. 166–67.
19. In an earlier work we attempted to rectify the subordination of spatiality by showing how time and space are co-primordially constitutive of human experience. Deformalizing time and space as abstracted and lifeless frames for conceptualization, we sketched an "existential coordinate of time and space" in which time and space are understood as living *horizon-forms* that mark out the concrete deployment of perception and embodiment. See Calvin O. Schrag, *Experience and Being: Prolegomena to a Future Ontology* (Evanston: Northwestern University Press, 1969), chapter 2: "The Temporality and Spatiality of Experience."

This peculiar mind-set of modernity, which grants more importance to time than to space, is a not unexpected consequence of the modern bifurcation of mind and matter, spirit and nature. From Descartes on, the rules of the game have called for an assignment of the category of space to the domain of matter and nature and the category of time to the domain of mind and spirit. This division of categorial labor was made particularly explicit in the philosophy of Hegel. As is well known, the net result in Hegel's metanarrative of the odyssey of Spirit is the sublation of time and space into the Absolute Idea. But what is equally clear is that in Hegel's narrative the temporal and historical determinations of Spirit keep the advantage. The travail of the Absolute Idea is a story of the victory of time over space. The ensuing "historical consciousness," for which Hegel was so profoundly responsible, quickly spread its mantle over subsequent philosophical developments in the nineteenth century and became a veritable defining feature of modernity.

The chronotopal abode or dwelling, wherein our figure of transversality is situated, emerges on the hither side of the epistemological and subject-centered construal of time-consciousness and its consequent devaluation of spatiality. It displays the time-space nexus within the heart of communicative praxis and its social and institutional practices. Socio-historical configurations antedate the episodical now-points of consciousness, and institutional constitution takes precedence over the phenomenological/transcendental constitution of the ego. In this chronotopal dwelling there is neither a "vertical coincidence" within the depths of an ever-present now nor a mere sequencing of a longitudinal progression of nows. Instead we find diagonals that cut across the variegated forms of life that make up the chronotopal communicative practices. The transverse mass of our praxial engagements consists of forms of life that lie across each other without coincidence; yet these forms of life do not dissolve into an indeterminate heterogeneity and "pure" incommensurability. Socio-historical practices display an interdependence and a "gathering" by dint of a transversal play of praxial critique, articulation, and disclosure. These moments of rationality, exhibiting a logos-effect of gathering, circumvent both the synchronic verticality of totalitarian hegemony and the diachronic horizontality of anarchic multiplicity. This enables us to speak of the transversal logos.

Edward S. Casey has also responded to the devaluation of space, particularly in discourses on memory. In his book *Remembering: A Phenomenological Study* (Bloomington: Indiana University Press, 1987), he carries through a detailed phenomenological analysis of the intertexturing of temporality and spatiality in what he names the phenomenon of "remembered space." In a highly suggestive passage of this work, he frames the issue as follows: "In actual experiences of remembering, the spatiality and the temporality of the mnemonic presentation are often correlated to the point of becoming indissociable. The 'when' and 'where' are inextricably linked—so that for example, to remember a scene from my grandparents' home is *ipso facto* to remember a scene that took place at a certain period of my childhood" (p. 70).

THE TRANSVERSAL LOGOS

Our explorations of the dynamics of transversal thought and action within a moving chronotope of assimilated times and places has led us to a reformulation of the classical concept of the logos. This classical concept, so despised in the literature of postmodernity because of its complicity in the misdeeds of logocentrism, is retrieved and refigured in our concept of transversal rationality. An assault on logocentrism does not entail a scuttling of the logos. Throughout we have attempted to show how the claims of reason remain in force, even though they no longer enjoy the metaphysical and epistemological guarantees that have been offered to them in the past. The universal logos of logocentrism is dead. The transversal logos of communicative rationality is alive and well.

The peculiar mark of the Occidental doctrine of the logos as it was taken over in the constructionist designs of metaphysics and epistemology was its putative claim for universality and necessity. Classical metaphysics called upon a doctrine of essence to insure such a claim. Essences were taken to be permanent, atemporal, and unifying determinations of both the human soul and its proper objects of cognition. The odyssey of reason thus came to be defined as an effort to recall the essential structures of mind and reality alike. The modern epistemological paradigm problematized the auspicious metaphysical architectonics that traveled with the classical concept of the logos and sought to locate the claims for universality and necessity within the structure of the human mind and within a criteriological concept of reason that found its legitimation in the quest for apodicticity.

In both these paradigms, classical metaphysical and modern epistemological, the presentation/representation of that which is universal and necessary finds its proper figure in that of a *vertical grounding*. There is either a grounding of such claims from above (from the vantage point of transcendent and ahistorical essences) or from below (the vantage point of transcendental, logically a priori, and equally ahistorical conditions). But whether grounded vertically from above or from below, we are proffered a perspective from the other side of history, a view from the perspective of an ahistorical subject that is nowhere and in no time.

The ahistorical subject, whether in the dress of classical metaphysics or modern epistemology, gravitates into the predicament of being unable to render an account of its own genealogy without undergoing reinsertion into the density of history from which it has sought to escape. Both the subject of social practices and the reason that it employs cannot escape their historical inherence. Subjectivity and reason alike arise from a complex networking of contingencies in communication-oriented existence.

Given the requirement for a communicative turn, we find Jürgen Habermas's project of devising "an alternative way out of the philosophy of the subject" by replacing "subject-centered reason" with "communicative reason" to be singularly suggestive.[20] Yet, at that very point where Habermas appears to have surmounted the perplexities in the traditional account of reason, he reverts to an epistemologically oriented doctrine of validity claims and continues to scrounge around in modernity's leftover holdings in theory construction and universalizability. His "theory of communicative action" continues an appeal to criticizable validity claims that have a universal grounding, designed to offer a "theory of rationality with which to ascertain its own universality."[21] Such ascertaining is purportedly accomplished through the exercise of validity claims that are built into the very structure of consensus formation, which "*as claims . . .* transcend all limitations of space and time, all the provincial limitations of the given context."[22] When all is said and done, validity claims are context-free, independent of the context of our socio-historical practices. We need, according to Habermas, something more—something more theoretical, more universal, and more validatable than the everyday know-how that enables us to make do in our quotidian practices. "The horizontal knowledge that communicative everyday practice *tacitly* carries . . . does not satisfy the criterion of knowledge that stands in internal relation to validity claims."[23]

Although Habermas's endorsement of communicative reason as a substitute for the subject-centered reason of modernity is to be commended, the fact remains that he has not taken his own project seriously enough. His notion of communicative reason remains lame and spineless, in need of the backing of validity claims that have the sanction of universality, claims that "transcend limitations of time and space." Habermas grasps clearly enough the importance of communication, but he needs to recognize a more robust, a more vibrant, and a more *full-bodied* notion of communicative rationality. What is required is a notion of communicative rationality that offers its own resources of critique, articulation, and disclosure, no longer requiring the epistemological guarantees of universality and necessity issuing from a vertical grounding.

That which we have found to be particularly instructive in the postmodern challenge is the problematization of such appeals to vertical grounding and claims for universality. Postmodernity has called our attention to the horizontal discontinuities in the flux of our changing and heterogeneous forms of discourse and social practices. Through this subversion of the metaphor of verticality by a persistent accentuation of horizontality, the search for a universal logos is indeed called into question. The unification and totalization promised by classical doctrines of es-

20. Jürgen Habermas, *The Philosophical Discourse of Modernity*, trans. Frederick Lawrence (Cambridge, MA: The MIT Press, 1987), chapter XI: "An Alternative Way Out of the Philosophy of the Subject: Communicative versus Subject-Centered Reason," pp. 294–326.
21. Jürgen Habermas, *The Theory of Communicative Action*, Volume 2: *Lifeworld and System: A Critique of Functionalist Reason*, trans. Thomas McCarthy (Boston: Beacon Press, 1987), p. 400.
22. *The Theory of Communicative Action*, p. 399.
23. *The Theory of Communicative Action*, p. 400.

sence, both of the idealist and realist varieties, come up short, and the a priori (universal and necessary) rules that governed the quest for certainty in the epistemological ventures of modernity are reduced to contingent strategies. Whereas the vertical grounding of metaphysically and epistemologically oriented modes of thought sought a view from the other side of history, the horizontal multiplicity celebrated in postmodernity offers only a fragmented vision from this side of history. This privileging of horizontality in postmodernism has its own disturbing consequences. It leaves us with a heterogeneity of socio-historical assemblages of discourse and action in which paralogy and incommensurability, rupture and overturn, have the final word. In such a scheme of things the relativization of all forms of thought and all contents of culture is difficult to avoid.

The problematization of the classical and modern claims for universality has sufficient reactive force to awaken us from our dogmatic metaphysical and epistemological slumbers, but this problematization does not require that we simply tune out the voices of classical and modern thought. After the overlay of philosophical constructionism has been pruned away, certain existential concerns about an understanding of self and world in the tradition of Occidental thought continue to solicit our interest. Indeed, as we have time and again emphasized, we cannot think and act except through an engagement with the tradition. The task is to stand in a *critical* relation to the tradition. It is thus that our project, simplified possibly to the extreme, comprises an effort to split the difference between the vertically grounded conceptions of reason and the horizontality of the postmodern anti-logos of becoming. We split the difference by calling upon the transversal logos.

The transversal logos requires a critical revision of the postulates of universality, both as essentialist prescription and criteriological a priorism. This critical revision, however, does not scrap the performance of the logos as rational comprehension. The logos is reconstituted but it is not left behind. It continues to register its effects (and it is discernible only through its effects) in a transversal binding or gathering of the multiplicity and flux of our socio-historical practices. The region in which this binding or gathering is operative is neither that of untrammeled essences nor a priori rules. Its proper region or arena is that of communicative praxis—a praxis that at once acknowledges the multiplicity of forms of discourse and action and discerns that the sense of the multiple does not reside in its historical specificities alone. The meanings that attach to our particular perceptions, speech acts, and local narratives are the result of a gathering and configuring of perceptual and discursive specifics against a background of the intrusion of alterities. As there is no perception at an instant, within an enclosed specificity, so there is no comprehension of a specific form of discourse or action without a background of other discourses and other actions that mutually define the figuration of each.

The overdetermination of the metaphors of verticality and horizontality leads in both cases to a blocking of the performances of critique, articulation, and disclosure, given that these phases of rationality are temporalized and spatialized "between" and "across" the orthodoxy of proclaimed unities and the heterodoxy of difference. Orthodoxy appeals to a vertical grounding to secure the universality and stability of "correct" and "right" opinion *(doxa)*. Heterodoxy valorizes the play of difference within the horizontal dimension of changing forms of thought and action. Framing the issue of rationality in terms of predilections toward orthodoxy and heterodoxy helps to make more explicit the role of *doxa* in the transversal performance of reason. The verticality of orthodoxy and the horizontality of heterodoxy comprise antipodal approaches to the delivered *doxa* of our communicative practices—be they scientific, ethical, aesthetical, or political. The challenge of the transversal logos is that of effecting a passage between orthodoxy and heterodoxy.

The privileging of verticality guides the effort to find within the extant *doxa* that which is "correct," "right," and "true," by virtue of it being grounded in some unimpeachable epistemic guarantee. The formalization and quantification of these epistemic guarantees leads to what Edmund Husserl had already suggestively described as "the despised doxa" of Western rationalism, in which the indigenous intentionality of everyday praxis is progressively occluded. Rationalism's obsession with correctness, grounded in atemporal conditions for universality and necessity, led to a disparagement of the contributions of doxa on the level of concrete lifeworld experiences. Husserl's celebrated "return to the lifeworld" was an effort to recover the concrete, functioning intentionality of lifeworld engagements and activities. Postmodernism radicalizes the Husserlian project of reclaiming the domain of doxa and finds in this domain *nothing but doxa*—nothing but a heterogenous succession of forms of life and modes of thought. We thus pass from the epoch of the despised doxa to that of the despised episteme and the despised logos.

This rite of passage, from verticality to horizontality, from orthodoxy to heterodoxy, from a "politics of reason" to a "politics of opinion,"[24] would seem to justify an identification of the entourage of postmodernists as the *new Sophists*. The prominence of Protagoras and Gorgias in Lyotard's definition of the *differénd*, as a conflict between two parties that remains insoluble because of the want of a rule of judgment, is quite plainly visible.[25] As did the Sophists of old, so do the new postmodernists privilege the way of opinion and disparage the claims of reason. The *epistēmē/doxa* dichotomy remains normative for both, and the right side of the virgule subverts the left. With the subversion of a logos-grounded *epistēmē*, all that remains is a succession of *hetero-doxa* in which each pre-

24. "There is no politics of reason, neither in the sense of a totalizing reason nor in that of the concept. And so we must do with a politics of opinion." Jean-François Lyotard, *Just Gaming*, trans. Wlad Godzich (Minneapolis: University of Minnesota Press, 1985), p. 82.
25. *The Differend: Phrases in Dispute*, pp. 6–16.

vailing opinion is countered by a new opinion within a conflictual rhapsody of "rhetorical agonistics" that has neither goal nor purpose.[26]

We find in this dispute between the vertical universalists, the friends of reason, and the horizontal pluralists, the friends of opinion, a double mistake that is shared by both parties. The one mistake is that of analyzing *epistēmē* into a universal logos, generating the theoretical construct of "epistemology," designed to provide a foundational support for every instance of knowledge. The second mistake, closely tied to the first, is that of bifurcating the realms of *epistēmē* and *doxa* and considering this matrix of bifurcation as a given. So long as one stays within a framework of inquiry that exhibits this double mistake, the oppositions of verticality versus horizontality, reason versus opinion, orthodoxy versus heterodoxy, universalism versus historicism, will remain in force and will be taken as normative. The battle lines will continue to be drawn between a logocentric epistemology and a doxastic flux of historical becoming, congealing into a differend that neither party can surmount.

That a philosophical resolution of this dispute has not yet been forthcoming is not all that puzzling. What is puzzling is that resolutions continue to be sought and that the problematic premises of the longstanding debate continue to go unrecognized. The dispute, in the end, remains a fight about the grammar of universals. Our response to this state of affairs is that of shifting the grammar and the questioning to see if one might get a better perspective on the issues at hand. The shift of questioning moves from an interrogation of metaphysical and epistemological postulates to the question about what goes on in the play of our quotidian speech and action, our discursive and institutional practices. The shift of grammar is that from the universal to the transversal. The notion of transversality, with its metaphorical resources to move across the disciplines and the differentiated culture-spheres, proves to be more productive in rendering an account of our multiple and interdependent social practices than is the metaphysically sedimented grammar of universality, which fixes the format of discussion in terms of an undecidable option between vertical grounding or horizontal dispersal. Seyla Benhabib points us in a fruitful direction for pursuing these matters when she remarks: "The oppositions within the confines of which much recent discussion has run—universalism versus historicity, an ethics of principle versus judgment in context, or ethical cognition versus moral motivation—are no longer compelling."[27]

The binding rationality of critique, articulation, and disclosure is transversal rather than universal in character. None of the moments of rationality, either singularly or in concert, yield universal validity. They do,

---

26. *The Differend*, p. 26.
27. Seyla Benhabib, "In the Shadow of Aristotle and Hegel: Communicative Ethics and Current Controversies in Practical Philosophy," *The Philosophical Forum* 21, nos. 1–2 (1989–90): p. 4.

however, enable the achievement of shared understanding and solidarity, which is to be distinguished from a consensus grounded in universalizable validity claims. This shared understanding and solidarity is the achievement of the hard struggle for communication across the spectrum of varying forms of life, attentive to the play of similarity within difference and the play of difference within similarity. In this struggle for communication, the myths of universalization and totalization (illustrated, for example, in Habermas's notion of the "ideal speech situation") may indeed continue to play a role, testifying of the inseparability of *mythos* and *logos* in our philosophical narratives. These myths, however, need to be recognized as *broken* myths, discharging their functions in the service of an open-ended process of unifying that does not congeal into a fixity of formal determinations and a closure of historical possibilities. Although the universal logos is problematized, this does not consign us to a *Walpurgisnacht* of irrationality in which all signifiers are black and in which every interpretation and every moral claim is as good as every other interpretation and every other moral claim. Both intracultural and transcultural judgments and assessments retain their efficacy. Indeed, such judgments and assessments are unavoidable given the transversal play of our beliefs and practices in responding to that which is said and done. It is precisely through this *response-dynamics* of communicative praxis, whereby we respond to the discourse and action that is thrust upon us, that the deployment of critique, articulation, and disclosure proceeds.

In chapter three we discussed the effect of the hermeneutical demand upon the claims of reason. We saw that interpretation enjoys a certain ubiquity, operative both in precognitive and cognitive world-comprehension, at work within the projects of understanding and explanation alike. The hermeneutical demand is inescapable; interpretation goes all the way down and all the way back. We now have the task of aligning in some manner the workings of interpretation with the dynamics of transversal rationality.

The alignment of the two, the grafting of the one onto the other, results in a mutual delimitation and reinforcement. Transversal thinking cannot outstrip the bounds of interpretation. The critique, articulation, and disclosure that extend over and move across the orthodoxy of congealed principles and rules and the heterodoxy of conflicting particularities of practice continue to ride the crest of the "hermeneutical as," geared to an understanding that is always that of understanding differently. In such understanding there is an evident circularity, a movement from one portion of discourse and event of action to another, against the backdrop of a whole that envelops them. This part/whole matrix that guides understanding privileges the circle as the root metaphor of rational comprehension. The transversal paradigm of rationality continues to call upon the services of interpretive understanding, but it also delimits the metaphor of circularity with that of diagonality. There is here a shift from the circle of understanding to a diagonal of thinking that intersects the surfaces of hermeneutical circles. Transversality delimits hermeneutics and resituates it within a wider space of rational circumspection. Not only does the diagonal of transversal thinking remain orthogonal to the various interpreted forms of discourse and action, it transversally extends beyond them to an infinity of "other" holistic complexes—an infinity that never congeals into a totality.[28]

The decisive feature in this transversal delimitation of hermeneutics is the intrusion of that which is other, the weight of alterity, the incursivity of disclosure. The directive of the transversal logos is to acknowledge the reality of the other. The effects of such are discernible across the spectrum of our variegated scientific and cultural communicative practices, in contending with an alien and incommensurable paradigm of scientific explanation as well as in negotiating disputes across political and religious lines of force. Disputes between Arab and Jew, Indian and Pakistanian, Irish Republican Army and British Crown, all of which exhibit a strong undertow of political and religious differences, become negotiable only to the degree that there is an acknowledgment of the reality and integrity of the other as other. The rationality of such negotiations resides in an understanding of the particular traditions in which each of the parties are situated and in a recognition of the need to make accommodations and adjustments through a transversal movement of responding to that which is at once other and alien.

Hermeneutical and transversal thinking, the circle and the diagonal, delimit each other. But in this mutual delimitation there is also a mutual enrichment and an expansion of resources, providing a wider perspective on the dynamics of rationality. It is within this wider perspective that the refiguration of universality is seen to occur, as "the universal" is transmuted into "the transversal."

Merleau-Ponty's suggestions for a refiguration of the classical and modern concepts of universality still await the full recognition that they deserve. Unfortunately, Merleau-Ponty's contribution toward a thinking beyond the stalemate that so often ensues from the confrontation of postmodernity with modernity tends to be lost in the philosophical shuffling of that which is deemed to be the most current and the most revolutionary.[29] We are particularly interested in Merleau-Ponty's thought experiments in refiguring the grammar of universals, in the process of which he designs what one might refer to as a "halfway house" in the journey from the universal to the transversal. He experiments with the vocabulary

28. On this topic see particularly Emmanuel Levinas, *Totality and Infinity*, trans. Alphonso Lingis (Pittsburgh: Duquesne University Press, 1969).
29. A notable exception to this neglect of Merleau-Ponty's thought as it pertains to issues relating to the current modernism/postmodernism controversy is Martin C. Dillon's recent work, *Merleau-Ponty's Ontology* (Bloomington: Indiana University Press, 1988). See particularly the highly provocative (in the sense of thought-provoking) concluding section "Abyss and Logos," pp. 224–44.

of "lateral universals," which he distinguishes from "overarching universals," universals that are grounded in a vertical and totalizing objectivity.

> This provides a second way to the universal: no longer the overarching universal of a strictly objective method, but a sort of lateral universal which we acquire through ethnological experience and its incessant testing of the self through the other person and the other person through the self. It is a question of constructing a general system of reference in which the point of view of the native, the point of view of the civilized man, and the mistaken views each has of the other can find a place—that is, of constituting a more comprehensive experience which becomes in principle accessible to men of a different time and country.[30]

That which solicits our particular interest in Merleau-Ponty's figure of lateral universals is his concrete contextualization of the achievement of such universals within the ethnological practice of coming to grips with differing points of view across the spectrum of cultural and historical diversity. Merleau-Ponty recognizes clearly enough the multiplicity and heterogeneity of discourses, actions, and institutions that define the region of ethnological study. This marks out the plane of horizontality with its cultural diversity and historical diachrony. But the projects of cross-cultural understanding and communication deliver the multiplex forms of life on the plane of horizontal diversity from an incommensurable otherness. The drive for understanding and communication experiments with "lateral universals," which perform the function of gathering the manifold social practices under study into "a more comprehensive experience which becomes in principle accessible to men of a different time and country." This gathering, however, proceeds not by way of appeals to overarching, synchronic, and vertically grounded universals but is rather the effect of a transversal rationality that is able to visit different times and places.

An additional feature to be noted in Merleau-Ponty's revisionary tactics in dealing with traditional claims of universality has to do with the implied requirement for a phenomenology of experience, through which the "comprehensive experience" of ethnological understanding is constituted. In the preceding chapters of our current study we too have argued for a phenomenological reclamation of experience, a return to the lifeworld of functioning intentionality and tacit knowledge, to enable us to deal with the vagaries of linguistic, textualist, and narratological closure. The experienced lifeworld resists sublation into semiotic systems, textual graphics, and narrational constructs. It retains its integrity and impinges on our discourse and action as the displayed referent of our communicative praxis. The task of transversal rationality is that of scanning the ter-

30. M. Merleau-Ponty, "From Mauss to Claude Lévi-Strauss," in *Signs*, trans. R. C. McCleary (Evanston: Northwestern University Press, 1964), p. 120.

rain of our lifeworld involvements, enabling a critique, articulation, and disclosure of the manifold forms of life that these involvements produce.

THE TRANSVERSAL AND THE TRANSHISTORICAL

Our refiguration of the universal logos as transversal provides us with a new perspective on addressing the issues spawned by the reactive stance of nineteenth-century historicism, the effects of which are still quite visible today. With its objectivistic attitude toward the past, relativistic attitude toward the present, and progressivistic attitude toward the future, historicism set in motion a plethora of oppositions that guided reflections on the topic of history well into the twentieth century. Chief among these were the oppositions of transcendentalism versus historicism; essentialism versus individualism; and absolutism versus relativism. The debates that moved within the play of these dichotomies were defined principally in terms of the use of the grammar of universals in our understanding of socio-historical reality. The garden varieties of transcendentalism, essentialism, and absolutism sought to find a haven of universally binding conditions of knowledge and regulative principles of action that transcend historical particularity. It was thus that the ahistorical, in the guise of a priori epistemic conditions, invariant essences, and universal principles, was pitted against the particularities and multiplicities of historical change.

The "new" historicism of postmodernity—if indeed the language of history and the historical still remains appropriate here—follows certain directions opened up by Nietzsche's "untimely" anti-historicist reflections, which problematized historicism's objectification of the past and its postulate of progressivism. In these Nietzsche-inspired postmodern developments some of the presuppositions and postulates of classical historicism are indeed undermined. Yet, for all that, the crux of the matter that occasioned the furor in the initial disputes between the historicists and the anti-historicists remains unprobed. This crux of the matter has to do with construing the difference between the historical and the ahistorical by collapsing the *a*-historical with the *trans*-historical. The new historicism of postmodernity continues to buy into a conceptual scaffolding in which the ahistorical and the transhistorical are conflated. It is thus that postmodern reflections on history have resulted in a peculiar paradox. On the one hand, the postmodern problematization of the tenets of the old historicism is suggestive and seems to offer a liberation from the dichotomous thinking in which it was caught up; but on the other hand postmodern reflection buys back into the original dichotomy by setting the universal, the metanarrational, and the consensual against the multiple, the local, and the dissensual. In such a scheme of things the ahistorical and the transhistorical are again fused, considered as partners in the crime against particularity, plurality, multiplicity, and the evanescence of a "present-becoming."[31]

The peculiar advantage of the grammar of transversality is that it facilitates a thinking beyond the dichotomies of transcendentalism versus historicism, the essential versus the contingent, the absolute versus the relative, and is thus able to avoid confusing the transhistorical with the ahistorical. The dynamics of the transversal logos, in its extending over and lying across the multiplicity of social practices and conventions, makes it possible for us to visit different times and places without either requiring a panoptic standpoint outside of history or having recourse to an incommensurability of local narratives. Understanding and communication across the variegated forms of life is achieved not via an appeal to an overarching or undergirding universal (whatever shape such a universal might assume) but rather through the hard struggle of a transversal communicative praxis that stays with the beckonings of the historical without being bound to the particularities of localized conventions. Transversal communication possesses the resources for transhistorical assessment, evaluation, and critique without the problematic appeals to atemporal essences or transcendental conditions. The performances of praxial rationality—critical discernment, articulation, and disclosure—achieve their efficacy in a transversal communication that is able to move from context to context, from one form of life to that of another. Socio-historical critique may indeed remain *context-dependent*, but this does not preclude an assessment, refiguration, or indeed overturn of different localized contexts as one discerns the play between and among them. Every context-dependency is situated within a wider context-interdependency.

A recognition of the enabling of transhistorical communication and critique within the economy of the transversal logos requires a double

31. The locution "present-becoming" is that of Claire Parnet, used in her dialogue with Gilles Deleuze. "Future and past don't have much meaning, what counts is the present-becoming; geography and not history, the middle and not the beginning or the end." *Dialogues*, trans. Hugh Tomilson and Barbara Habberjam (New York: Columbia University Press, 1987), p. 23. See also Gilles Deleuze and Félix Guattari, *A Thousand Plateaus: Capitalism and Schizophrenia*, trans. Brian Massumi (Minneapolis: University of Minnesota Press, 1987), chapter 10: "1730: Becoming-Intense, Becoming-Animal, Becoming-Imperceptible," pp. 232–309. The effort to hang everything on a "present-becoming" results in a somewhat bizarre twist or wrinkle in the new historicism. History is shorn of its past and future, any sense of beginning and end, and is subordinated to geography. Time is read back into space, into a topography of rhizomatic multiples, pulverized into an evanescent present-becoming. It is indeed questionable whether such a thin sense of the historical can support a "historicism"—either old or new. Clearly, such a pulverization of the present, devoid of past and future, nullifies any project of historical understanding that would proceed transversally, reclaiming the past whilst anticipating the future. It is precisely the sense of historical presence as the chronotopal intersection of a continuing tradition and a yet-to-be-shaped future that is threatened by the new historicism of postmodernity. Although Deleuze and Guattari have found a place for the dynamics of transversality in the institutional life of humankind, their weak sense of the historical, their preference for geography over history, and their spatialized view of time keeps them from acknowledging the chronotopal texture of the play of transversal forces.

shift—a shift away from the domination of verticality in modernity and the domination of horizontality in postmodernity. This peculiar splitting of the difference between modernity and postmodernity gives rise to a transfigured performance of reason "between" them. The subject-centered and criteriological conception of rationality of modernity had its sights set on a vertical grounding of the claims of reason in ahistorical epistemic conditions for universality and necessity. Given the paucity of resources for a determination of universality and totality within the horizontality of historical becoming, principles of epistemic justification were located on the other side of history. The reactive stance of postmodernity turned the tables, privileged horizontality, abandoned the quest for universalization and totalization, and valorized the flux and multiplicity of "present-becoming." Within such a perspective, we are proffered only a fragmented and fractured vision from this side of history. The history at issue for postmodernity, shorn of any recollection of the past and any reality of the future, is too thin and fragile to comport a logos that can transcend its specificities and particularities through transhistorical discernment, assessment, and critique.

Both the privileging of verticality in the interests of securing an untrammeled universality and the privileging of horizontality bent toward a random, diachronic pluralization occlude the distinction between the ahistorical and the transhistorical. Indeed, the one is seen to collapse into the other. The integrity of transhistorical comprehension can be secured only through the installment of a praxial rationality transversally defined. In this transversal historical understanding and comprehension neither the metaphorical weight of verticality nor that of horizontality become dominant. It effects a passage between the orthodoxy of sedimented belief-systems and institutional forms and the heterodoxy of changing beliefs and practices, between normativized rules and procedures and revolutionary thought and action.

The transversal extending over and diagonally lying across the interplay of conjunctions and disjunctions of thought and action in their localized differentiations and constituted idealizations, between the standpoints of heterodoxy and orthodoxy, provides the motivation for transhistorical communication. Neither dissensus nor consensus, neither agonistics nor an unbroken communitarianism, provide the proper ends of human discourse and action. The transversal time-space of our communicative practices yields an interplay of dissent and consent, occasioning shared understanding and cooperative endeavors, but only against the background of a recognition of the integrity of the thought and action of the other. From this there emerges a dialectics of achievement and breakdown of communicative projects, in which there is a struggle to communicate in spite of misunderstanding and irremediable differences.

Lyotard may indeed have a point in questioning Habermas's assumption that "the goal of dialogue is consensus." But simply to replace this assumption with the counter-assumption that the "end" of dialogue and discussion "on the contrary, is paralogy" does not advance matters all that much.[32] The limitations of dialogue, some of which are admittedly disconcerting, need to be made known; however, the installation of dissensus and paralogy as the proper end of human discourse suffers its own limitations. What is required is a continuing effort to articulate the communicative event as one that illustrates a dialectics operating between the solidarity of consensus and the heterogeneity of dissensus.

Our delineation of the workings of transversal communicative rationality, in what amounts to an end run, either to the right or to the left, around the transcendentalism/historicism aporia and its mistaking of the transhistorical for the ahistorical, provides us with some new perspectives on the rationality of socio-historical criticism and its implied ethical-normative content.

The concrete concerns that motivate any social critique of delivered forms of life and institutions issue from an uneasiness in accepting the stock of taken-for-granted beliefs and practices, even when these congeal into a unanimity of convention. There is no guarantee that the unanimity of convention coincides with ethical requirements for justice, defensible claims concerning rights and duties, and the good life as both a personal and corporate achievement. Justice is not to be identified with the unanimity of convention; rights and duties are not simply historically specific; and the good life exceeds the parameters of any particular tradition. Because of these concrete concerns that motivate ethical behavior, various appeals to rationality, the rationality of both thought and action, have been made. Our own appeal has taken shape as an appeal to a *praxial* rationality, communicatively situated and transversely postured, displaying interdependent moments of discernment, articulation, and disclosure. Against this background the ethical requirement falls out as the performance of a "fitting response."

In a previous work, *Communicative Praxis and the Space of Subjectivity*, we sketched the outline of an ethics of the fitting response, contextualized against the backdrop of what we called "the rhetorical turn," involving revisionary perspectives on the ancient Greek notions of *kathakonta*, *ethos*, and *polis*. We saw an ethics of the fitting response as providing an alternative to the traditional theory construction of teleological, deontological, and utilitarian ethical systems.[33] In this previous work our specific interest was that of locating the ethical requirement within the responsivity of an engaged and decentered moral self as it responds to the prior thought and action already inscribed within a historicized polis. An ethical way of life is not an interior construct of a centered and sovereign

32. See Jean-François Lyotard, *The Postmodern Condition*, trans. Geoff Bennington and Brian Massumi (Minneapolis: University of Minnesota Press, 1984), pp. 65–66.
33. *Communicative Praxis and the Space of Subjectivity*. See particularly chapter Ten: "Ethos, Ethics, and a New Humanism," pp. 197–214.

subject. It is achieved in and through a responsiveness to alterity, to the reality of the encountered other, who intrudes upon one's subjectivity and solicits responses that are proper for discourse and action.

What was implied throughout this discussion, but was never made sufficiently explicit, was the role of rationality in the fitting response of the ethical. The principal aim of the current work has been that of elucidating and describing the role and dynamics of rationality as it operates transversally across the practices in the cultural spheres of science, morality, and art by dint of praxial critique, articulation, and disclosure. It is by calling upon the resources of this praxial rationality that the conventions of our thought and action are tested and contested and become subject to assessment and evaluation.

It is thus again that a possible rejoinder to the postmodern challenge can be offered, and more specifically to the point of Lyotard's willingness to sacrifice a "politics of reason" for a "politics of opinion." In sketching his politics of opinion, Lyotard distinguishes his understanding of opinion *(doxa)* "from the overly empirical context that many Sophists (and even Aristotle) have given to it."[34] This we consider to be a notable advance. In his own way, Lyotard has rescued what Husserl had already referred to as the "despised doxa" of Western rationalism from certain accumulated distortions. What remains problematic, however, is Lyotard's hurried scrapping of the resources of rationality, whereby the despised doxa of modernity is simply replaced with the despised logos of postmodernity. Indeed, our general continuing argument has been that a reclamation of the concrete intentionality of our doxastic lifeworld engagements does not entail a scuttling of the claims of a praxis-oriented logos. In the sphere of ethico-political involvement, a revitalized "politics of opinion" works hand in glove with a revitalized "politics of reason." As the *doxa* of the tradition needs to be pruned of its empiricistic distortions, so also the *logos* of the tradition (both ancient and modern) needs to be shorn of its pretensions for universalization and totalization and refigured within the texture of transversal communicative praxis.

In the expanding current literature on the uses of reason in social and political criticism, the explorations by Kai Nielsen merit particular attention. He has formulated an approach and strategy that he names "wide reflective equilibrium." We are particularly interested in Nielsen's broadened perspective on reflection because it displays remarkable similarities to our own understanding and use of transversal rationality and offers similar potential for transhistorical critique. Nielsen's proposed "wide reflective equilibrium" borrows features from Rorty's anti-foundationalist neo-pragmatism as well as from Habermas's accentuation of emancipatory interests in his critical theory of society.[35] Indeed, Nielsen's approach

34. *Just Gaming,* p. 82.
35. See particularly Nielsen's article "Searching for an Emancipatory Perspective: Wide Re-

effects an imaginative synthesis of these two dominant current strands of thought on the issue, which on first reading are not all that similar. Habermas is intent on continuing the conversation with modernity; Rorty shifts the terrain of discourse and speaks the language of postmodernity. It is thus that Nielsen's project of synthesizing certain features of the thought of Rorty and Habermas offers its own response to the postmodern challenge, marking out possible moves toward sociopolitical critique within a space between the modernist proclivity to despise doxa and the postmodernist tendency to despise the logos.

Nielsen's notion of reflection as it plays in "wide reflective equilibrium," it soon becomes evident, has little commerce with the use of reflection in the subject-centered paradigm of modern epistemology. Reflection is no longer construed as an interior mental event, issuing from a sovereign cogito intent upon forging an access to an exterior world. Reflection, according to Nielsen, is from bottom up social, always situated within the density of world-engagements. Reflection takes on a sociopragmatic orientation, bent toward a discernment of the intercalation of knowing and doing, thought and action, within the panoply of social practices.

In articulating the dynamics of reflection, Nielsen makes much of the need for a "shuttling back and forth" as we engage in efforts toward "rebuilding the ship at sea." These well-placed metaphors enable him to articulate what we would be disposed to call the transversal play of rationality as it moves across the multiple configurations of thought and action.

> We shuttle back and forth between considered convictions, moral principles, ethical theories, social theories, and other background empirical theories and those considered judgments (at least some of which must be distinct from the initial cluster of considered judgments) that are associated with or are constitutive of or partially constitutive of the moral principles, social theories or other background theories.[36]

This shuttling back and forth between convictions and judgments, moral principles and empirical theories, ethical perspectives and institutional forms, illustrates at once the dynamics and wide scope of the workings of reflection that Nielsen advances. This wide scope encompasses the separated culture-spheres of modernity (science, morality, and art), and the dynamics of wide reflection enables one to move across these spheres, effecting a binding of sorts, whereby each functions as a background for the other. The canvassing of these spheres, moving back and forth be-

flective Equilibrium and the Hermeneutical Circle," in Evan Simpson, ed., *Anti-Foundationalism and Practical Reasoning* (Edmonton, AB: Academic Press, 1987).
36. *Anti-Foundationalism and Practical Reasoning*, p. 148.

tween them, occasions adjustments and modifications of theories and practices in each of the spheres and sometimes leads to a disavowal and abandonment of them in the forging of new and untried perspectives.

> In such shuttling we sometimes modify or even abandon a social theory or other background or even come to construct a new one. We move back and forth—rebuilding the ship at sea—modifying and adjusting here and there until we get a coherent and consistent set of beliefs. When we have done that, then we have for a time attained wide reflective equilibrium.[37]

We find Nielsen's strategy of wide reflective equilibrium helpful for fleshing out our portrait of the transversal rationality of praxis. The reflection at work in "wide reflective equilibrium" possesses features that we highlighted in our explication of the performance of reason as a dynamics of discernment, articulation, and disclosure.

Yet, in continuing the conversation with Nielsen on the matter at hand we are disposed to offer a friendly critique of his construal of reflection. This critique may indeed have something to do with the epistemological sedimentations in the very concept of reflection—sedimentations that are difficult to dislodge. These sedimentations reappear in Nielsen's overdetermination of a "belief-system" orientation in defining the accomplishments of reflective equilibrium. We attain the sought-after equilibrium, says Nielsen, when "we get a coherent and consistent set of beliefs," and we achieve this coherence and consistency of beliefs by shuttling back and forth between clusters of "theory" (empirical, social, ethical, and aesthetical). It is this heavy accent on the role of beliefs and theories that occasions for us certain concerns.

To be sure, beliefs, connected with theory either explicitly or implicitly, play a role in the forms of life that make up our communicative praxis. They comprise, however, only a part of the web of lifeworld engagements, which fall out more globally as a networking of social practices, habits, and skills, in which beliefs and theories are later arrivals. The lifeworld, as we have seen, is properly portrayed as an amalgam of configurations of discourse and action, configurations of praxis including speech acts, gestures, habits, skills, and social competencies that comport their own insight and understanding, irreducible to a belief structure and a theory-grounded definition of rationality.

One might formulate the requirement for dealing with the issue at hand as one that calls for an even "wider" wide reflective equilibrium than that proposed by Nielsen. This would refigure and expand the range of reason, making its alignment with the social sources of thought and the practices of everyday life more explicit, and provide a corrective to recurring tendencies of privileging a belief-centered approach to rational-

---

37. *Anti-Foundationalism and Practical Reasoning,* pp. 148–49.

ity. Throughout the pages of this work our project has been that of showing how a praxis-oriented rationality, illustrating a transversal dynamics in the interdependent workings of discernment, articulation, and disclosure, meets this wider requirement.

Works Cited

Apel, Karl-Otto. *Analytic Philosophy of Language and the Geisteswissenschaften*. Trans. Harold Holstelilie. Dordrecht: Reidel, 1967.
———. *Charles S. Peirce: From Pragmatism to Pragmaticism*. Trans. John M. Krois. Amherst: University of Massachusetts Press, 1981.
Aristotle. *De Interpretatione*. In *The Basic Works of Aristotle*. Richard McKeon, ed. New York: Random House, 1941.
———. *Rhetorica*. In *The Basic Works of Aristotle*. Richard McKeon, ed. New York: Random House, 1941.
Bachelard, Gaston. *The Poetics of Space*. Trans. Maria Jolas. Boston: Beacon Press, 1969.
Bakhtin, Mikhail M. *The Dialogic Imagination*. Trans. Caryl Emerson and Michael Holquist. Austin: University of Texas Press, 1981.
Barbour, Ian. *Myths, Models and Paradigms*. New York: Harper & Row, 1974.
Baudrillard, Jean. "*Modernité*." In *Encyclopaedia universalis*, Vol. 12. Paris: Encyclopaedia universalis France, 1985.
Becker, Carl L. *The Heavenly City of the Eighteenth-Century Philosophers*. New Haven: Yale University Press, 1932.
Benhabib, Seyla. "In the Shadow of Aristotle and Hegel: Communicative Ethics and Current Controversies in Practical Philosophy," *The Philosophical Forum* 21, nos. 1–2 (1989–90).
Bernstein, Richard J., ed. *Habermas and Modernity*. Cambridge, MA: The MIT Press, 1985.
Bitzer, Loyd F. "The Rhetorical Situation," *Philosophy and Rhetoric* 1, no. 1 (1968).
Black, Max. *Models and Metaphors*. Ithaca: Cornell University Press, 1962.
Blumenberg, Hans. "An Anthropological Approach to the Contemporary Significance of Rhetoric." In *After Philosophy: End or Transformation?* Kenneth Baynes, James Bohman, and Thomas McCarthy, eds. Cambridge, MA: The MIT Press, 1987.
Burke, Kenneth. *Language and Symbolic Action*. Berkeley: University of California Press, 1968.
———. "The Rhetorical Situation." In *Communication: Ethical and Moral Issues*. Lee Thayer, ed. New York: Gordon and Breach Science Publishers, 1973.
Caputo, John. *Radical Hermeneutics: Repetition, Deconstruction, and the Hermeneutic Project*. Bloomington: Indiana University Press, 1987.
Carr, David. *Time, Narrative, and History*. Bloomington: Indiana University Press, 1986.
Casey, Edward S. *Remembering: A Phenomenological Study*. Bloomington: Indiana University Press, 1987.
———. "The World of Nostalgia," *Man and World* 20, no. 4 (1987).
Cassirer, Ernst. *The Philosophy of Symbolic Forms*. Trans. Ralph Mannheim. New Haven: Yale University Press, 1953.
Cavell, Stanley. *The Claim of Reason*. New York: Oxford University Press, 1979.
Cheatum, Robert, et al. "Lexicon: Guide for the Perplexed," *Art Papers* 10, no. 1 (1986).
Connor, Steven. *Postmodernist Culture: An Introduction to Theories of the Contemporary*. Oxford: Basil Blackwell, 1989.
Cox, J. Robert. "Cultural Memory and the Public Moral Argument." *The Van Zelst Lecture in Communication*. Evanston: Northwestern University School of Speech, 1987.

Cumming, Robert D. *Starting Point: An Introduction to the Dialectic of Existence*. Chicago: University of Chicago Press, 1979.

Dallery, Arleen B., and Scott, Charles E., eds. *The Question of the Other*. Albany: SUNY Press, 1989.

Dallmayer, Fred R. *Critical Encounters: Between Philosophy and Ethics*. Notre Dame: University of Notre Dame Press, 1987.

Dauenhauer, Bernard P. *Silence: The Phenomenon and Its Ontological Significance*. Bloomington: Indiana University Press, 1980.

Deleuze, Gilles. *Différence et répétition*. Paris: Presses Universitaires de France, 1968.

———. *Nietzsche and Philosophy*. Trans. Hugh Tomlinson. New York: Columbia University Press, 1983.

———. *Proust and Signs*. Trans. Richard Howard. New York: George Braziller, 1972.

Deleuze, Gilles, and Guattari, Félix. *Anti-Oedipus: Capitalism and Schizophrenia*. Trans. R. Hurley, M. Seem, and H. R. Lane. Minneapolis: University of Minnesota Press, 1983.

———. *A Thousand Plateaus: Capitalism and Schizophrenia*. Trans. Brian Massumi. Minneapolis: University of Minnesota Press, 1987.

Deleuze, Gilles, and Parnet, Claire. *Dialogues*. Trans. Hugh Tomlinson and Barbara Habberjam. New York: Columbia University Press, 1987.

Derrida, Jacques. *Dissemination*. Trans. Barbara Johnson. Chicago: University of Chicago Press, 1981.

———. *Margins of Philosophy*. Trans. Alan Bass. Chicago: University of Chicago Press, 1982.

———. *Of Grammatology*. Trans. G. C. Spivak. Baltimore: Johns Hopkins University Press, 1974.

———. *Speech and Phenomena*. Trans. David B. Allison. Evanston: Northwestern University Press, 1973.

———. *Writing and Difference*. Trans. Alan Bass. Chicago: University of Chicago Press, 1978.

Descartes, René. *Discourse on Method and Meditations*. Trans. Laurence J. Lafleur. New York: The Liberal Arts Press, 1960.

Dillon, Martin C. *Merleau-Ponty's Ontology*. Bloomington: Indiana University Press, 1988.

Donato, Eugenio, and Macksey, Richard, eds. *The Languages of Criticism and the Sciences of Man*. Baltimore: Johns Hopkins University Press, 1970.

Feyerabend, Paul. *Against Method: Outline of an Anarchistic Theory of Knowledge*. Atlantic Highlands: The Humanities Press, 1975.

———. *Farewell to Reason*. New York: Verso Press, 1987.

Fisher, Walter, *Human Communication as Narration: Towards a Philosophy of Reason, Value and Action*. Columbia: University of South Carolina Press, 1987.

Foucault, Michel. *Discipline and Punish: The Birth of the Prison*. Trans. Alan Sheridan. New York: Random House, 1979.

———. "Final Interview," *Raritan: A Quarterly Review* 5, no. 1 (1985).

———. *Herculine Barbin*. Trans. Richard McDougall. New York: Random House, 1980.

———. *Politics, Philosophy, Culture: Interviews and Other Writings*. Lawrence D. Kritzman, ed. London: Routledge, Chapman, & Hall, 1988.

———. "The Subject and Power." In *Michel Foucault: Beyond Structuralism and Hermeneutics*. Hubert L. Dreyfus and Paul Rabinow, eds. Chicago: University of Chicago Press, 1982.

Gadamer, Hans-Georg. *Philosophical Hermeneutics*. Trans. David E. Linge. Berkeley: University of California Press, 1976.

———. *Reason in the Age of Science*. Trans. Frederick G. Lawrence. Cambridge, MA: The MIT Press, 1981.

————. *Truth and Method.* New York: The Seabury Press, 1975.

Genette, Gerard. *Narrative Discourse: An Essay in Method.* Trans. Jane E. Lewin. Ithaca: Cornell University Press, 1980.

Goodman, Nelson. *Languages of Art: An Approach to a Theory of Symbols.* Indianapolis: Bobbs-Merrill, 1968.

Guattari, Félix. *Molecular Revolution: Psychiatry and Politics.* Trans. Rosemary Sheed. New York: Penguin Books, 1984.

Guthrie, W. K. C. *A History of Greek Philosophy,* Vol. I. Cambridge: Cambridge University Press, 1962.

Habermas, Jürgen. "The Hermeneutic Claim to Universality." In *Contemporary Hermeneutics.* Josef Bleicher, ed. London: Routledge & Kegan Paul, 1980.

————. *The Philosophical Discourse of Modernity.* Trans. Frederick Lawrence. Cambridge, MA: The MIT Press, 1987.

————. *The Theory of Communicative Action.* Volume One: *Reason and the Rationalization of Society.* Trans. Thomas McCarthy. Boston: Beacon Press, 1984.

————. *The Theory of Communicative Action.* Volume Two: *Lifeworld and System: A Critique of Functionalist Reason.* Trans. Thomas McCarthy. Boston: Beacon Press, 1987.

Harvey, David. *The Condition of Postmodernity: An Enquiry into the Origins of Cultural Change.* Oxford: Basil Blackwell, 1989.

Heelan, Patrick A. *Space-perception and the Philosophy of Science.* Berkeley: University of California Press, 1983.

Heidegger, Martin. *Being and Time.* Trans. John Macquarrie and Edward Robinson. New York: Harper & Row, 1962.

————. *Der Satz vom Grund.* Tübingen: Verlag Gunter Neske Pfullingen, 1957.

Hesse, Mary. *Models and Analogies in Science.* Notre Dame: University of Notre Dame Press, 1966.

Husserl, Edmund. *Cartesian Meditations: An Introduction to Phenomenology.* Trans. Dorion Cairns. The Hague: Martinus Nijhoff, 1960.

————. *Die Krisis der europäischen Wissenschaften und die transzendentale Phänomenologie.* Walter Biemel, ed. The Hague: Martinus Nijhoff, 1954.

————. *The Phenomenology of Internal Time-Consciousness.* Trans. James S. Churchill. Bloomington: Indiana University Press, 1964.

Hyde, Michael. "Rhetorically Man Dwells: On the Making Known Function of Discourse," *Communication* 7 (1983).

Hyde, Michael, and Smith, Craig. "Hermeneutics and Rhetoric: A Seen but Unobserved Relationship," *The Quarterly Journal of Speech* 65 (1979).

James, William. *Essays in Radical Empiricism.* New York: Longmans, Green and Co., 1942.

Jaspers, Karl. *Reason and Existenz.* Trans. William Earle. New York: The Noonday Press, 1955.

Johnstone, Henry. W., Jr. *Validity and Rhetoric in Philosophical Argument.* University Park: The Dialogue Press of Man and World, 1978.

Kant, Immanuel. *Critique of Judgement.* Trans. James Creed Meredith. Oxford: The Clarendon Press, 1952.

————. *Critique of Practical Reason.* Trans. Thomas K. Abbott. Sixth Edition. New York: Longmans, Green and Co., 1909.

————. *Critique of Pure Reason.* Trans. Norman Kemp Smith. London: Macmillan and Company, 1953.

————. *Religion within the Limits of Reason Alone.* Trans. T. M. Greene and H. H. Hudson. LaSalle, IL: The Open Court Publishing Co., 1934.

Kierkegaard, Søren. *The Journals of Søren Kierkegaard.* Trans. Alexander Dru. New York: Oxford University Press, 1938.

————. *The Sickness Unto Death.* Trans. Walter Lowrie. Princeton: Princeton University Press, 1951.

Kuhn, Thomas. *The Structure of Scientific Revolutions.* Chicago: University of Chicago Press, 1962.

Lakoff, George, and Johnson, Mark. *Metaphors We Live By.* Chicago: University of Chicago Press, 1980.

Leitch, Vincent B. *Deconstructive Criticism: An Advanced Introduction.* New York: Columbia University Press, 1983.

Levinas, Emmanuel. *Totality and Infinity.* Trans. Alphonso Lingis. Pittsburgh: Duquesne University Press, 1969.

Luckmann, Thomas, and Schutz, Alfred. *Structures of the Life-World.* Trans. Richard M. Zaner and Tristram Engelhardt, Jr. Evanston: Northwestern University Press, 1973.

Lyne, John R.; and McGee, Michael Calvin. "What Are Nice Folks Like You Doing in a Place Like This?" In *The Rhetoric of the Human Sciences: Language and Argument in Scholarship and Public Affairs.* John S. Nelson, Allan Megill, and Donald N. McCloskey, eds. Madison: The University of Wisconsin Press, 1987.

Lyotard, Jean-François. "Adorno as the Devil," *Telos* 19 (1974).

———. *Driftworks.* Roger McKeon, ed. New York: Semiotext(e), Inc., 1984.

———. *The Differend: Phrases in Dispute.* Trans. Georges Van Den Abbeele. Minneapolis: University of Minnesota Press, 1988.

———. *The Postmodern Condition: A Report on Knowledge.* Trans. Geoff Bennington and Brian Massumi. Minneapolis: University of Minnesota Press, 1984.

———, and Thébaud, Jean-Loup. *Just Gaming.* Trans. Wlad Godzich. Minneapolis: University of Minnesota Press, 1985.

MacIntyre, Alasdair. *Whose Justice? Which Rationality?* Notre Dame: University of Notre Dame Press, 1988.

Madison, Gary B. *The Hermeneutics of Postmodernity: Figures and Themes.* Bloomington: Indiana University Press, 1988.

———. "The New Philosophy of Rhetoric." In *Texte: La rhétorique du texte.* Toronto: Les Editions Trintexte, 1989.

McCloskey, Donald N. *The Rhetoric of Economics.* Madison: The University of Wisconsin Press, 1985.

McGee, Michael Calvin. "On Feminized Power." *The Van Zelst Lecture in Communication.* Evanston: Northwestern University School of Speech, 1985.

Merleau-Ponty, Maurice. "Cezanne's Doubt." In *The Essential Writings of Merleau-Ponty.* Alden L. Fisher, ed. New York: Harcourt, Brace & World, 1969.

———. *Phenomenology of Perception.* Trans. Colin Smith. London: Routledge & Kegan Paul, 1962.

———. *Signs.* Trans. R. C. McCleary. Evanston: Northwestern University Press, 1964.

Miller, David James. "Immodest Interventions," *Phenomenological Inquiry* 2 (October 1987).

Nielsen, Kai. "Searching for an Emancipatory Perspective: Wide Reflective Equilibrium and the Hermeneutical Circle." In *Anti-Foundationalism and Practical Reasoning.* Evan Simpson, ed. Edmonton, AB: The Academic Press, 1987.

Nietzsche, Friedrich. "On Truth and Lies in a Nonmoral Sense." In *Philosophy and Truth: Selections from Nietzsche's Notebooks of the Early 1870's.* Daniel Breazeale, ed. Atlantic Highlands: The Humanities Press, 1979.

O'Neill, John. "Postmodernism and (Post)Marxism." In *Postmodernism—Philosophy and the Arts.* Hugh Silverman, ed. New York: Routledge, 1990.

Porritt, Ruth. *A Textual Dialogue: Bakhtin and Derrida on Meaning in Philosophical and Poetic Texts.* Doctoral Dissertation, Purdue University, 1989.

Richards, I. A. *The Philosophy of Rhetoric.* New York: Oxford University Press, 1965.

Ricoeur, Paul. "Explanation and Understanding: On Some Remarkable Connections among the Theory of the Text, Theory of Action, and Theory of History." In *The Philosophy of Paul Ricoeur*. Charles E. Reagan and David Stewart, eds. Boston: Beacon Press, 1978.

————. *Freud and Philosophy: An Essay on Interpretation*. Trans. Denis Savage. New Haven: Yale University Press, 1970.

————. *Interpretation Theory: Discourse and the Surplus of Meaning*. Fort Worth: Texas Christian University Press, 1976.

————. *The Conflict of Interpretations: Essays in Hermeneutics*. Don Ihde, ed. Evanston: Northwestern University Press, 1974.

————. "The Hermeneutical Function of Distanciation." In *Paul Ricoeur: Hermeneutics and the Human Sciences*. John B. Thompson, ed. Cambridge: Cambridge University Press, 1981.

————. *The Rule of Metaphor: Multidisciplinary Studies of the Creation of Meaning in Language*. Trans. Robert Czerny. Toronto: University of Toronto Press, 1977.

————. "The Task of Hermeneutics." In *Paul Ricoeur: Hermeneutics and the Human Sciences*. John B. Thompson, ed. Cambridge: Cambridge University Press, 1981.

————. *Time and Narrative*, Vols. 1 and 2. Trans. Kathleen McLaughlin and David Pellauer. Vol. 3. Trans. Kathleen Blamey and David Pellauer. Chicago: University of Chicago Press, 1985–88.

Rorty, Richard. "Habermas and Lyotard on Postmodernity." In *Habermas and Modernity*. Richard Bernstein, ed. Cambridge, MA: The MIT Press, 1985.

————. *Philosophy and the Mirror of Nature*. Princeton: Princeton University Press, 1979.

————. "Postmodernist Bourgeois Liberalism." In *Hermeneutics and Praxis*. Robert Hollinger, ed. Notre Dame: University of Notre Dame Press, 1985.

————. "Science as Solidarity." In *Rhetoric and the Human Sciences*. John S. Nelson, Allan Megill, and Donald N. McCloskey, eds. Madison: The University of Wisconsin Press, 1987.

Said, Edward W. *Beginnings: Intention and Method*. New York: Basic Books, 1975.

Sallis, John. *Being and Logos: The Way of Platonic Dialogue*. Pittsburgh: Duquesne University Press, 1975.

————. *The Gathering of Reason*. Athens: Ohio University Press, 1980.

Sartre, Jean-Paul. *Being and Nothingness: An Essay on Phenomenological Ontology*. Trans. Hazel Barnes. New York: The Philosophical Library, 1956.

————. *Existentialism*. Trans. Bernard Frechtman. New York: The Philosophical Library, 1947.

————. *The Emotions: Outline of a Theory*. Trans. Bernard Frechtman. New York: The Philosophical Library, 1945.

————. *The Transcendence of the Ego: An Existentialist Theory of Consciousness*. Trans. Forrest Williams and Robert Kirkpatrick. New York: The Noonday Press, 1957.

Schrag, Calvin O. *Communicative Praxis and the Space of Subjectivity*. Bloomington: Indiana University Press, 1986.

————. *Experience and Being: Prolegomena to a Future Ontology*. Evanston: Northwestern University Press, 1969.

————. "Rationality Between Modernity and Postmodernity." In *Life-World and Politics: Between Modernity and Postmodernity*. Stephen K. White, ed. Notre Dame: University of Notre Dame Press, 1989.

————. "Rhetoric Resituated at the End of Philosophy," *The Quarterly Journal of Speech* 71 (1985).

Schutz, Alfred. *The Phenomenology of the Social World*. Trans. George Walsh and Frederick Lehnert. Evanston: Northwestern University Press, 1966.

Seigfried, Charlene Haddock. *William James's Radical Reconstruction of Philosophy.* Albany: SUNY Press, 1990.

Shapiro, Gary, ed. *After the Future: Postmodern Times and Places.* Albany: SUNY Press, 1990.

Shusterman, Richard. " 'Ethics and Aesthetics Are One': Postmodernism's Ethics of Taste." In *After the Future: Postmodern Times and Places.* Gary Shapiro, ed. Albany: SUNY Press, 1990.

Taylor, Charles. "Overcoming Epistemology." In *After Philosophy: End or Transformation?* Kenneth Baynes, James Bohman, and Thomas McCarthy, eds. Cambridge, MA: The MIT Press, 1987.

———. "Rationality." In *Rationality and Relativism.* Martin Hollis and Steven Lukes, eds. Cambridge, MA: The MIT Press, 1982.

Turbayne, Colin Murray. *The Myth of Metaphor.* New Haven: Yale University Press, 1962.

Welsch, Wolfgang. *"Vielheit ohne Einheit? Zum gegenwärtigen Spektrum der philosophischen Diskussion um die 'Postmoderne',"* *Philosophisches Jahrbuch* 94 (1987).

Wheelwright, Philip. *Metaphor and Reality.* Bloomington: Indiana University Press, 1968.

Wilshire, Bruce. *The Moral Collapse of the University: Professionalism, Purity, and Alienation.* Albany: SUNY Press, 1990.

———. *William James and Phenomenology: A Study of "The Principles of Psychology."* Bloomington: Indiana University Press, 1968.

Zaner, Richard M. *Ethics and the Clinical Encounter.* Englewood Cliffs: Prentice Hall, 1988.

Name Index

Subject Index

absence, 47, 111
absolute, 4, 45, 163, 173
absolutism, 75
aestheticism, 71, 96, 127
affirmation, 66, 68–76, 127, 139
agonistics, 57, 129, 152, 174; of language, 55; partisans of, 123, 125, 132; rhetorical, 123, 125, 168
aletheia, 71
alienation, 127, 132–133
alterity, 11, 91, 111, 112, 113, 114, 132–133, 158, 166, 170, 175. *See also* the "other"
anti-logos, 8, 20, 166
archaeology, 46, 95, 96
archē, 65, 94, 95, 127
Aristotelianism, 1
art, 14, 54, 61; as culture-sphere of modernity, 3, 4–5, 18, 24, 28, 50, 52, 99, 177
atomism, 87, 108, 128, 131; linguistic, 87; logical, 87

capitalism, 27
chronotope, 83–85, 88, 92, 94–95, 157, 158
cogito, 64, 128, 134, 136, 149
coherence, 70, 178
coincidentia oppositorum, 76
collectivism, 128
communication, 35, 49, 81, 117, 123, 130, 134–135, 136–137; distorted, 47; negativities in, 134–135; transhistorical, 173; transversal, 155
communicative praxis, 8–10, 63, 66, 72, 100, 125, 130, 132, 138, 140, 146, 151, 153, 155, 159, 163, 166, 169
community, 35, 48, 88, 117, 130–132, 135, 139, 140; and praxial critique, 62–67
consciousness, 148–151, 159–160; alienated, 9; existentialist theory of, 150, 153, 162; historical, 163; proletarian, 73; subject-centered, 149, 153, 161; transcendental, 25; unhappy, 48
consensus, 33, 34, 123, 125, 126, 134–135, 152, 169, 174, 175
constitution: active and passive, 160; eidetic, 104; institutional, 131, 163; intersubjective, 104; objective, 104; subjective, 104; transcendental, 104
criteria, 52–57, 59–61, 99
criteriology, 53–55, 59
critical theory, 82, 176; school of, 34, 51–52

"death of God," 96
"death of the author," 93
deconstruction, 15, 29, 31, 112, 123

deontological, 175
desire, 35–42, 46, 82; assemblages of, 41; "desiring machines," 41; politics of, 35–36, 40–42, 128
dialectics, 102; existential, 65; Hegelian, 45, 65; linguistic, 82; of participation and distanciation, 63–66, 70, 139; of repetition and disavowal, 138–139; socio-pragmatic, 66
dialogue, 35, 49, 83–84, 87–88, 123, 130–132, 152, 174; partisans of, 123, 125, 132
différance, 6, 9, 25
difference, 30, 47, 87, 125, 152
différend, 26, 123, 132, 134, 153, 167, 168
Dionysian, 70
dissensus, 33, 125, 126, 134–135, 152, 174, 175
distanciation, 63–66, 68
dogmatism, 2
doxa, 19, 138, 167, 168, 176; despised, 19, 167, 176; Sophistic, 176; versus *epistēmē,* 167, 168

ego, 25, 85; transcendental, 23, 108–109, 149, 150, 150*n,* 160, 161
ego-cogito, 23
egology, 160, 161
Eleatics, 30
emancipation, 27, 35, 39–40
embodiment, 82, 85, 158*n,* 162*n*
empiricism, 24, 85, 108; abstract, 113; British, 23, 44, 50, 108; radical, 108
"end of philosophy," 5, 5*n,* 17, 31
Enlightenment, 2, 20, 27, 34, 52
epideictic, 118
epistēmē, 23, 167, 168
epochē, 64*n*
eristics, 118, 119
Erkenntnistheorie, 27, 28
eschatology, 46, 47, 95, 96
essence, 21, 24, 88, 124; and existence, 65, 133; doctrine of, 164, 165
eternal recurrence, 21, 44
ethics, 39, 39*n,* 175*n,* 176, 177, 178
ethnology, 171
ethos, 9, 135, 175, 175*n*
existentialism, 15, 44–45
existential-phenomenological, 9
explanation, 28, 86*n,* 101

fitting reponse, 9, 175
forensic, 118, 119
foundationalism, 5, 5*n,* 10, 23, 35, 50, 54, 59, 92
freedom, 128
French Revolution, 3

CALVIN O. SCHRAG, George Ade Distinguished Professor of Philosophy at Purdue University, is author of *Experience and Being* (1969), *Radical Reflection and the Origin of the Human Sciences* (1980), and *Communicative Praxis and the Space of Subjectivity* (1986).

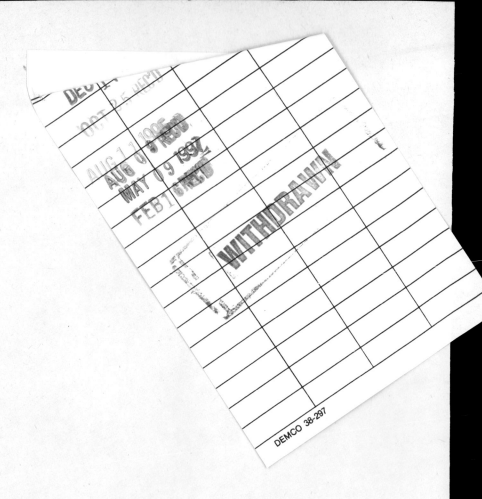